THE FAR FROM COMPLEAT ANGLER

Tom Fort

Foreword by Jeremy Paxman

Merlin Unwin Books

First published in Britain by Merlin Unwin Books, 1995
Published in paperback 2021

ISBN 978-1-913159-31-3

Text copyright © Tom Fort

All rights reserved. No part of this publication may be reproduced, stored in a retrieval system or transmitted in any form or by any means, electronic, mechanical, photocopying, recording or otherwise, without the prior permission of the publisher:

Merlin Unwin Books
Palmers House, 7 Corve Street, Ludlow, Shropshire SY8 1DB
www.merlinunwin.co.uk

The author asserts his moral right to be identified as the author of this work.

British Library Cataloguing-in-Publication Data:
A catalogue record for this book is available from the British Library.

Designed and typeset in Times by Merlin Unwin Books.

To My Brothers

Contents

Foreword by Jeremy Paxman	iv
Author's Preface	vi
1. In the Beginning	1
2. On Being Coarse	7
3. Ancient and Not-so-modern	17
4. Great Men	23
5. The Way We Live Now	45
6. A Ragbag, Medley or Pot-pourri	61
7. Cold Feet in Poland	87
8. Trials and Small Triumphs in Bohemia and Slovakia	101
9. Nothing, and Something Ugly, in Hungary	113
10. Trout, Bears and other Amusements in Romania	127
11. South of the Danube: Interludes in Bulgaria and Croatia	143
12. Brazilian Gold	147
13. Sometimes a Salmon	155
14. Morality and Other Matters	163
15. Across the Water	177
16. Kennet Days	189
17. Other Chalkstreams	199
18. In Eden	208

FOREWORD BY JEREMY PAXMAN

I first met Tom Fort when he emerged from the Brazilian jungle wearing *It Ain't Alf Hot Mum* shorts and a straw hat which looked as if it had once belonged to Vita Sackville-West. 'What about these Dorado, then?' The voice was simultaneously quizzical and bossy. The Dorado, dubbed the 'Golden Salmon' by Major Hills in the 1920s, was what had brought us both seven thousand miles. Within an hour of his arrival, having seen the arsenal of ironmongery in his luggage, local people had dubbed Tom 'El Professor'. Professor of fishing. The impression of effortless angling superiority was somewhat undermined by the way they fell about laughing at the extraordinary collection of flies, spoons, rappallas and devons which fell out of his *Financial Times* carrier bag.

But the Professor isn't an entirely unfair name for Tom. All fishermen are full of preposterous talk. Tom is no more full of it than the rest of us. But he has a persistence and dedication which sometimes means that he knows what he's talking about.

Most anglers are one thing or the other – flyfishermen, sea-anglers, monster carp chasers. Doubtless there are even whitebait specialists. But Tom Fort is an enthusiast for all forms of fishing. Although he now spends as much time trout fishing as his employers and his bank manager allow, he has never lost his early joy in chasing tench, priming barbel swims or dead-baiting for pike. My most recent fishing expeditions with him have been, in order, a day on a

Foreword

chalkstream, an afternoon barbel-hunting, a morning's pike-fishing, a couple of days' early-season salmon spinning and an afternoon nymphing for trout in the Cotswolds.

In *The Far From Compleat Angler* you will read of fishing exploits from the Scottish Highlands to the Danubian Plain. It is tempting to see such feats as examples of flyfishing brilliance. Do not be deceived. As readers of his column in the *FT* know, he's as likely to get his fly caught in an overhanging willow as the rest of us. But what he has in abundance is that essential prerequisite for any fishing success, boundless enthusiasm. Fishing with Tom – either on the riverbank or in these pages – is fun.

In Brazil, we soon gave up our naive ideas about spinning or flyfishing and took up the local custom of chucking livebait upstream and waiting for a passing set of jaws to clamp themselves around it. In one hundred degree heat and ninety percent humidity it was not the sort of technique which made undue demands on the dry fly purist. Our boatman, who had a bullet stuck in his head from a bungled bank-job and a set of false teeth he'd been sent through the post from Sao Paolo, grimaced in benign astonishment. The river, twice the width of the Danube, rolled beneath in muddy indifference.

After three or four days of this brain-addling torment, we had advanced the time of the first beer of the day from 12.30 to 8am. I had more-or-less abandoned hope. But Tom battled on until, finally, he found a way of hooking the Dorado on a spinner. In the space of half an hour he hit four of them. That was the fruit of persistence and competence and it put those of us who preferred a cold tinny to shame.

Author's Preface

One morning in early spring seven years ago, my brother Matthew, who was then writing about foodyish matters in the *Financial Times* weekend section, telephoned me to say that the paper's respected angling correspondent, John Cherrington, had died. He suggested to me that I should apply to be Mr Cherrington's successor. 'You're always banging on about fishing,' he said. 'Here's a chance to get paid for it.'

In fear and trembling, I rang the man then running the Weekend *FT*, the redoubtable J.D.F. Jones. 'I know nothing about fishing,' he boomed at me. 'But it's amazing how many people on this paper have been into my office to tell me that they do, and that they should be writing about it. So what do you think you have to offer?' I gulped, searching for an answer. 'Well,' he continued briskly, 'send me something and I'll look at it.' So I sent him a piece about some curious characters I had observed at an auction of old fishing tackle, and that was the start of it.

Occasionally, I return to the question JDF asked me, and I still have no wholly convincing answer to it. I can, however, put my finger on one or two aspects of fishing about which I have almost nothing of value to say. This may be useful in saving potential readers from the pain of disappointment.

Anyone who reads anything I have to say in the hope that it will assist him or her to catch more fish, bigger fish or better fish

Author's Preface

is barking along the wrong river bank. I should like nothing better than to be one of those visionary thinkers - a Skues, a Halford, a Goddard, a Dick Walker - who, by the power of observation and intelligence, unlock one or more of the mysteries which make the sport so endlessly absorbing. But it is not so. My mediocre level of competence has been acquired slowly, clumsily and painfully through experience, and through an indifferent application of the bright ideas of others. I cannot claim to have made a single original observation of a technical nature.

Nor do I have stories to tell of the great fish I have caught; at least, not true ones. As a hungry reader of writing about fishing, I love that sort of stuff, if it is well done. There are a few technical treatises which I regard as having been of real worth to me: Walker's *Still Water Angling*, Falkus and Buller's *Freshwater Fishing*, J.R. Harris' *An Angler's Entomology*, Goddard's *Waterside Guide* among them. But I like better those stirring accounts of monsters lost and conquered: of Bishop Browne's Tay salmon, of the vast seatrout of the Em, of Zane Grey's swordfish and Walker's record carp, Mitchell Hedges' sinew-stretching battles with shark and sawfish, and a host of others.

My own record in the big fish department is not so much scanty, as non-existent. I have caught but one 20-pound salmon, and that by a method (harling) which denies the angler any credit whatever. My biggest pike is a respectable but un-newsworthy 23 pounds. I have caught decent chub and barbel, but nothing which would rate a paragraph in the *Angling Times*. My best trout is a measly 4¼ pounds (though I have lost two leviathans, either of which would have been worth having stuffed - if I could have landed them). I once caught an eel of over 4 pounds, which is as close as I have come to a true specimen fish.

None of this has brought us any nearer to answering that nagging question. If pressed, I suppose I could explain why I write about fishing (apart from the money, of course, a sordid consideration which I do not propose to investigate further). The clue is contained in my school reports, those faded records of the academic endeavour of thirty years ago.

The Far From Compleat Angler

It was an article of faith among us that those who taught us - those aged, absurd figures in tweed jackets and twills - knew nothing of us. They hardly seemed to belong to the same species, so ancient and unreal were they. Yet there is a common thread through their comments about me which suggests that they may have been more perceptive than I imagined. The judgement is constant, though its expression varies: 'Fond of the sound of his own voice... fluent in writing and speech, perhaps excessively so... if only he would *think* before opening his mouth... to him there is no music sweeter than the sound of his own...' and so on.

Here, I fear, is the nub of it. That affection for my own tones persists into middle age; and will doubtless become a tedious adoration as the years roll on. And the great joy of writing about something - as opposed to shouting about it in the pub or around the dinner table - is that NO ONE CAN SHUT YOU UP. Just think of it. It is the dream of the expert, the self-proclaimed authority, the intolerable bore: to be able to go on and on, without fear of interruption. What a drug, what an addiction, that is.

So that is why I do it. Why anyone should wish to read it is quite another matter; and one with which, if you don't mind, I'd rather not grapple.

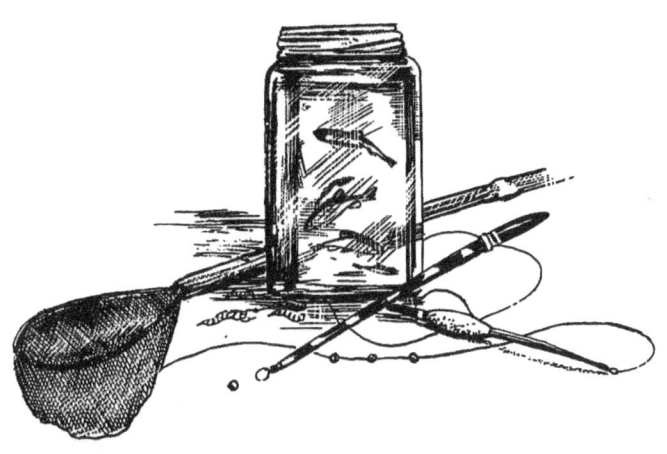

1. In the Beginning

'When I became a man,' St Paul says in that high-minded way of his, 'I put away childish things.' I did not; not all of them, anyway. You need a few to stay sane in this grown-up world. And my favourite childish thing is fishing. By 'childish', I do not mean infantile or ill-becoming an adult, as the dictionary has it. In my view it becomes an adult very well. Once I know someone is a fisherman - whether it be Hemingway, Neville Chamberlain or Ranjitsingh - I know I have identified one redeeming feature in him. I suppose what I mean by childish is that it is an enthusiasm most easily acquired in childhood.

The urge to fish springs from the instinctive fascination which water exercises on boys. I would go so far as to say that there is something wrong with the boy who can pass a pond without wanting to dip a net in it, inspect its margins for tadpoles, or - at the very least - chuck a stone into it. But there is a great divide between that general urge to muck about, and the particular longing to pull fish out of the water. My own elder son is a case in point. He will go fishing,

The Far From Compleat Angler

can catch fish, and will be happy doing so for an hour or so - but would rather play football. The truth is that, in his heart, he is not a fisherman; not yet anyway. This matters not a jot to him or me. For - while you can teach your child or anyone else's to fish - you cannot persuade them to want to fish. The spark, the magic of the passion, is a gift from somewhere.

If the bug does bite in childhood, it usually does so deep, and the fever is fierce. My father was no fisherman, but by the time I was eight or nine I had become aware that two of my elder brothers were thoroughly infected. They had been given elementary instruction by my grandmother, afloat on Windermere. They had learned the nasty but necessary techniques of sticking a hook through a worm and subduing the perch which grabbed it. This knowledge they took to the banks of our local river, and there developed it. And eventually I was allowed to go too.

We were blessed in our river, the Loddon, which flows into the Thames at Wargrave in Berkshire. We had friends who lived in a large house beside it, and we had the run of the water. There was the Loddon itself, and what we called the Second Stream, which was once gloriously overgrown and fish-filled until the old Thames Conservancy blighted it with a typically barbarous act of dredging and bank clearance. But the main river was untouched and, summer, autumn and winter it was our playground.

It is many years since I fished it, and I would not care to do so now, for there is too much of a tangle of memory attached to it. Then, thirty years and more ago, it ran clear and was rich in weed and fish. Chub thronged the quicker water, with barbel as well; while the quieter holes held perch and roach and the odd pike.

I was passionate about fishing at once, and it is a sign of the depth and power of the passion that it endured at all, for it was two years before I caught anything more significant than suicidal bleak and bristly ruffe. The first great event took place, not on the Loddon, but at the mill on the Thames at Sonning. Its great grinding wheels have been silent for many years. It is now a pretty theatre, and the millpool is silted and lifeless. But then the water surged and roared, and shoals of chub and barbel gathered to feed on the tasty waste from the milling.

Chapter One - In the Beginning

It was a tricky place to fish. You had to stand on the road bridge, with the morning traffic at your back, and cast with a heavy weight towards the white water foaming out from beneath the mill. The bottom was strewn with snags, and many a week's pocket money was swallowed up on the hooks and leads we left there. The best time was early morning, and we would bicycle over from our home along the murky lanes with rods and bags precariously arranged, and the aluminium worm bucket clanking on the handlebars.

There were big fish at Sonning. One morning we arrived to find a gnarled Thames fisherman poised on his stool on the far bank, with a sack at his feet which was stuffed with barbel, at least one of them over eight pounds. But my first proper fish was not of this order. It was a chub, and it took my worm near the willow on the right side of the mill pool. It may have weighed a pound-and-a half; big enough to put a bend in my cane rod and to require one of my brothers to scramble down onto the bridge support to net it. I felt that I had joined the big boys.

Not long after I caught a bigger chub on the Loddon. It came up and seized a piece of floating breadcrust, dived into several weedbeds, and reduced me to an utter lather before giving itself up. By then the fire was well and truly lit. Waking and sleeping I dreamed of toothy pike, fat-lipped chub, round-mouthed carp. I pored over books of instruction, buried my head in the *Angling Times*, learned to revere Richard Walker above all other men, longed in vain to become a proficient catcher of big fish. I remained as incompetent as I was obsessed.

Painful adolescence brought a temporary remission in the disease. This is common, and many youthful victims find themselves wholly cured, and able to progress to golf, gardening, DIY or some other more mature pastime. My eldest brother, for instance, gave up fishing altogether, preferring village cricket and service on the committees of worthy local bodies. But I, having emerged from the waking sleep of university and the catharsis of having to earn a living, began to fish again in earnest. And around that time I entered a new world, inhabited by trout and decorated by flies.

As a boy, I used occasionally to wonder why people made such a fuss about trout. I knew nothing of fly fishing. I dug worms, tore

The Far From Compleat Angler

loaves of bread into bite-sized pieces, moulded balls of cheese paste, and kept live bait in buckets. The notion that you could catch anything worthwhile on a confection of feather, fur and tinsel would have struck me - had I ever considered it - as most improbable. Little by little I became aware of trout, as a species which might be caught on a worm, and eaten. The first was almost black, with a few faded crimson spots near his grey little belly. He lived in the shadows beneath a stone Lakeland farmhouse, where the tumbling beck had long ago turned some wheel or other. He dashed at the worm as soon as I flicked into his cavern, and kicked and wriggled mightily as I swung him into unfamiliar daylight.

For many years the trout was a holiday fish, always pursued with a worm. There was a beck high above Windermere which required a tremendous scramble to reach the best pools, in one of which I once caught a trout close on three-quarters of a pound. There was another stream - a burn, this time - which cut its way through a tangle of forest to a lonely shore of a Scottish sea loch. Here the pools were bigger, but the trout just as small and famished as their Westmorland cousins; although, in a spate, the silver sea trout would run, and give us prodigious excitement.

I cannot remember the first fish I caught on a fly. It was certainly on the Eamont or Eden near Penrith, where indulgent friends let us roam at will over many miles of glorious water; and certainly on a wet fly, fished downstream. I was captivated by these fish, the violence of whose struggles made my beloved chub seem tame. And I was enraged and dismayed by my clumsiness as a caster, and by the knots, snapped casts and lost fish which tormented me. Slowly and painfully, I acquired necessary wisdom and a mediocre degree of efficiency. I graduated from the downstream wet fly, to the upstream dry fly, and was entranced by the new discipline.

Thus I have arrived at this time of life - a little way beyond forty, a time for self-examination. Although I no longer have the fanatical dedication of extreme youth, I find I love the sport as much as ever. But the passion is mitigated by the restraints typically imposed by middle age. I do not like fishing in the rain - it is uncomfortable. I do not like fishing all day - it is boring. I do not like sitting in boats

Chapter One - In the Beginning

for hours - it makes my bottom hurt. I prefer dry fly to wet, summer to winter, fair days to foul, wild brown trout to rainbows. Give me a river rather than a lake, for I like the feel, look, sound, rhythm of moving water.

What I like most of all in fishing is success. You meet anglers, mainly in books, who expatiate on the birds, the insects, the flowers and trees, the bounty of nature. These are all very well, and they help to fill books. But they do not make up for absence of fish. They may console, but they do not compensate. The essence of the business is catching fish. Non-anglers sometimes ask: what do you think about when you're fishing? The answer, most of the time, is: fishing. If you are kneeling beside a stream when the rise is on and the trout are on the feed, and your mind is on the cost of borrowing or whither New Labour, you're most unlikely to able to put your fly accurately over that fat fellow guzzling by the weeds, or to be able to hook him when he takes you.

At that moment, you must want to catch him more than anything in the world. Indeed, there is no other reality then. After he has risen and broken you, scaring every other fish in the pool and signifying the end of sport for the day, by all means relax by chewing over a few eternal philosophical truths. But the moment at which the contest between you and the trout is decided is simple and pure.

Behind that simplicity, nourishing it, is the wonderful, immense complexity of the science of angling. No other sport has inspired such expenditure of high-grade brainpower. There is theory and practice enough to sustain a university faculty. Great men have pondered the mysteries of fishing, and offered their solutions and theories. Yet mysteries they remain.

I have, in my time, dreamed of being a good fisherman. Now, I know this will not be. Good fishermen are born, not made. I have advanced, but only within the category of the moderate, and I know I will never get any higher. And that is fine by me. I do not want to be too good. Speaking analytically, I value disaster as highly as triumph. I want those heady moments of conquest to be earned, painfully. I do not care for the idea of being an expert, and am consoled by the knowledge that I am in no danger of it.

The Far From Compleat Angler

It is good for each of us to be fervent about something which does not, in universal terms, matter; and further, that it should be something incapable of being mastered. Gardeners need to be beaten by blight or black fly. Every now and then a sculptor should chip off a nose or ear. Sailors must fall in, horsemen fall off, crack shots miss, batsmen get ducks, golfers go mad in bunkers, fishermen break rods and lose monsters. It is not failure we must fear, but perfection.

2. On Being Coarse

By the time I reached thirty-five I was, in my own estimation of myself, a trout fisherman. I no longer day-dreamed of chub and barbel. June 16th, the opening of the coarse fishing season and at one time a date of overwhelming and mystical importance, had become nothing more than mid-June, prime time on the chalkstreams. If pressed on the subject, I would probably have said something faintly pompous about growing out of coarse fishing, or the higher art of the dry fly, or some such humbug.

My only concession to the past was the three or four days pike fishing I had each winter on a most beautiful lake in the grounds of a startling neo-Gothic pile not far from Reading. But although there was pleasure to be had in those short, grey days, in the march around the reedy shore, spinning rod in hand, in the slap of the wavelets against the sides of the grimy fibreglass boat, in the bob and dive of the float and the jagged tug as the sprat was seized, in the cry of triumph as my old Polish friend, Adam, dragged another olive-backed victim to the net, reaching as he did so for the cosh to beat it over the

The Far From Compleat Angler

head - although there was a pleasure, it was a little melancholy and pallid, a touch lacking in red blood. In my heart, I suspect, I yearned for moving water, rather than the still breadths of the lake.

Thus, in the main, did my old rods - the Mark Four, the Kennet Perfection, the Fred J. Taylor roach rod - hang untroubled in their bags on their nails, gathering cobwebs; and the Mitchell fixed spool reel, which had so thrilled me when I had bought it twenty years before, lay neglected in the wicker tackle box. Then I had some rare good fortune. I stumbled upon a fishing paradise; and having had that good fortune, applied myself to securing it. A man I then knew hardly at all, but who has since become a friend indeed, had bought a house on the lower Kennet, with the river running beneath it out into the most perfect millpool imaginable. I had a casual invitation to come over one November afternoon, caught a pike from almost every hole into which I lobbed a sprat, and made myself as pleasant to my host as I knew how. He - generous and saintly man that he is - told me I could fish whenever I liked. I don't know whether in the subsequent years, he has ever repented the invitation, for I have never asked him. I trust that he has not, nor ever will.

On the map it doesn't amount to much, this bit of river, for it is no more than quarter of a mile from the point at which it leaves the canal to the bridge which marks the bottom boundary. But within that short stretch is an amazing richness and variety of water. One stream runs under the house, through the millpool, down to the bridge. Another breaks off above the house, bursts over a weir into a wide racing pool, before narrowing and curving through the gardens to rejoin its companion. A third, man-made and miniature, snakes back and forth through the wood, tumbling over a succession of tiny falls, until it, too, rejoins its fellows. When I first knew it, the place had not been fished seriously for twenty years and more; apart from by the gardener, that is. Mr Hughes was a stringy, wiry old man, with a voice and a face ravaged by the effects of a lifetime of unbroken cigarette smoking. Before he died, we got to know each other pretty well, for - once he had realised how I had fallen for the water - it cheered him to break off from his labours to tell me where lurked the big pike, where were the gravel runs beloved by barbel, below which chestnut tree was to be found the most fruitful roach swim.

Chapter Two - On Being Coarse

Very soon the old affections were rekindled, as it dawned on me that I had done my former friends, the so-called 'coarse' fishes, an injustice. Of course, I like to think of myself as a refined and sensitive soul; and therefore I should either dispute the fairness of attaching the adjective 'coarse' to species other than salmon, trout and grayling, or I should have nothing to do with the business of trying to catch them. But I scorn these empty dilemmas. I actually do think there is a coarseness about the bullying pike, the thick-scaled chub, the cunning, placid carp and the golden-green tench; and a coarseness about the fishing for them. And further, I would confess that it is a coarseness which I like.

It lies as much in the fishing as the fish. In dry fly fishing, it suffices to carry a little rod and reel, a net, and a shoulder bag for flies and accessories. But he who has serious intent towards, say, carp or tench will have a twelve foot rod with a big, fixed-spool reel. There will be buckets of ground bait, electric bite alarms, chests containing floats, weights, rigs and the rest of it. There will be a keepnet and a long-handled landing net, rod rests, a basket with provisions for a lengthy stay. There will be a chair, quite possibly a tent and a bed. The dry fly man approaches his task like a scout, the coarse fisher as if he were preparing to lay siege.

There is, too, a certain absence of refinement in the eating habits of these fish. Not for them the delicate wisp of feather and fur. They want something solid and meaty - balls of high-protein paste, cubes of luncheon meat or cheese, garden worms, bunches of maggots. Greasy luncheon meat I regard as an unappetising necessity, but I have a soft spot for lobworms; and as for maggots, they may smell rather nasty, but when sport is slack, you can organise a diverting race between a pair of them on the palm of your hand.

The rebirth of this long dormant enthusiasm has given me such intense pleasure that, on occasional summer evenings, I have found myself neglecting my expensive trout fishing in favour of sitting beside the foaming outflow into the millpool, still and expectant, awaiting the snatch at my bait and the battle with the bull-like barbel. But the best of it has been in the banishment of that doleful hibernation which the end of the trout fishing season used to impose. Now, from October to March, I continue to be a riverbank haunter, impaling

The Far From Compleat Angler

worms and maggots and sweaty lumps of meat, and catching these useless, inedible fish in order to admire them and put them back. In short, I do as I did when I was a boy.

A Boxing Day morning should have a keen, healing quality, capable of repairing swiftly the damage sustained by the system the day before. The reeds and hedgerows should be white with frost, the sky pale blue, the air still. Your breath should hang in clouds, your cheeks should glow, and there should be much stamping of feet and vigorous rubbing of hands. But sadly this species of Christmas weather seems to have followed other traditional aspects of the festive season into extinction. And there was nothing in the character of the Boxing Day just gone to drive away the dreadful sensations of biliousness and self-disgust which afflicted me as a result of frenzied feasting. It was warm and grey and meteorologically mediocre.

It could, however, have been worse. I could, instead of going fishing, have been preparing for another bout of gluttony. And this soft mildness seems to suit the pike, keeping their appetites constantly keen; whereas extreme cold brings on torpor and indifference to the angler's artifices. I had arrived bearing the Christmas dinner of which the pike's dreams must be made. As food for humans, I cannot say much for the rank and oily sprat. But as pike bait it is first-rate - cheap, easy to procure, easy to fish with, and deadly.

I met Stevie at the waterside. He was accompanied by a nephew of his, an engaging but impudent boy who had not fished for pike before. When I confided to him that I had left the scissors at home, he recommended that in future I make a list, to avoid such errors. I repressed a desire to stake him in the weirpool, as ground bait, and instead directed him and his uncle to the second-best spot, a turbulent eddy at the side of the pool. I myself went a little way on to the best spot, a hole formed where the sidestream prepares to meet the main current. One afternoon Mr Hughes had taken five fish from it, weighing between fifteen and twenty-seven pounds. Its green, slow-moving water was pregnant with promise.

Chapter Two - On Being Coarse

A juicy, stinking sprat was soon dangling beneath a cheerful, tubby float, and the ensemble lobbed into the middle of the hole. This float-fishing for pike can be a gripping affair when the fish are in the mood. In my youth I would use livebait, which is a barbarous business. The dead bait is just as effective, and indeed, hardly had my float hit the water than it shot away towards the roots of the willow, and my rod bent in answer to the strike. I turned to shout for Stevie's help, only to see him in a similar fix. But the nephew scurried about with the net to good effect, and both fish were soon thrashing around in a large keepnet immersed in a quiet corner.

By the time I had landed a second fish from the same hole, I was aware that my inner being was on the mend. Nausea had fled, and I felt almost human again. My brother - he at whose table I had gorged myself so grossly the day before - arrived bearing dark, potent Calabrian wine and legs of turkey. An hour or two before, I would have dismissed with a shudder the suggestion that I could ever again have a meaningful relationship with a turkey. Now I fed and drank, and agreed with my comrades that this was how Boxing Day was meant to be spent.

I spent an hour or two of the early afternoon trying to catch a chub. I cast my luncheon meat into the smooth water below the ash tree where, a fortnight before, I had caught three fat fellows up to four pounds. This time, though, there was no jerk at the rod tip, no pluck at the bait. Perhaps the chub had been overdoing the Yuletide feasting, too. But there was just time, before the gloom gathered into darkness, to return to the hole and dispatch another sprat therein. Again my float went away and again my reel made its protesting music.

We had ten for the day, the best just over eight pounds. Although the big ones stayed aloof, we had enjoyed almost ceaseless action of one sort or another. And they fight respectably, these river pike, and with their predatory lines and muted colours, make a pleasing sight together on the grass. The impudent boy caught his first one and was heard to ask if it was always so easy. He was sternly admonished - but try explaining to a ten-year-old that it would stop being fun if it happened every time.

The Far From Compleat Angler

The epic account of the epic battle is a staple of fishing literature. These descriptions are almost always variations on a standard theme: 'The rod bucked like a wild horse in my hands... the reel shrieked/screamed/howled/whined... the fish leaped skyward, lit by the sun, like a bar of silver... the huge tail lashed the water into foam... a final, desperate bid for freedom...'

This kind of thing becomes wearisome. The trouble is that, while the outcome and the incidentals vary, one struggle with a big fish is pretty much like another. The fish pulls. The angler pulls. The fish dashes around. The angler dashes after it. One side or the other comes out on top. If it is not the angler, he swears. It is all rather predictable.

I would not deny that the fighting of the fish is an integral, thrilling part of the sport. It stirs deep responses, and is the necessary prelude to the glow of triumph or the bleakness of despair. But the purest, most intense excitement precedes the fight. It comes while the angler is still, while he is waiting and watching. It is the moment of the take. And I would further suggest that, in its highest form, it must engage the visual rather than just the tactile sense. This is not to disparage the heart-stopping moment at which a salmon or trout grabs a sunken fly. But, more often than not, this is felt, not seen. It may be that, when it happens, you are concentrating hard on your fishing. But you may equally well be ruminating on the excesses of the gutter press or the wisdom of privatising the railways.

Contrast this with the responsibilities of the dry fly man addressing a trout which is on the feed. He must be aware of where the fish is, cast in the right place, spot his fly, chart its progress towards his quarry, and then - as the surface is broken and it vanishes - be ready. Should his mind wander, he will be lost, and so will the fish. It is a sure bet that the moment he starts pondering the issue of the female priesthood or the expansion of the European Union, the trout will rise and he will miss it.

However I sometimes feel that fishing with the humble float offers an even purer joy. Pleasing in appearance, even more pleasing in disappearance is how H.T. Sheringham put it with

Chapter Two - On Being Coarse

exquisite pungency. The glory lies as much in the variations in the manner of that disappearance, as in the fact itself. The float may tremble awhile, then move off with steady purpose before slanting into the depths. It may do no more than dip. It may stir almost imperceptibly, then glide away. It may bob for minutes before being pulled under. Or it may, almost as it meets the water, be jerked from sight. All the fisherman can do is watch, shaking under the strain of powerful emotions.

These reflections came to me as I watched my favourite crimson-topped pike float circle that dark green hole beside the weirpool. It was a glorious day to be out, with a clean breeze blowing through the bare trees. The river, as if tired of its trick in turning most of the surrounding countryside into a lake for the previous two months, had retreated within its banks for the time being. But it was still running high, and the little backwater was the only place quiet enough for my float. It, and the sprat beneath, had travelled no more than a couple of yards down from a tangled willow, when the crimson top stopped, vibrated for a second as if conducting an electric current, and went under. I could see it beneath the surface, whizzing towards the roots of the willow, and I struck.

The rod bucked, the old centrepin reel whined, the great tail..... no, after what I said earlier, I'd better leave that bit out. Suffice it to say that after a stern contest, I netted a magnificent, small-headed, fat-bodied, female pike; gawped at it; thrust it into the keepnet; and ran off to the house to find witnesses. Plastered in mud, dripping with pike slime, reeking of sprats, I hurtled upstairs in search of the infinitely indulgent couple who let me have the run of the place. 'I've caught a monster,' I bawled. 'You've got to come and look at it.' Michael followed me, dressed for a smart lunch in suit and natty Italian shoes, and hopped about in the mud, whooping with excitement, when he saw the creature.

I slipped it back into the weirpool, and watched as - with a flick of its tail - it went off to resume its life's work of terrorising lesser species. One does not fish on after such a triumph, so I went home, singing. The pike weighed twenty-three pounds and was, by half a pound, the biggest fish I have ever caught.

The Far From Compleat Angler

One of the attractions of this Kennet fishery, for a non-specialist non-specimen hunter such as myself, lies in the diversity of species. I no longer have the stamina or the inclination to spend hours in one spot waiting on the whim of a single quarry. I like to roam and vary methods. If the pike are sullen, the chub may well be feeding. If the perch are not tempted by a float-fished worm, a little spinner with a tuft of red wool at the tail sometimes rouses them. A biteless hour poised over the legering rod is enough for me, and my thoughts wander to the roach reputed to inhabit the deep swims upstream.

There was a November day, deep autumn verging on winter. The river ran clear, rid at last of the rubbish swept down by floods and gales. We were a party of four: myself; the proprietor, who was distracted by turmoil in the business world, although he did emerge briefly to drag a fifteen pound pike from the millpool; Stevie, who immediately after he arrived from London announced that he had to return there to ingratiate himself with a client; and my brother Matthew, who devoted himself to tiddler-snatching. As befits a serious angling correspondent, I angled seriously, beginning with a pike of seven pounds or so from the weirpool. Lunch was excessively protracted, and the sun was already beginning to sink when I caught a four pound chub from the millpool, and - a little further down - a bristly-spined, black-banded perch of close on two pounds.

By now the light was fading fast. But there was still half an hour left to try for a barbel in the run beside a Portuguese laurel above the house. A lump of luncheon meat was sent on its way, and I had hardly made myself comfortable when there was a violent wrench at the rod tip and the fish was on. I knew at once it was a barbel, for there is a fierce, muscular determination to its fight which is unmistakeable. Head down, great tail driving, it bored this way and that, seeking weedbeds and tangled roots. By this time Stevie had returned, and at last, bug-eyed with envy, he netted it for me: a glorious, golden battler of eight pounds, by far the biggest I had ever caught.

Such days of multifarious success are suitably rare. On the other hand, I know of no piece of water which offers a better chance of catching something. This applies whatever the conditions, barring roaring flood, and whatever the season. As a result the river has become a constant presence in my mind, forever trespassing across

Chapter Two - On Being Coarse

the line between the subconscious and the conscious, its rhythms elbowing aside mundane considerations. Thus, one March morning, I was toiling at my desk - or, more probably, staring into mid-air with the end of my pen in my mouth - when a thought struck me. At once it sabotaged whatever tedious task it was on which I was engaged, for it demanded immediate attention.

It was that if I didn't go fishing there and then, I would have no further opportunity to do so before the coarse fishing season ended in a few days' time. Outside the sun was shining, the birds were chirruping, the daffodils were about to bloom, and the river was calling me in insistent, irresistible tones. The internal debate between duty and inclination was brief, and within the hour I was beside the water. I had decided that, since it was my last chance, I needed to pack a lot in. I would therefore begin by catching a perch or two, spinning; move on to the elusive roach, which I would lure with bread; and bring proceedings to a resplendent coda with a barbel, undone by a helping of Sainsbury's breakfast slice, which a friend had assured me was the barbel bait of the moment.

At five o'clock - with an hour of daylight left - I had caught neither perch, nor roach, nor barbel, nor anything else. In catching nothing, I had also suffered a series of misfortunes, each in itself trifling, but cumulatively demoralising in the extreme. The fact that they were self-inflicted offered no comfort. Of course I should have remembered to bring a stool, and not relied on the ground - for a damp backside in chill March is no laughing matter. And, yes, I know I should have bought a new pair of gumboots - although it seems a bit much that the leak in the right one which I knew about should have been matched by a new and unsuspected gash in the left one which looked like the work of a maniac with a butcher's knife. All right, I should have been alert enough to prevent Bertie the spaniel stealing most of the packet of breakfast slice; and I should not have been so careless as to cast most of what was left into the upper branches of the alder opposite.

I could have risen above all these irritants, if only I could have caught something. This is what most aggrieved me - the obstinate, unreasoning, ungrateful refusal of the fish to bite. As the evening drew in, so my scowl grew darker. Then I had an idea. I should be

The Far From Compleat Angler

after fish which were always hungry. That meant chub. Only the chub could save me.

I hastened to the millpool. And there, on the fragments of meat which the blasted Bertie had left me, I caught five fine, fat chub. The bites were bold, the fights in the foaming water strong and satisfying. I avoided any more absurd blunders, applied myself intently, and was rewarded. All the love for the chub which I had had as a boy - as a fish which could be depended on - returned. The last was the best, a good four pounds. As I slid the net beneath its gleaming flanks, I murmured my thanks for the inspiration which had taken me from my desk that morning, and for a day redeemed from disaster.

3. Ancient and Not-so-modern

Auctions

Anglers are, on the whole, comparatively decent and virtuous souls. They love children and other living things. They can make dutiful spouses, are respectful to their parents, and are good workers. Their sins tend to be the minor ones of omission: a box of maggots left in the fridge or a tin of worms in the pocket, a dinner engagement overlooked in the excitement of the evening rise. They are characterised by humour, modesty and intelligence. In short, there has never been a greater calumny than Doctor Johnson's celebrated jibe about 'a worm at one end and a fool at the other' - if indeed the Doctor ever said anything so foolish, which I doubt.

If fishermen do have a collective fault, it is perhaps that of acquisitiveness. However adequate their store of equipment for the efficient pursuit of their sport, they long for more. They sigh for the bewitching melody in the swish of the latest graphite fly rod, and the soft click of the newest Hardy reel. This urge to accumulate

The Far From Compleat Angler

clobber now extends as much to the treasures of the past as to the technological advances of the present. There is an undiscriminating fever for old fishing tackle, and curious and quaint memorabilia associated with the sport.

For these days it is not sufficient for image-conscious sportsmen simply to practise their sport. You must be a collector as well. The cricket lover should have a shelf or two of Wisdens, a brace of Spy cartoons, and a bat autographed by the 1934 Australians. The golf man should have acquired a set of Bernard Darwin first editions and Bobby Jones's hat. I'm not sure what would be appropriate for the tennis enthusiast - perhaps a broken string from a racket used by Helen Wills Moody, or a sweatband discarded by Fred Perry.

No sport has spawned more baggage than fishing. There is the tackle itself, made by craftsmen to last; the thousands of books, each written in the hope of containing an eternal truth; and the stuffed fish, the prints and the paintings, evidence of the endearing desire for a permanent memorial of that catch of a lifetime. My own chief hunger is for books, of which I have an absurd number. Next to them, I love stuffed fish, even though I possess no more than one example, and that a rather small, anonymous, weary-looking roach.

When we were boys we used to buy our maggots at Messrs Perry and Cox, a dim and dusty cavern of a shop in Reading. On the wall was an amazing and beautiful sight, a display of rare golden tench, five of them, exquisitely mounted in a broad, bow-fronted case by the great taxidermists, Cooper and Sons. I would stand before it, staring at these gleaming creatures suspended timelessly among the waving weed. And I would see them in their element, gliding through their own mysterious domain. So faithful was the detail that this took no effort of the imagination, even though I had never seen a golden tench alive, nor have I since.

I recall another glass case, in which resided - and still resides, I trust - a mighty trophy known as the Parrot Pike. I first saw it at the top of the stairs at Bonhams in Chelsea, and was so staggered by it that I nearly tumbled down the way I had come. This beast, 12 inches deep, a foot thick, 42 inches long, and weighing almost forty pounds, was caught by a London silk merchant named Parrot on the Dorset Stour in March 1909. Someone who saw it on a fishmonger's slab

Chapter Three - Ancient and Not-so-modern

before it was stuffed described it as immense and perfect, which it is. It was bought early in the 1950s by a member of the Finchley Anglers for two pounds. At Bonhams it fetched £4000.

I would love to have been kept company by the Parrot pike and a few of his comrades. But I concede that there might be a problem with the displaying of them. Such a fish, glaring from the wall with its teeth glinting in the lamplight, might well be inimical to social intercourse. I was told once that the owner of the stuffed remains of Richard Walker's record carp, Clarissa, was facing a similar difficulty. His wife, oppressed by Clarissa's overbearing presence, had told him that either her rival went, or she did. The last I heard, he was still thinking about it.

The most straightforward way of obtaining these treasures is to attend one of the specialised auctions, of which the biggest and best-known takes place annually near Winchester. The first time I went, I spent a good deal of time observing the dealers, who bought most of the decent lots at prices which might have seemed mind-boggling if it hadn't been for the assumption that they would resell them for even more. The women were smart, the men - with a few exceptions - amazingly scruffy. Several had unkempt beards, and they all needed a haircut. Their faces seemed to have been shaped by long years of talking out of the sides of their mouths. Their most expansive gesture was the half-inch lift of the bidding card.

A wary camaraderie prevailed among them, a cloak for bitter and sometimes obsessive rivalry. I met a young German called Dirk who was returning to Hamburg with a hoard of old rods and reels. 'Your dealers they are so polite to each other,' he said. 'They smile and laugh and tell jokes, and really they wish to roast each other alive.' Among their prime targets was Joe from Connecticut, attending the auction for the sixth year running. Joe was disappointed not to get an ancient copper bait kettle. He wanted it as a spittoon, but considered £200 a bit steep. Outside the hall he was to be seen in deep and conspiratorial congress with a dealer from Devon, the upshot of which was that he parted with several thousand pounds for a deep sea outfit made by Hardy for the cowboy writer and pre-eminent fishing fanatic, Zane Grey. The smile on the face of the dealer from Devon, and the scowls of envious loathing with which he was regarded by his colleagues, were a pleasure to behold.

Myself, I bought nothing. I lusted after the books and the stuffed fish, had a brief urge to acquire a fork for stabbing eels, and came close to bidding for a pair of waders four sizes too small for me. But I was conscious of having behaved indiscreetly at previous sales. There had been a landing-net with holes in it (I trust my meaning is clear), and a rod so broken-backed that you could not have beaten a dog with it, and assorted other piscotat distinguished neither by elegance nor usefulness. So, for once, I stayed my hand.

Rods

To me, it is more beautiful than anything in the Uffizi or the Louvre. The dominant colour is a warm honey, broken at pleasing intervals by the gleam of stainless steel rings attached by emerald whippings edged in scarlet. The reel is fixed by a golden ring on a base of walnut. Above curves a smooth handle of cork, as shapely as a fine Havana. The full length of this exquisite creation is eight feet six inches - no metrical nonsense here. It tapers to a most delicate slenderness, yet is pregnant with power and resilience. It is, as you may have guessed, my new fly rod and already I am enamoured of it.

To the dry fly man, the acquisition of a new rod is an event of vast, quasi-spiritual significance. The bond between them is, I imagine, similar to that between a violinist and his Stradivarius or Guaneri. Poverty would inhibit me from buying a first-class airline seat for my rod, as Isaac Stern is said to do for his violin. But if I could, I certainly would.

The loss of such a friend can be appallingly painful. I remember an ill-fated nocturnal excursion to a remote, midge-infested Scottish burn - seatrout were the theoretical quarry - which ended abruptly when my blundering search for whoever had the only torch was interrupted by the splintering sound of my wader crushing my brother's beloved Sharpe's Scottie. Thirty years and more on, I am still awaiting full forgiveness.

For a great many years my own best chum was a Sharpe's Featherweight. In its youth it was eight-and-a-half feet long, and

Chapter Three - Ancient and Not-so-modern

straight. Then a tussle with a thistle beside the Evenlode necessitated a three inch truncation. But we stayed together, season in season out. It saw me develop from an inept tyro into the moderately competent operator which is all I shall ever be. It was forgiving towards early maladroitness and quietly encouraged the slow growth of skill. It was with me on the Eden and Eamont, on forays to Devon and Hampshire, and on a three month exploration of the rivers of eastern Europe, and - over many years - on the Kennet.

It was on this river that the little rod first displayed intimations of mortality. The details of the incident are still painful to recall, among them a big fish rising purposefully, a clumsy cast delivering fly into clinging vegetation, an impatient yank, and sharp, tragic crack. There are few more dispiriting experiences than trudging away from a river full of feeding trout with a piece of fractured cane in your hand.

I had the Featherweight repaired, but in doing so it lost that sturdy straightness. Like the discourse of the elderly, it wandered before getting to the point. But we were old friends, and I vowed to treat it more humanely. Alas for good intentions! We travelled together to the Teign in Devon, and I got my fly caught up on a branch. Like most branches, it was just out of reach, so I turned the rod round to hook the reel over it. As I pulled towards me, the tip entered the breast pocket of my waistcoat, bent and broke. I still feel a shudder of guilt to think that I repaid such service with such oafishness.

There was another rod, even more ancient. My eldest brother had bought it in Paris in the late 1950s, unaware that it embodied the abstruse dynamic theories of that demon French fisherman, Charles Ritz. Eventually it came into my possession, the Pezon et Michel 8ft 5in, 5½ ounce Ritz Super Parabolic FFP Fario Club, to give its full, imposing title. It was designed to give practical effect to the doctrines of High Speed/High Line propounded with such passion by its inventor; but these I never came close to understanding, nor did I need to in order to recognise the rod for the wondrous piece of engineering and craftsmanship it was.

With the demise of my Sharpe's, I used the Pezon for a time, and I have it still. Despite a pronounced set, it throws a decent line, but has, I fear, lost something of its inner strength, its backbone. Hence the need for a new rod, which I wanted to be of split cane.

The Far From Compleat Angler

Now, anglers are curious creatures. They are neophiliacs, entranced by the latest invention, the newest theory, always hoping that it will be the key which unlocks the door leading from mediocrity to expertise. But they are also tremendous sentimentalists, devoured by nostalgia for the days when the rivers ran cleaner and clearer, the fish were less discerning, anglers were fewer, hatches of fly were more prolific, and the world was generally a quieter and more congenial place.

The first split cane rods reached England from the United States not much more than a century ago. To anglers accustomed to arm-wearying materials like whalebone, ebony and greenheart, these wands were a revelation. The way in which they combined power and precision was a chief factor in the development of dry fly fishing as we now know it. Cane ruled the rod world for half a century and more, until man-made substances intruded - glass fibre, hollow glass, carbon fibre, boron, and graphite. These rods married strength with lightness to an incredible degree, and seemed to threaten their burnished, hexagonal predecessors with extinction.

However, the lovers of cane survived. In my own case, penury and meanness may have had something to do with it, because I could not bear to discard my old rods while there was life in them. And I suppose a fogeyish sentimentality is at work, in the same way that I like a cricket bat which needs oiling, and prefer sheets and blankets to a duvet. All I know is that graphite does not engage me at a spiritual level; split cane does. So, for my new rod, I went to see Edward Barder, who makes them in a draughty shed in Berkshire.

I used to fish with Edward's father, Dick, until he was seduced from angling by clocks. The piscatorial passion, though, burns brightly in the son. He understands the qualities of the dense natural fibres of cane; and, more important, how much these rods mean to their owners. Thus a business, small and not hugely profitable was born; and thus I have my new rod. I will say no more of it than that it is a thing of beauty, an exciter of envy in others, and a most splendid subduer of fish. Our relationship, I would say, is already a close one, although - no doubt - there will be tiffs and misunderstandings. But it is good to have a new friend.

4. Great Men

Izaak Walton

Before travelling to the ancient city of Winchester for my exclusive 400th birthday interview with the man we call 'The Father Of The Angle' I took the precaution of reading, for the first time, the book which secured his immortality. Never before had I got far beyond the Compleat of the title, and wondering about the old chap's spelling.

Without wishing to sound condescending, it isn't half bad. It's true that the 'Venator...Piscator' format palls after a time, that the songs and ditties and toasts and proclamations of loyalty to King Charles are a trifle wearisome. But all this is as nothing against the easy, unforced sweetness of the Waltonian tone, the combination of eloquence, passion, and joy which suffuses almost every page. When you think what else was on offer to lovers of English prose in the 17th century - the desiccated prosyletizings of Milton, for instance - it is hardly surprising that Izaak Walton's musings on

The Far From Compleat Angler

fish, milkmaids and the pastoral beauties of England became a bestseller.

I tracked him down to a fine old house in the cathedral close, where he lives quietly with his son-in-law, Prebendary Hawkins. Outside, the sun shone fitfully on a pleasing garden enclosed by high, antique walls. Beyond rose the great church itself, with its stained glass window and memorial: 'In Memoriam Piscatorum Principis Isaaci Walton Hanc Fenestram Posuerunt Piscatores'.

As the chief Piscator himself showed me into his study, I mentioned Milton. 'As a man, I did not love him. He was as a pike, a tyrant melancholy and bold, a pertinacious schismatic and Republican. For you should know, Master Thomas, that I was ever for the King and the established Church. But he was the chief poet of the land, and I a mere chronicler of the lives of men greater than me.'

He nodded, his watery blue eyes on the floor, and was quiet for a moment, then added: 'And my *Compleat Angler*, if I am not much mistook, has been published in nigh on four hundred editions in this country, and in many scores more in America and even in distant Jappon; and they have societies named after me; which, I trow, is a fate unenjoyed by that tedious and mischievous *Areopagitica*.'

I asked him about Sam Johnson, whose enthusiasm for *The Compleat Angler* inspired its revival after a period of comparative neglect. 'Johnson was a man of prudence, deep learning and piety, a sound Royalist filled with virtue and wit and vigour of the mind. True, he was an abomination to behold, dropsical and ever a-twitch. He was, I fear, unquiet in spirit and given to melancholy. I believe angling would have been more beneficent medicine to him than the tea he drank in such immoderate volume.'

Inside the front door, I had spotted, hung from a brass knob, a bulbous leather container which I assumed to be Walton's creel. Stretched along the wall above was a rod, six yards of ash and hazel bound together, with a tendril of horsehair attached to the thin end. 'Dost thou,' I began, then corrected myself. 'Presumably, Mr Walton, you don't do a great deal of fishing now?'

'I am too old and infirm, Master Thomas,' he replied with a little shake of his thin, white locks. 'And, besides, it would fill my heart with sadness to see the streams I remember from my young manhood

Chapter Four - Great Men

as they are now. What fate has overtaken the Wandle, whence Thos Barker and I would walk of a Maytime morn to ply the angle?'

'It runs by Youngs Brewery in the London borough of Wandsworth, Father Izaak.'

'And what of its trout? I recall one of more than twenty inches, which I caught on a caterpillar. Its belly was as yellow as marigold, and part as white as a lily. We, Barker and I and Doctor Donne - who was no fisher but loved abundantly the eating of them - had it in a sauce of marjoram, sweet thyme, winter savory, anchovies and sweetened butter.'

At the memory, he licked his thin, dry lips. I did not care to tell him that the Wandle is now dark and lifeless, strewn with supermarket trolleys and discarded beer cans, its trout belonging as much to the past as the old man's leggings and buckled shoes. 'I know not of the trout, sir. Though they do make a fine ale at its banks.'

'And what of the lovely Lea?' he inquired. 'And of the Dove, where so oft I angled with my beloved friend Cotton?'

'There are still trouts in the Dove,' I replied. 'And, marry, the cottage which Cotton built for you still stands, with its motto *Piscatoribus Sacrum* above the door, and the initials of yourself and Cotton intertwined on the keystone.'

He sighed. 'Ah, Charles, I loved him as a son. Doubtless he was, as they told me, a roisterous soul and dubious versifier. But to me he was ever gentle and filled with reverence; and in the matter of angling with the fly for trouts and graylings he was a master of guile. He was patient with me, for I was too old to learn this new practice of the fly. I liked better the worm, slug or frog, or some other natural bait made by God.'

There was much else I wished to ask him; for, after all, it is the best part of four hundred years since *The Compleat Angler* came out, and his comments on the evolution of the sport since then would have been illuminating. But I could tell he was growing weary, and I knew I had to hit him with the controversial question now. I asked: 'Forgive me for vexing you, Mr Walton, but I must put to you the charge that *The Compleat Angler* was not your own work, but that you took other people's ideas and, without acknowledgement, presented them as your own.'

The Far From Compleat Angler

'Master Thomas, Master Thomas,' he chided. 'He who turns his back on the wisdom of others is no wise man, but a fool. This complaint of yours was first made against me by one Richard Franck, a trooper in the army of the detested Cromwell, and, as befits a republican, a right cribbed and dolorous soul. And how many editions are there of his dreary tales, I wonder?'

'And what about the allegation that you were - sorry, are - a credulous dupe? Believing that pike were bred from a special weed, and that eels were spawned by dew, and that frogs eat fish's eyes and so on?'

'Peradventure I was wrong. Many matters are known now which were not known then. But for all this knowledge, Master Thomas, are we more contented now? Is not the world more troubled, noisome and pestilential than ever it was in my young days? I have a word of counsel for thee, for I have remembered what I wrote of my friend Sir Henry Wotton, Provost of Eton College, with whom I oft fished and conversed. I said that to him, after tedious study, angling was a rest to his mind, a cheerer of his spirits, a diversion of sadness, a calmer of unquiet thoughts, a moderator of passions, a procurer of sadness; that it begot habits of peace and patience in those that professed and practised it.'

'So what is your advice to me, Father Izaak?'

'Be quiet and go a-angling.'

And I did as I was bid.

G.E.M. Skues

I doubt if there has ever been a cleverer, more clear-sighted trout fisherman than the dry-stick legal eagle, G.E.M. Skues. The initials stood for George Edward Mackenzie, but he wasn't the sort of chap you hailed with: 'George, old man, how's it going?' Emotionally he kept himself to himself, living with his sisters in Croydon, working for the same firm of solicitors for sixty years. Whatever passion was contained within his spare, unindulged frame was devoted to a Hampshire chalkstream and its residents.

Chapter Four - Great Men

Skues was a scholar at Winchester, and there he first encountered the Itchen. I find it a consoling thought that during his first summer's fishing he caught nothing at all. But the river, its limpid water, its emerald weed, its refined and discriminating trout, fastened a grip on his intellect and imagination which never slackened over the seventy years or so that he fished it.

His great gift was to see through the surface, into the water. He observed, analysed, calculated, produced solutions. He was not, in my view, a writer of the first rank; for his sympathies were narrow, and he did not concern himself with the humanity and philosophy of the sport. But he was a stylist, in his dry, precise way, with a lawyer's sense of humour. And he was a brilliantly original thinker about fishing.

As such, Skues made enemies, for the English treasure mediocrity and conventionality. His crime was to question the canons which prevailed on the chalkstreams; in particular, the doctrine expounded by Halford and preached by his followers, that trout should be caught on an imitation of the floating fly, or not at all. Skues examined the matter from the point of view of the trout, and stood the sport on its head.

His discovery was that chalkstream trout gained the greater proportion of their nourishment from eating insects below the surface, rather than waiting until they were floating on it. Skues took the nymphs the fish liked, created imitations of them, caught vast numbers, and presented his conclusions in a succession of clever, lawyerish articles and books. In doing so, he brought down a storm on his head, for daring to challenge the Halfordian dogma.

The prevailing code was long on hypocrisy, myopia and snobbery, distinctly short on commonsense. But its devotees, the sport-loving gentry, clung to it with all the fierce, obstinate prejudice of their breed. And Skues, a thousand times brainier than they, and just as obstinate, danced rings round them. The climax was a long time coming, for Skues' first book - *Minor Tactics of the Chalkstream* - was published in 1911, and it was not until 1938 that his opponents had their revenge.

The setting was the Flyfishers' Club, of which Skues had been a member for fifty years. The occasion was the Nymph Debate. The accused defended himself with characteristic brilliance, mocking the

The Far From Compleat Angler

long-dead high priest of the dry fly, Halford, in deadly fashion. His enemies argued that nymph fishing was too easy, that it frightened the fish. But the core of their position - which could not be argued, being based on naked prejudice - was that in some mysterious way, nymph fishing was an offence to decency. It was simply not cricket. In such circumstances, the words of that great fisherman and writer, J.W. Hills - that the art of the upstream nymph was a far higher one than that of the dry fly - were ignored.

There was no vote, of course. Being gentlemen, they shook hands at the end and agreed to differ. But it was a savage blow to Skues. The feeling against him had, by now, infected his own club on the Abbots Barton water, where his unrivalled skill and superior ways had made him increasingly unpopular. Eventually snobbery and intolerance drove the old man away from the river he loved, and he never returned.

Were he to do so now, he would find the charms of Abbots Barton much diminished, I think, but far from completely erased. The fishery lies just beyond Winchester's city walls, where the roar of the traffic on the bypass overwhelms the chimes of the bells of the cathedral in which Walton's bones lie. The peace and sylvan beauty of Skues' day have perished in the creeping advance of the city. But between the road, and the housing estate, and the factories and warehouses looming through the trees, are spread the water meadows, much as they ever were, dotted with copses and spinneys and intersected by the Itchen and its carriers.

The fishing is still good, though not so good as in that golden era. The hatches of fly are comparatively plentiful, the water is clean and pure. Most of the fish are stocked - a practice Skues abhorred - and I doubt if they are as educated as they used to be. The main river is sadly silted as a result of dredging, but the little carriers are in cracking condition. Much of the credit for this goes to a man as unlike the stuffed shirts of yore as is possible to imagine. Roy Darlington is unmistakeably a Midlander, square-jawed, blunt speaking. Moved by the spirit of Skues, he came to Abbots Barton some years ago, found it horribly neglected, and - with the help of a brother and a band of companions - set about clearing the little streams and allowing the crystal water to move once more.

Chapter Four - Great Men

On the evening of my first visit, he directed me to the main river. As I strolled across the meadow, I was thinking about the old days, when a system of irrigation ditches led the flood water of winter to soak the land. I was vaguely wondering what had happened to these ditches when I fell into one. I squelched on, passing by a seat dedicated to Skues. The water was dark and unpromising, and not a trout rose in earnest. I met another angler, who advised me to go upstream, to a shallower stretch, where the current quickened.

There, in the deepening dusk, I came upon a cluster of fish feeding on a sparse hatch of blue-winged olives. Oh Skues of blessed memory, I thought, as I knotted on an Orange Quill. For, although his great work was done with the nymph, he also discovered that this fly, with its body of hot orange, was an unsurpassable imitation of the BWO in the late evening. The first fish I covered took it like a lamb, and fought like a tiger. When darkness fell, I made my way back through the meadow, my two-and-a-quarter pounder in my bag. And I raised my hat reverentially to the shadow of a remarkable man.

H.T. Sheringham

It was well over a quarter of a century ago that my eyes were first opened to the possibility that there might be more to fishing than catching - or, more commonly in my own case - failing to catch fish. One of my elder brothers and I, browsing in a second-hand bookshop in Reading, came upon a case of books on angling. We were passionate fishermen, but of a severely non-spiritual kind, and this was reflected in the few books we possessed. Among them, I remember a volume called *Coarse Fishing With The Experts* and a series of little manuals on catching perch and roach and the like.

Among the books we bought that day was one bound in faded red cloth. Its spine was decorated with two crossed fishing rods, between which were a net and a fat basket with lid raised to display a fish, a carp or chub. It cost two and sixpence and was called *An Open Creel*. The author's name, H.T. Sheringham, was, as it happened, faintly familiar to us. For, in addition to our handful of practical treatises, we

The Far From Compleat Angler

did have another book - BB's *Confessions of a Carp Fisher* - which includes an immortal account of a battle royal with a big carp at Cheshunt Reservoir written by this selfsame Sheringham.

I read *An Open Creel* straight through, with a swiftly swelling sense of wonder and delight. Even now, I can remember the condition of hilarity to which I was reduced by the chapter entitled 'A Day Of Tribulation', in which Sheringham describes a succession of calamities which overtook him during a day's wet fly fishing, presumably on the Exe. I was at that time making my own early, cack-handed attempts to educate myself in the use of a fly rod. It was a great solace to find the despair which unfailingly overwhelmed me as I sought to deliver my flies in the teeth of gales, mirrored in this light-footed but deeply felt prose. Thus we have Sheringham, having left his cast in a bush over deep water, sitting down to contrast his misfortunes with those of Job; and a while later, having contrived to lose the big trout on which his heart was set, pondering on 'Job and his exaggerated griefs'.

Having devoured *An Open Creel*, my brothers and I (for a third of us had also become a devotee) rushed back to the shop in Reading and snapped up Sheringham's *Elements of Angling* and *Coarse Fishing*. These are both works of instruction and much of the content is inevitably dated. But each is beautifully written, awash with humour and good sense, and well worth the trouble of tracking down.

There were no more Sheringhams in the Reading bookshop. But by now the fire of our enthusiasm was lit, and we wasted no time in obtaining *Trout Fishing: Memories and Morals* from a dealer (alas, at a dealer's price). *An Angler's Flours* took a little more hunting down, and with that the oeuvre was almost complete (I exclude from the essential Sheringham his *Fishing: Its Cause, Treatment and Cure*, whose drolleries now seem somewhat laboured, and his whimsical novel *Syllabub Farm*). This burst of buying laid the foundations of a collection which now amounts to over six hundred fishing books.

I cherish them all, even the ones I have never got round to reading. And there are writers to whom I return again and again: J.W. Hills, Zane Grey, Roderick Haig-Brown, BB, G.D. Luard, Frank Barker, F.A. Mitchell-Hedges, Richard Walker, Chris Yates, Negley Farson, Arthur Ransome, Harry Plunket Greene, to name but a few.

Chapter Four - Great Men

Yet, for all the hundreds of fishing books I have read since those distant days of enlightenment, I have never had occasion to change the opinion I must have formed then: that Hugh Tempest Sheringham was the finest of them all.

The Sheringhams were a family of strong clerical leanings. His father was vicar at Tewkesbury, and his grandfather Archdeacon of Gloucester. The flavour of his childhood and the dawning of the passion for rivers, are exquisitely captured in the opening chapter of *An Open Creel*, 'Waters Of Youth'. The affection for the chub - whether caught on worm, or cheese, or, best of all, fly - was born on the Severn and Avon and their tributaries, and was never to leave him. While his grandfather, the stern Archdeacon, endeavoured to bend him to the discipline of Latin verse, the boy's imagination ran on water meadows, the play of sunlight on moving water, the tantalising mysteries of the depths beneath the hanging branches of willows. But the young Sheringham was a gifted scholar and that strict classical education - apart from leaving him with an occasionally excessive affection for Latin tags - was to stand him in good stead when it came to developing his graceful, easy style of writing.

In 1903 Sheringham became angling editor of *The Field*, a job he held until his early death from cancer twenty-seven years later. Had he gone into the Church, or the diplomatic service, or to the British Museum - which was apparently his first ambition - he might well have joined the great throng of us whose immortal masterpieces remain firmly locked inside our heads. As it was, by subjecting himself to the constant, nagging demands of journalism, he produced a mass of writing which made him the most cherished and respected authority on fishing of his day. What is more, in his role as editor, he encouraged, cajoled, flattered and browbeat a host of friends, acquaintances and complete strangers into putting pen to paper. Plunket Greene's *Where the Bright Waters Meet* is merely the most celebrated of the books to which Sheringham acted as midwife.

Sheringham was an atheist and a socialist, at that time an unusual combination for one of his class. And his attitude to fishing clearly reflected his political convictions. His friend John Moore - with whom he collaborated in editing *The Book of the Fly Rod* - wrote of him: 'It was chiefly the humbler angler that he loved, and by whom

The Far From Compleat Angler

he was loved in return. He always preferred that a river should be bought by a large angling club than by a single millionaire or a syndicate of plutocrats'.

Although Sheringham relished his days on preserved stretches of the Itchen, Test and Kennet, he always fished them as a guest and was never to be counted a member of a syndicate of plutocrats. The kind of fishing club he liked was the one he celebrated in 'A Suburban Fishery' in *An Angler's Hours*, where a man might stalk a trout, then a cast a fly for a chub, and finish his day watching his float circle a shaded eddy in the hope that the perch or roach might bite.

It was in his passion for coarse fishing that Sheringham's democratic instincts are most apparent. He wrote in his introduction to *Coarse Fishing*: 'Salmon fishing is good; trout fishing is good; but to the complete angler neither is intrinsically better than the pursuit of roach, or tench, or perch, or pike'. Put like that, it sounds so reasonable. Yet, in those days and coming from a man of Sheringham's social background, the creed was almost heretical. The gods of the age - men like Halford - did not demean themselves by considering the ways of chub. Only the salmon in his Scottish torrent, and the noble trout of the chalkstream, were considered worthy of a gentleman's time and study. Sheringham's partiality for floats and spinners, worms and cheese, an 18-foot rod and Nottingham centrepin reel, made him an object of curiosity among his friends. Plunket Greene, for instance, portrays him 'diggling for sticklebacks' and 'sitting in a punt watching a float for hours at a time on the chance of flicking a two-inch pinkeen over his shoulder'.

As a trout fisherman, he was clearly no mean performer, and he was as thrilled as the next man by a great hatch of blue-winged olives on the Test, or the spectacle of mighty Kennet trout gorging themselves on mayfly. But he seems to have been happier still battling his way up some inconsequential, overgrown brook or weed-choked carrier, employing every conceivable minor tactic to winkle out a brace or two of wild, wary trout.

Sheringham loved rivers like the lower Kennet, the Colne and the Evenlode, where democracy reigned and the fish which rose to his fly was as likely to be a chub or dace as a trout. As for salmon,

Chapter Four - Great Men

he caught his share, mainly from the Welsh Dee and the Coquet in Northumberland. But he maintained an air of lofty indifference to the famous rivers of Scotland, and appears to have believed that those who fished them and nowhere else were not truly to be counted of the brotherhood.

He was, by all accounts, a gentle and lovable man. His friends prized him for the humour of his conversation, his scholarship, his immense knowledge of angling's traditions and literature; for his proverbial insistence on being supplied with afternoon tea; for his ability to conjure a brace from an improbable spot on an impossible day. Above all, he inspired through his writing respect and affection from friends and unknown subscribers alike. In his heyday, before the Great War, there was only one question to be asked on the day *The Field* came out: 'Has HTS anything in this week?'

Sheringham's son-in-law, H.D. Turing, deftly analysed the nature of his originality as a writer on fishing. Roughly speaking, before him there were two mainstream styles. One - exemplified by Halford - was that of a teacher addressing his pupils, a colossus condescending to address mere mortals. The other - with a deplorable tendency towards the sentimental, contrived and verbose - attempted to sustain the fiction that the capture of a fish was of no consequence at all, compared to the ecstasy derived from communing with nature as found on the river bank.

HTS's voice came as a fresh breeze, dispersing the tired old conventions. He spoke of fishing as other fishermen find it, of rare triumphs and frequent reverses, of the joy of escape which is at the heart of the sport's allure. He subscribed wholeheartedly to the axiom that it is better to catch fish than not to do so - but knew well enough that, for ordinary folk, success in fishing as in other matters could never be easily won. He defined the angler's season thus: 'Of the total number of his days, probably two-thirds will give him no results worth mentioning. Three-quarters of the rest will be of the type conveniently labelled 'fair to middling'. And there may be two or three days of really fine sport about which he at once writes articles. An article or two may be written about days of the second class, but about those of the first there is a grim silence'.

The Far From Compleat Angler

That grim silence he broke, and he also left an incomparable record of those days of the second class. Sheringham did not preach from the mountain top, compelling an envious awe for his fish-catching expertise; but spoke to his fellows as equals, in a manner wise, funny, unaffected, fresh and elegant.

The curious thing is that I feel I have known him a long time - almost, that I have fished with him. He lived for several years in a house not far from my own. He fished the same Kennet millpool which is now my favourite haunt when the mood is on me for a couple of hours after chub or barbel. Ever since I first read the books, I have enjoyed his company, and do so still - as Eric Parker described him 'an angler gay and wise, an eager comrade, humorous scholar, truthful and loyal friend'.

B.B.

Rising 85, a little rocky on his pins, enslaved to a regime of thrice-weekly dialysis, 'BB' - the supreme chronicler and illustrator of the mysteries and joys of the English countryside and its sports - has by no means lost the hunger for the kill. Sitting amid the clutter of the living room in his circular home in the flatlands of Northamptonshire, he explained that if someone would lend him a Land Rover, he thought he could manage one last wildfowling expedition to Scotland, alternating between shooting geese and having treatment for his defective kidney in Aberdeen.

I asked him if the time might come when he would no longer wish to shoot. He clearly considered the idea ridiculous. Though the very antithesis of the pheasant-slaughtering country gent, BB's view of the outdoorsman is simple and unshakeable: that without a gun on the wall, a collection of fishing rods in the corner, and a dog to trot at his heels, he is no more than an impostor.

BB is probably best known for his children's stories - among them *Brendon Chase*, *Wild Lone* and *The Little Grey Men* - and for the mass of his writing on shooting. But I had come to talk to him of fish, fishing and fishermen; for since boyhood I had held him as

Chapter Four - Great Men

an idol. BB himself is the first to admit that he was never an expert angler. One of the innumerable charms of his writing is the openness with which he relates tales of his incompetence - several of them involving the discovery, as the big fish plunges at the end of his line, that he has left his net somewhere else.

His gift, far rarer than mere technical accomplishment, has been to capture something of the essence of the sport, the magic at its heart. In fishing terms, BB's spiritual home is beside a quiet, reedfringed pool buried deep in leafiest England; his quarry, carp or tench. Seated still beside the dark water, awaiting the tremble of his crimson tipped float, his mood is one of intense peace, heightened by expectation, as he contemplates and observes the beauties of his waterside world.

He was, of course, responsible for outstandingly the best angling anthology ever compiled, *The Fisherman's Bedside Book*. Characteristically, BB took his time. Not content with picking and choosing from published literature, he went to immense lengths to track down fishermen devoid of literary aspirations, but with a tale to tell; none more memorably than J.L. Webb of Reading, whose account of how he fought and lost the great barbel in the meadow below the French Horn at Sonning is an immortal classic. The work was done during BB's years as an art master at Rugby school, which he remembers more for his frequent escapes to fish or shoot than for any notable success as a teacher.

His masterpiece, though, was *Confessions of a Carp Fisher*. This was first published in 1950, and technically is as redundant as the blunderbuss. But no one has approached BB in the way he distilled the spirit of the obsession, and captured the nature of the men driven by it. The prose is delicious in its lack of pretension, as here: 'Most carp fishers I have known are big, still men, slow of movement, soft footed and low voiced; many have nagging wives (I hasten to add that I am not so afflicted), and it is by the calm secluded waters that they have found peace and quietness for their troubled lives'.

It is a continuing source of delight to BB that this little book, with the exquisite scraperboard illustrations executed under his true name, Denys Watkins Pitchford, should have become an essential spiritual textbook for carp fishermen over the decades. Although he did write two other fishing books, *Be Quiet And Go A-Angling* (under

The Far From Compleat Angler

a different pseudonym) and *Wood Pool*, neither has the unique quality of *Confessions*. It is difficult to imagine that, while men continue to pursue carp, it will be forgotten.

Until he suffered kidney failure a year ago, BB was still doing a little carp fishing in a pond near his home. 'There are big ones there, but I've never managed to catch one,' he says in his typically self-deprecating way. Indeed, he remains heart-warmingly active despite age and infirmity, painting, writing fortnightly pieces for *Shooting Times*, and working on what he says will be his last book, a collection of wildfowling reminiscences.

In the garden outside the round house are three ponds, dug by BB in days long gone. He showed me them, pointing out the perch and tench and his favourite, a fat carp called Big Boy; and I remembered how he'd written somewhere that he had trained a previous pet to come to the surface and take worms from his fingers. Beside the water stands a painted heron on permanent guard, warning his mortal brethren to look elsewhere for their breakfast. I bade BB farewell, and he gave me a copy of what he regards as his best book, *Brendon Chase*. It is the story of three boys who, rather than return to their boarding school, escape to the forest and live and learn there for a year. He signed it D.J. Watkins Pitchford MBE, with 'BB' in brackets. A great and modest man, he is proud of the honour. I think he should be a knight, at the very least.

A few months after this interview, BB died, unknighted

Arthur Ransome

I believe it was Evelyn Waugh who remarked that one of the advantages of going senile was to be able to read the same detective story again and again without having any idea who the murderer was. We lovers of fishing books, too, return to our favourites repeatedly. But I would hope that our pleasure is of a higher order than that associated with feeble-mindedness. It is derived from the companionship that

Chapter Four - Great Men

true anglers instinctively feel for each other, and their shared heritage. When we talk to each other of fishing - even as complete strangers - there is at once that bond which confers immediate intimacy.

So it is with the books we love. We hear the voice of the writer. Much may separate us in time, technique, attitude, locality, the detail of the subject matter. But what links us is far more powerful. With those books to which we return, it is as if we had conducted a conversation across time which - after a year, or two years, or ten - is resumed. With it comes the warming glow of picking up an old friendship and finding new life breathed into it.

It is clear from the pamphlet on fishing books which Arthur Ransome wrote at the behest of the National Book League that he understood the peculiar quality of fishing literature more deeply than most. This is how he identifies it: 'We do not think of them as books but as men. They are our companions, and not only at the riverside. Summer and winter they are with us, and what a pleasant company they are'.

No one would dispute the right of Ransome himself to be included in that gallery of pleasant men. Away from the waterside, he was henpecked, inclined to melancholy, capable of harbouring violent grudges over trivial misunderstandings, restless, full of self-doubt. His fame rested on his books for children. Yet - as Malcolm Muggeridge acutely observed - 'he never seemed to care much for children... Most adults like children because they are different from them; a childlike adult like Ransome dislikes them and is bored by them precisely because he is like them'.

But we are concerned with Ransome the fisherman, and here we see the best of him. Fishing is a great promoter of humility. Men who trample their fellows underfoot in the boardroom are reduced in their pride by the circumstances which confront them at the waterside. If a man behaves badly when fishing - hogging the best spots, boasting, sticking a maggot on his fly, marching downstream and frightening every trout in sight - you may be pretty sure that he bullies his wife, tyrannises his children, and is loathed and despised by his workmates.

As a fisherman, Ransome was properly humble. Rarely does he dwell on his own catches, and he never boasts. He is also entirely

The Far From Compleat Angler

free of that curse of English angling, snobbery. His clear preference is for trout, grayling and salmon. Yet his writing is shot through with his affection for the so-called 'coarse fishes' and his admiration for those who pursue them. Ransome's contempt is reserved, not for any species of fish, but for a species of angler - the one who, from arrogance and ignorance, appoints himself as an arbiter of what is, and is not, proper fishing.

There are two aspects to Ransome's writing on fishing which I particularly envy and admire. One is his tone, his voice, the way he addresses you as an equal, in a manner humorous, slightly gruff, rich in understanding of our foibles and in thoroughgoing commonsense. The other is literary. He is, simply, an outstanding writer of English; witty, ironic, devoid of pretentiousness, a master of the telling descriptive phrase. Only his friend H.T. Sheringham matches him, and none has surpassed him.

I have said that Ransome was a democrat as an angler. But he was not free from prejudices. The principal of these was against the south of England, for he was - wherever he happened to be living - a north countryman to his marrow. This bias is clearly reflected in his essay on fishing books. It is not that Ransome has any animus against writing inspired by the chalkstreams, any more than he objected to receiving invitations to fish them. He is generous in his appreciation of men like Grey of Falloden, J.W. Hills, Sheringham, J.W. Dunne and others whose spiritual homes lay by the Itchen, Test or Kennet.

But Ransome's warmest affection is for men of the north - John Younger the St Boswells shoemaker, John Beever of Coniston, Stoddart, William Nelson of Appleby, and that tireless Lakeland wanderer, Stephen Oliver. He liked them best because they shared the same tradition. They knew and loved the same open landscapes of tawny windswept hills and sweeping vistas; and the same species of river; rough, rockstrewn, free from Man's civilising influence. Essential fishing, to Ransome, was with three lightly-dressed wet flies for trout which might run three to the pound; or, in winter, for grayling with the float-fished worm.

Of the books he discusses in some detail, I am ashamed to say that several I have never read. Of course, I know Grey's *Fly Fishing*

Chapter Four - Great Men

(which I admire less than Ransome did) and Stewart's *The Practical Angler*, and Stoddart (whom I confess to finding a little tiresome). Sheringham and Martin I have long loved, and Nelson's *Fishing in Eden* is quite as delightful as Ransome maintains. But I do not have Younger's *River Angling for Salmon and Trout*, nor Beever's *Practical Fly Fishing*, nor Oliver's *Scenes and Recollections*. I should like to have them, for Ransome's recommendation is good enough for me. But sadly, his suggestion as to how they may be obtained ('the young fisherman putting together a library for himself should by no means neglect the secondhand bookshops') is of little use. The days when the standard general secondhand shop was likely to hold a useful stock of worthwhile fishing books are long past. Now - barring the very occasional triumph - the specialist dealers hold sway, and a decent copy of any of these old treasures will set you back a couple of hundred pounds or so.

When we come to the library recommendations which follow Ransome's essay, it becomes clear how well-informed he was. Ransome was an old man - seventy-one - when the pamphlet was published, and one might have expected him to be turned back to the past, and against the moderns. Yet Ransome misses very few of the notable books published in the decade after the Second World War. Here are Ivens' *Still Water Fly Fishing*, Waddington's *Salmon Fishing: A New Philosophy*, BB's *Confessions of a Carp Fisher*, Walker's *Still Water Angling*, Harris' *An Angler's Entomology*, Frank Sawyer's *Keeper of the Stream*.

Naturally there are significant omissions. It is surprising that Patrick Chalmers fails to appear. There is no mention of G. D. Luard's lovely books of reminiscence (*Fishing Fortunes and Misfortunes* and *Fishing: Fact or Fantasy*), nor of Corney O'Gorman's priceless *The Practice of Angling Particularly as Regards Ireland*. Books from America are wholly ignored, so no Haig-Brown, Negley Farson, nor Zane Grey. Sea fishing is unrepresented - therefore nothing of one of my own favourites, the irrepressible story-spinner F.A. Mitchell-Hedges.

In many cases the works of instruction suggested by Ransome have been superseded, except - as in the case of Richard Walker, for instance - they are of exceptional originality. But these are trifling cavils. In general, Ransome's selection represents as sound a basis for a fishing library now as it did forty years ago. Anyone who took the trouble to track down the books Ransome mentions, and to read them, would - even today - find their understanding of the sport, and pleasure in it, mightily enhanced.

Two Irishmen

J.R. Harris

Lewis Douglas, who was American ambassador to London from 1947 to 1950, was evidently a man of discrimination. In addition to his accomplishments as businessman and diplomat, he was a passionate trout fisherman, and could recognise a good thing when he saw it. He said this of a book first published nearly half a century ago: 'It so extraordinarily enlightens the art of fishing that it should be a piece of the equipment of every intelligent angler'. I am relieved to say that the book in question - J.R. Harris's *An Angler's Entomology* - is indeed a piece of my equipment.

For an ignoramus such as myself, the study of Harris's great work is a source of shame and enlightenment in about equal measure. The first is derived from my own realisation of personal inadequacy; the second from the easy display of rich and useful learning. It is an inquiry into the inexhaustibly fascinating subject of the insect life of our waters. It tells of the births, habits and brief lives of these creatures, of when and where they are found or not found, and - above all - of how they may be identified. From this, if we attend to the lesson, we may learn how to catch the trout which eat them.

Any fisherman will testify that, of the many frustrations he must endure, among the very worst is being unable to tell which type of fly to use (the worst of all, perhaps, is having that knowledge and not having the fly). The sequence is usually thus: the trout are rising keenly and confidently; the angler attacks them with a likely pattern which they ignore; he peers at the insect life around, and puts on

Chapter Four - Great Men

another fly, then another, then another. All are treated with equal disdain, so he reverts to the one he tried first. The trout move aside to let it pass; the angler retreats, or throws a brick at the trout.

I am not ass enough to suggest that close reading of *An Angler's Entomology* will abolish such nightmares, for there is a gap between the printed page and life as it is lived on the river bank which can never entirely be bridged. But it helps, and the man who provides such assistance is to be prized. So, on a recent visit to Dublin, I went to visit Dick Harris. He is a powerfully-built, affable man with a sharing attitude towards his whiskey, and a colourful way of expressing his trenchant views on fishing, fishermen, the trustworthiness of journalists, Irish rugby, life and other matters.

Now 79, he has had a varied career. He was described in the book as a demonstrator in limnology - it means the study of bodies of water - in the department of zoology at Trinity College, where he spent many years inquiring into the life cycle of the tapeworm. He has been a fishing consultant, a director of Dublin's best-known tackle shop, Garnett and Keegan, a journalist, a salesman. It never mattered greatly so long as it was either connected with fishing, or afforded ample opportunity for it.

The passion gripped Dick Harris early. His father, a solicitor, was keen; and at the age of 10 he caught his first trout on a pattern he had tied himself. Long summer holidays were spent on Achill Island in the far west, where he learned to catch seatrout. As he travelled Ireland, and fished, Harris became increasingly obsessed by the secret life of the insects he observed. He found that no one had addressed the subject coherently since Alfred Ronalds published his *Fly Fishers' Entomology* in 1836, so he set to work.

The importance of Harris's book was recognised as soon as it was published, and it has continued to exercise a potent influence, even though the last of its seven impressions was released as long ago as 1977. Niall Fallon - who wrote by far the best recent book on fishing in Ireland, *Fly-fishing For Irish Trout* - called Harris 'perhaps the greatest living Irish angler-entomologist'.

These days, because of age and a certain disenchantment with what he regards as the despoilation of the waters he loved by polluters and other criminals, Dick Harris hardly fishes any more. But the love of the sport endures. As we spoke, his flytying vice was before him; and he still responds gladly when presented by an old friend with some thorny problem of identification. For many years he has also been working on a second book, which - he told me - contains the four fundamentals of flyfishing. Innocently I asked him what these were. He asked me if I thought he was 'eejit' enough to tell me; then reached for more whiskey.

As I tottered out into a grey Dublin afternoon, I was a trifle fuddled. But I could remember one thing Dick Harris said: 'I know a lot about fishing, and the most important thing is that the more you know, the more you know how little you know'. I'm still thinking about that one.

Dick Harris died in 1994, his second book still unfinished.

Liamy Farrell

I had sad news in Ireland this autumn. I heard it in a fitting place, beside the finest and most challenging trout river in the land, the Suir in County Tipperary. It was of a man who had, in a quiet, unintended way, made himself a legend of that stream.

We had driven over to Cahir from the Blackwater, seeking respite from fishless hours after salmon. The Suir promised balm, and we were soon striding through the meadows downstream from Swiss Cottage, the pleasure house built by the Charteris family to decorate their estate. Beside the broad water was a tiny figure, immediately recognisable. It was Jean-Pierre, a dentist from Paris, a man with a deep, sustaining love for the Suir and its discriminating trout. He embraced my friend Niall, and shook my hand warmly. Then he told us that Liamy Farrell was dead, and the afternoon at once seemed a little greyer and more chill.

Liamy was a big man, with short-cropped white hair and a rubicund face. Many years before any of us had known him, he had been employed (there was doubt as to whether work was the right

Chapter Four - Great Men

word) by the Post Office. He had had some kind of accident, and been invalided out of the service with a disability pension and a limp which did nothing to inhibit his sprightly progress up and down the river.

The Post Office's loss was much to the benefit of the Suir and its fishermen. Liamy gave to the river as he took from it. He was a fierce defender of it against those he identified as its enemies - poachers, polluters, rough types from Cork. For many years he acted as a highly conscientious secretary for the Cahir Angling Society, issuing absurdly cheap permits for its many miles of prime fishing with immense courtesy, and a word or two of advice which the visitor was wise to heed.

Although Liamy occasionally strayed as far away as the Blackwater, the Suir was his passion. He had a genius for water, to a degree I have only encountered in one other fisherman; and he, too, was an Irishman. Through his almost daily communion with the river, Liamy acquired a vast knowledge of its weed-rich depths, blessedly abundant fly life, and its teeming trout. And he had as well a rare and blessed instinct that whispered to him - in the absence of any identifiable visual data - about where a fish was, what it was taking.

Even more remarkable than Liamy's watercraft was the way he chose to fish. He used only the one rod, and it was not a thing of beauty: a severely functional cane spinning rod which looked as if it could subdue a smallish shark. With it, Liamy spun for salmon and trout, and wormed for them. And with it he also contrived as quiet and delicate and efficient a presentation of a dry fly as I have ever witnessed.

The trout of the Suir demand a finesse which is generally beyond me. Their larder is well-stocked and rarely do they do more than pick at the olives floating above their heads. Persuading such well-fed canny creatures to take an artificial seems to require something beyond mere skill, akin to magic. You must present the correct fly in the correct size softly, without drag, again and again, as often as not in a fierce downstream wind, and keep at them; and if you are dogged, one may at last rise, and you will probably miss him. It is, to say the least, testing stuff; and it brings home to you in a way unimaginable

The Far From Compleat Angler

with the slow-witted stockies of the English chalkstreams wherein lies the true art of the dry fly.

Day in, day out, Liamy limped tirelessly up and down the Suir, duping those epicureans with the whispy little badger hackle flies which he ran up in the shed at the back of his council house. As his fame spread, he gathered a band of disciples, youngsters who fished Liamy's way, employing their ten foot spinning rods as if they were wands. It was as if a great golfer had opened a coaching school, at which the pupils were encouraged to use croquet mallets instead of clubs.

Though the disciples caught fish, Liamy caught more and bigger. He was a quiet, slightly secretive man, helpful in the extreme in generalities, sensibly parsimonious with information about the particulars of his triumphs; ever modest and self-deprecating in his soft, murmuring Tipperary accent. At the end of April he had caught a wild brown trout of six-and-three-quarter pounds on one of the bends below Swiss Cottage. A month later he was dead, of a heart attack.

The day he died, the mass of trees along the river were coming into leaf. The day we heard, they were just turning, showing autumn's gold. Beneath, the Suir ran as clear and bountiful as Liamy Farrell would have wished to remember it, with those damnably difficult trout still rising merrily away.

5. The Way We Live Now

I caught my first salmon on a breathlessly hot August afternoon over a quarter of a century ago. Expert opinion held that conditions on the Cumberland Eden were hopeless: the water low and scummy, the few fish stale and sulky. But I was keen, and it was easier to keep me quiet than to listen to me, so the keeper thrust a spinning rod at me and bid me do my worst. It took me a little time to acquaint myself with the workings of a multiplier reel. But, at length, a respectable cast sent the Toby beyond a line of rocks below a dub, and it was seized. When the keeper saw my six pounder he raised a hairy eyebrow, muttered something about beginner's luck, and shook me warmly by the hand.

Since then I suppose I have caught about a dozen salmon. Since four of them came in one morning, also on the Eden, and three during one brief stay in Ireland, you will see that I am not a salmon fisherman at all. In fact, speaking purely as a catcher of fish, I could without salmon. They are simply too much trouble. I haven't the money, the connections, or the hunger to pursue them seriously - although I

The Far From Compleat Angler

admit there have been times, standing in big, beautiful rivers with the fifteen foot rod doing its stuff over my right shoulder, when I have felt that I could develop a taste for them.

I love them, you see, even if they swim at the very margins of my fishing dreams. The thought that this wonderful creature, epic wanderer of the seas and rivers, might one day be lost is intolerable. It is no more than a cliche, but nonetheless true: that we would all, salmon fishermen, trout fishermen, non-fishermen, members of the League Against Cruel Sports, be diminished by such a loss. A few years ago it seemed that, by our folly, we might manage it. At last the bitter harvest of years of unrestrained netting in the North Atlantic was being enjoyed. West, north and east around the British Isles, the story was broadly the same. Stocks of fish were pitifully low, catches unprecedentedly low. In Scotland, the lamentations reached a new pitch of rage and despair, for great efforts and large sums of cash had been expended there to buy out the estuary netting stations - only for the decline to accelerate.

In the nick of time, a saviour strode onto the stage, an Icelander called Orri Vigfusson, a man of demonic energy and magical persuasiveness who had made the salvation of the Atlantic his personal moral crusade. His chief triumph, among many, was to convince a vast gaggle of disparate interests that the salmon *could* be saved, and that it was worth their while to pay to do it. Vigfusson and his disciples talked the Faroese in to giving up their netting, then negotiated the suspension of the Greenland driftnet fishery. Remorselessly they badgered government agencies, persecuted pirate factory ships, waved collection bowls under the noses of anglers and river boards until, at last, a pale ray of light made itself visible at the end of the tunnel.

All that can safely be said at this time is that there is hope for our salmon. There are respected authorities who maintain that its fate will be determined by forces which are hardly within our control, and that Vigfusson and the other campaigners are merely nibbling at the fringe of the matter. One theory holds that the numbers of salmon have waxed and waned on a cyclical basis throughout the ages, that climatic changes enforce mass migration of the food on which salmon grow fat at sea, and that if we are patient the balance will tilt

Chapter Five - The Way We Live Now

again, possibly within our lifetimes, and possibly not. The advantage of blaming ourselves is that it offers the hope - maybe an illusory one - that something can be done. Look at how difficult we make it for the fish. We destroy its spawning grounds with acid rain, and poison the estuaries through which it must swim. We net it in those estuaries, and out at sea. We steal one its main sources of nourishment, the sandeel, for use as fertiliser or heating oil. We pollute the waters, and destroy what lives in them. Oh, and we anglers catch a few.

What is absolutely certain is that if we, the British section of humankind, do have the ability to affect the salmon's destiny, we would be well advised not to leave it to our government. We come here to the infamous case of the north-east England driftnet fishery. For years the fishing interests in Scotland - where this atrocious practice was banned years ago - have gnashed their teeth at the interception of tens of thousands of salmon bound for east coast rivers such as the Tweed and the Spey. A while ago, the then Minister of Agriculture, John Gummer, ceased his humming and hawing on the matter and announced that this fishery was to be phased out. I'm sorry to say that I, among others, hailed this as an important, if grudging and belated, step in the right direction. It has proved to be nothing more than a empty gesture, a fine example of the sort of trick ministers play to disguise their inertia and indifference. The arrangement allowed the existing holders of netting licences to continue their depredations until death intervened.

I have no particular urge to join the lengthy queue of those itching to put the boot into Gummer, who has now moved on to higher things. The fact remains, though, that driftnet fishing for salmon is now outlawed off the coasts of the United States, Canada, Norway, Iceland, Greenland and Iceland. The only legal fisheries for Atlantic salmon in the civilised world are those off the north-east coast of England and the west coast of Ireland - and even the Irish government seems at last to be waking up to the realisation that vastly greater economic benefits spring from exploiting salmon as a sporting resource, than from selling them to supermarkets.

Is it too much to hope that one of Gummer's successors, Gillian Shephard, will rouse herself and erase this small, shameful blot from the government's conservation record? Far too much, I fear. This

The Far From Compleat Angler

government, like most others, prefers words to deeds. Action is taken only when what the ministry paper-shovellers regard as 'conclusive evidence' is furnished - and usually not then. The problem when dealing with something as complex as the survival of a species is that the only conclusive evidence tends to take the form of extinction.

Mercifully, we are still a long way short of that. The patient's condition remains serious, but is stable, with some signs of returning health and strength. A good few of the premier Scottish salmon rivers, given decent rainfall, have fished better than for years. There are exceptions, of course - particularly with those traditionally dependent on the now almost-vanished spring run. And in England the situation is bleak indeed, with famous rivers like the Eden and Lune ghosts of their former selves. The Test, Itchen and Avon can hardly be counted salmon rivers at all, while in Wales the Severn and Wye are also sadly reduced in stature. Ireland, on the other hand, continues to furnish evidence of reasonable well-being, with consistently plentiful catches on the Blackwater, Moy and lesser rivers.

At last proper attention is being given by some fishery owners to putting their own houses in order. At Delphi, in the far west of Ireland, for instance, the exertions of an enlightened proprietor and dedicated helpers in carrying out a carefully organised stocking programme has seen a prodigious rise in salmon catches (though the seatrout fishing which made this glorious place famous has yet to emerge from the darkness of near annihilation). Great work has also been done on the Connon and Beauly in north-east Scotland, while a massive programme to improve and enhance spawning grounds on the tributaries of the Tweed holds out the prospect of this mighty river regaining at least some of its old glory.

But as always in these matters, the proportion of those actively involved is miniscule. Lethargy, indifference, meanness, ignorance, prejudice, hopelessness - these depressing vices shape, and will continue to shape, the response of the vast majority of anglers to the suggestion that the sport which they passionately love is worth a little effort and money to protect. The task of conversion to the cause will continue to be a thankless one.

In addition, it is also often agonisingly difficult to decide what is worth doing and should be done, where the limited resources

Chapter Five - The Way We Live Now

available should be directed. Our knowledge of the salmon and its world is so disablingly incomplete. Yes, we know something of its life cycle, of its great journey - enough, the cynic would comment, to organise the mass premature end to that journey. But the nature of its inherited instincts, its genetic constitution, its breeding habits, the understanding of how we may help rather than hinder it - this science is in its infancy. And, necessarily, much of the effort expended is misguided.

An arguable example is the long-running campaign to restore a run of salmon to the Thames. Now, it is pleasant, when sauntering across Southwark Bridge to or from that palace of culture and learning which is the headquarters of the *Financial Times*, to reflect that somewhere in the soupy swirling water beneath one's feet, the silver Atlantic salmon is on the move. Of course, you are no more likely to see a salmon there than a mermaid. But not far upstream, at Molesey, the evidence may be inspected in the National Rivers Authority fish trap.

It is a minor miracle, in view of the fact that, for a century and a half, London's filth had blocked the salmon's way. By early Victorian times the river was little more than an open sewer. Nor, because of the tides, was it a particularly efficient one. What was washed down with the current was forced up again by the tide. Eventually, their minds concentrated by the abominable stench from a huge raft of suspended faeces which had come to rest beneath the windows of Parliament, MPs authorised the construction of the capital's first sewage system. But it was not until after the Second World War that the marvellous transformation of the Thames was undertaken in earnest; an achievement which should compel admiration throughout continental Europe, where, by and large, the degradation of the great rivers has continued unabated.

Having made the river clean enough for salmon, the old Thames Water Authority decided that salmon there should be. Its return would be an outward and visible sign of what had been done. It was an understandable, if vainglorious, ambition. The task was immense, demanding far more than merely tolerably clean water. The fish has to be able to forge its way upriver to spawn, and to find suitable spawning grounds when it gets there. But standing in the way were

The Far From Compleat Angler

more than forty weirs. More than half of these are situated between London and Reading, while most of the decent spawning streams enter the Thames above Reading. Each weir would require a fish-pass to allow the salmon through, and each fish-pass would cost up the sixty thousand pounds. A charity, the Thames Salmon Trust, was set up to raise the money and thus far a good dozen-and-a-half of the passes are in place. At the same time the NRA has continued its work of enhancing the spawning beds, clearing obstructions, and introducing juvenile stock.

How very admirable and plausible it all sounds. But a closer examination of the scheme throws up grave doubts. Its long-term target is to establish a self-sustaining run of one thousand fish. When you consider that on a much smaller river, the Moy in the west of Ireland, something like ten thousand salmon are caught each year on rod and line, the projected total for the Thames seems footling. Yet, footling as it may be, it has come nowhere near being realised. In the best year, 1988, the run approached five hundred. It has been as low as sixty.

This is no fault of the scientists nor of the Thames Salmon Trust. Everyone involved has done their utmost. But they are powerless to reverse the overall decline in stocks; powerless, too, to mitigate the droughts which have compounded the already formidable difficulties facing the Thames salmon. However, it is worth asking what the benefits would be if a run of a thousand fish were established. In sporting terms it would be nil, since the salmon would far too scarce to repay serious angling, except for the handful of committed souls happy to grow old spinning for them in the weirpools. The value would be symbolic. The presence of the salmon would tell people that something had been done, encourage them to believe that the consequences of Man's disgusting habits are not necessarily irreversible.

At what cost, though? The fish-passes up to Reading will have cost around a million pounds when they're finished. The NRA is planning to spend a further million over ten years, from a desperately hardpressed budget. And all this to nurture and cosset a fish which even those living on the river's banks are most unlikely ever to see. One cannot help speculating whether there are not

Chapter Five - The Way We Live Now

worthier beneficiaries. Whole rivers might have been saved from extinction.

And yet, and yet. Having raised the objections, I confess that I am still undecided. Reason proclaims that the whole idea was a typical piece of Sixties conceit, gross and unrealisable. But I can see that, having come so far and having expended such effort, from such pure motives, it would be a terrible shame to give up; even if, in the end, it amounts to no more than a glorious and costly failure. And yes, it is cheering, even inspiring, to think of this astonishing creature fighting its way through the heart of London, against the odds and the current, just as it did two centuries ago.

The smaller scale of trout rivers, and the fact that their populations are resident rather than itinerant, make them thoroughly vulnerable to adversity. One moment of carelessness by a farmer with his slurry, by a lorry driver with his load of liquid ammonia fertiliser, can annihilate a stream. Water abstraction compounding drought kills as surely, though slower. But the consolation is that the rebirth of the little rivers is always possible, and once engineered, its progress can be marvellously swift. With the salmon, we must deal with vast imponderables: events far out in oceans, industries, communities fighting for life, airborne pollution on a continental scale. It is a mammoth undertaking, to seek to tilt such scales. In contrast, a stream is a microworld. Unkind treatment will bring it to its knees; tender, informed care will restore it to health, and keep it there.

A few years ago, the curse of south-country rivers was lack of water. One afternoon, in January - note the month - I was near the village of Bucklebury, in Berkshire. The Ordnance Survey map showed a ribbon of blue looping down from Blewbury Down towards the Thames at Pangbourne. The map maintained this was a river, the Pang, but this was a falsehood. I stood in the ford upstream from Bucklebury, where the gauge is marked up to four feet. My feet were dry. A couple of hundred yards below me were a couple of puddles, but no moving water.

The Far From Compleat Angler

To the north, the course of the river wound away towards Frilsham and Hamstead Norreys, pleasing names for pleasing places. There were willows by its banks, and it was crossed by little brick bridges. But beneath those bridges was not the merest trickle of water, even the map had me believe that the Pang extended for a further five miles above Bucklebury, and that its source was a spring above Hamstead Norreys. There was a time, not much more than twenty years ago, when the little stream was alive in these upper reaches. It was only a baby, too small for trout fishing, and in dry spells inclined to disappear. But once the winter rains had replenished the subterranean chalk aquifers, the springs would bubble again and the crystal water would sparkle down the valley. Flyfishing began at Frilsham, and at Bucklebury the Pang was a classic small chalkstream, pellucid, alive with shrimp and insect, full of wild trout. And there were still six miles of good fishing below, until it met the Thames.

The Pang's troubles began when a pumping station was built near its source, in the downs above Hamstead Norreys. The Thames Water Authority, faced with demands from expanding Didcot and the great power station on its outskirts, thrust its boreholes deep into the chalk to suck the water stored therein. The Pang began to shrink. Mile by mile it diminished, then vanished. The bed at Hamstead Norreys became dry for most, then all of the year. The flow became intermittent past Frilsham, then ceased altogether. Below Bucklebury what had been a delicious stream was reduced to a pitiful rill.

As so often, the fishermen were the first to complain. But fishermen are constantly complaining, so no one paid much attention. Gradually, however, it dawned on a wider public that something which they knew as a river was becoming a former river. The fishermen made an alliance with the conservation groups, and together the mobilised the parish councils and the landowning bigwigs. They clamoured at the National Rivers Authority, which had been created to prevent such things happening. The NRA made noises at Thames Water, now a privatised water company. And Thames Water, bending before the breeze, eventually announced with considerable smugness that, as a result of developing new boreholes near Goring, it would be able to reduce its pumping from the Pang station by two thirds.

Chapter Five - The Way We Live Now

Unfortunately, the altruism of water companies is a limited commodity. Thames Water has retained its licence to abstract, and, legally, there is nothing to stop it returning to its wicked ways. Its first duty remains to supply water to its customers, and should there be a renewed surge in demand resulting, most probably, from one or more of the 'new villages' which developers are clamouring to dump on us, the Pang could well become a casualty again. For the time being, the situation on the river has shown a significant improvement - partly because of the diminution in abstraction, but principally because our weather has at long last woken up to its responsibilities, and reverted to supplying decent quantities of water.

In those years of drought, it sometimes seemed that it would never rain properly again. The land cracked and baked, the rivers shrank until they were rivers no more, and the merchants of doom - of whom I was one - wrung their hands and prophesied catastrophe. For me, the nightmare was most intense on the Kennet. Early in the 1980s, I had received my rudimentary self-education in the art of the dry fly on a gorgeous stretch of the upper Kennet, between Ramsbury and Marlborough. In those days it was a truly lovely piece of water to behold, crystal clear, bright with weed and golden gravel, seething with right sort of insects, alive with fine, canny trout. At the height of the drought, I went back, and it was as if a plague had struck. The bed of the stream was dark and dead, the weed and gravel smothered in silt. The water itself was thick with gobbets of algae, the surface still and scummy. The trout which remained darted through the murk, as if searching in vain for the river's innocent past.

The curse was lack of water. The aquifers had been sucked dry, and the springs were defunct. What water there was hardly moved. Without current, the river had ceased to be a river and had become something else - a ditch. But even then the keeper, John Hounslow - while making no attempt to disguise the scale of tragedy - had never despaired. Give me two or three winters of rain, he implored, and I will see my river reborn. And rain it did, and three years on I went back again, to see if those hopes had been fulfilled.

It was a grim autumn day, with a sky the colour of coffin lead, and as we made our way down to the river, the heavens opened and remained open. In his youth, John explained, riverkeeping had been

The Far From Compleat Angler

a simple game. You kept the banks clear, cut the weed, stocked the fish, cleared the hatchgates, and listened politely to the anglers. Now, of necessity, he had become a self-taught hydrodynamic engineer. His problem was this. A chalkstream must have the right sort of weed if the insects and trout are to flourish. The right sort of weed is ranunculus, and it will grow only on gravel bottom kept clear of silt by an adequate current. He showed me where, with back-breaking labour, he had narrowed the watercourse to increase the flow; and where he had placed tons of rock on the river bed to create little groynes, or underwater breaks; anything to accelerate the passing of the water.

It was working. Everywhere were signs of returning life: in some places, a mere trail of ranunculus; in others, true beds of weed, thick green masses nourishing shrimp and nymphs, creating larders for trout. The water, as pure as ever, was moving again, although with nothing like the volume and force which I remembered when the fishery was in its prime. The springs at the Kennet's source were still too depleted to guarantee wellbeing. The patient had returned from near death to convalescence, its strength returning, but slowly, slowly. It had a dedicated carer in the shape of John Hounslow, to cosset it. But its ultimate fate was beyond the power of mere men to determine. It was up to nature to do its stuff, to let the gentle rain drop from heaven, and keep dropping.

More often, though, the blight afflicting a river is the work of men, and nature can do no more than stand as a witness, awaiting the opportunity to repair the damage. It is in these circumstances that the angler, whether acting singly or in a band, can change the way things are, can be a force for good. Metropolitan campaigners against field sports sneer that this concern springs from self-interest: you want to keep the rivers clean so there are more fish for you to kill. Wearily, you may attempt to explain that a clean river is, of itself, better than a poisoned one; add that if the self-interest of anglers brings this about, then that self- interest is, of itself, beneficial. On the other hand, you might be better advised to keep silent, and reserve your energies for doing something about our world, rather than wasting them on those who spout, and do nothing.

Chapter Five - The Way We Live Now

There is a river in Surrey, the Wey, of which - until I saw it - I knew nothing beyond its name, and the fact that, 130 years ago, eggs were taken from its trout and successfully shipped to New Zealand, Tasmania and the Australian mainland. It is a little stream, and it follows a sinuous, leisurely course through a hidden, wooded valley, a cheerful, modest, sweet water. But the morning I saw it, there was something horribly wrong. The surface was unbroken by any sign of life. A human shadow over the water provoked no answering scurry across the gravel bottom. It was a trout stream, without trout.

A few weeks before, it had been the picture of vitality. Inside an hour during the mayfly season, the owner, Peter Whitfield, had caught and returned six wild brown trout, weighing between one-and-a-quarter and one-and-three-quarter pounds. Whitfield has cherished and nourished his two miles of river for 25 years. His pleasure, as a wealthy man, is to maintain his property as a sanctuary for the wild creatures of the countryside. His river is for indigenous brown trout and there are no stocked arrivistes. Whitfield was a witness to the consequences of the outrage of that August morning. As was his custom, he had paused on the bridge near his farmhouse to pay his respects to the half-dozen well-fed and sophisticated trout resident in the pool below. On this occasion, the water was manure brown. A few coarse fish thrashed at the surface in de-oxygenated death throes. The trout, almost all of them, were already dead.

The source of the pollution was the sewage treatment works a couple of miles upstream at Bordon. Whitfield summoned officials from the National Rivers Authority, who took samples. There was talk of a prosecution, but Thames Water took refuge in a pernicious piece of nonsense known as the 95 percent rule, under which a sewage treatment plant could fail up to five percent of the quality checks carried out by the NRA without being hauled up before the courts. The message had, however, got through: that Peter Whitfield was not a man to stand by and allow something he treasured to be fouled. Money was spent on improving the sewage works, the water in the Wey was returned to its former purity, and nature was left to tilt the balance back. Now the Wey is restored, and once again the

The Far From Compleat Angler

native trout raise their noses to sup the mayfly in the pool below Peter Whitfield's bridge.

In Ireland, the horrors of pollution have a grossness and brutality which is unusual in England. The Irish are blessed with a wealth of waters. But landowners like Peter Whitfield, with the muscle and determination to stand up for a little trout river, are virtually unknown. By and large, the fishing is in the hands of clubs which pay trifling rents, collecting trifling sums in subscriptions, and are weak against the power of the poisoners. But this is not to say that Irish anglers are unconcerned. They have the same passion for their waters as anywhere else, and every now and then a minor triumph is achieved against the odds.

The Suir is the most magnificent trout river in Ireland, wide, deep, rich, bursting with food, with an astounding stock of highly selective, well-fed trout. The best of it flows through County Tipperary, the Republic's agricultural heartland, and as a result it has been the victim of an endless succession of crimes. In the main, these have been incidents, acts of ignorance, carelessness, recklessness, spite, and downright criminal intent; and the river, like an indestructible boxer hit by a low blow, has staggered, then fought on, sustained by its own, miraculous fertility.

But the first time I visited the Suir, a more insistent force was at work. We were on the stretch below the friendly country town of Cahir. It is known as Swiss Cottage, after the pleasure house which was built beside it by the Charterises, when they owned the estates. It is a simply superb piece of water, with great beech woods on one bank, and open meadows on the other, framing a succession of broad pools, each of which has a variety of water and head of fish sufficient to keep the angler occupied for a day, if not a week. On this September day, though, there was something rotten in the air. There was a sweet, sickly smell hanging over the river. The great beds of weed were pale, as if infected; and the gravel runs between were clogged with something vile.

It was fat, animal fat, a foul layer of grease coating the bed of the river as if it were an unwashed frying pan. The stink was that of the abattoir. There was a factory on the edge of town, producing meat pies, black pudding and the like; and the unused muck was

Chapter Five - The Way We Live Now

being spewed untreated into the clear water of one of the finest trout river in Europe. The factory owners had told the Cahir Anglers, who control many miles of the Suir, that they couldn't afford to install equipment to deal with the fat. It would compromise the viability of the plant, on which many local people depended for jobs. It was a lie, of course. The Cahir Anglers kept up the pressure, we added our voices to the clamour, the newspapers took it up - and now, many years later, the factory is still going, and a comparatively low-fat Suir is continuing to provide some of the best and most testing trout fishing that I know.

Sometimes, however, it is not that simple. Sometimes the angler, having done his best and made his pitch, has to acknowledge that his interests cannot always be paramount; that there are other, competing interests which may be as legitimate as his own. This was brought forcibly home to me in the case of possibly the most celebrated and lovely piece of chalkstream fishing in southern England, the Bourne in Hampshire. Its song was sung in one of the masterpieces of angling literature, Plunket Greene's *Where The Bright Waters Meet*.

For a decade before the Great War, he had made his home in the village of Hurstbourne Priors. It lies across the meadows from the Bourne - 'in those days,' Plunket Greene wrote, 'unquestionably the finest small trout stream in England.' Small is the word, for the average width is perhaps twelve to fifteen feet. It is deeper than it looks, though, the impression of shallowness being intensified by the amazing clarity of the water, in which every stone, every trail of weed, and every trout can be seen. There is nothing miniature about the trout of the Bourne. Fish of a pound upwards abound, while two-pounders are reasonably common, and three-pounders are there. They prosper because conditions for them are just about ideal. The water is pure, the volume constant, and the feeding prodigiously rich.

But there is one part of this exquisite fishery where no such plenty is found - no shrimp, no caddis, no trout. It is at the top, immediately below the viaduct which carries the railway towards Salisbury, where the river is split into two tiny channels. Plunket Greene begins his book by recalling the view, and the capture one August day of three wild trout from the left-hand channel (looking downstream) which weighed between one-and-a-half and three-and-a-quarter pounds.

The Far From Compleat Angler

Nowadays, the view from the viaduct is pretty much as it was in Plunket Greene's golden era - with one significant difference. Immediately upstream, where in his day the Bourne wound its way towards St Mary Bourne, is a great, green expanse of watercress. It is owned by a company called Hampshire Watercress, which sells its product under the name Vitacress, and is the biggest producer of the stuff in Europe. Sales of watercress have boomed in the age of health consciousness. It looks healthy eating, and is. But, naturally enough, there has to be a refinement of it between its condition in the wild, seething with freshwater shrimp and larvae of one sort or another, and its bug-free neutrality on the shelves at M&S or Safeway. In short, it has to be dosed to get rid of the insects and crustacea. It is also vulnerable to an ailment known as crook disease, which is akin to club root and requires the application of zinc sulphate to control it.

The Bourne anglers first noticed in 1981 that there was something wrong with the channel which emerges below the cress farm. By 1987 it was virtually devoid of fish. The scientists investigated, and found that the shrimp and other invertebrates had disappeared, and with them the trout. The depopulation had coincided with a steep increase in production at the cress farm. But, try as they might, the boffins could not establish a correlation between whatever chemicals were being sprayed on the cress, and the exodus below. They could do nothing more than express their suspicion that a factor might be the presence of zinc, deposited in the silt washed down from the farm.

The Company, Hampshire Watercress, did everything asked of them. They were meticulous in observing effluent standards, and installed traps to collect the silt. When I approached the Managing Director, he asked helplessly what more he could do. The only solution - to restore for the benefit of half-a-dozen trout fishermen a short stretch of river - would have been to shut down the farm altogether, putting several score of employees out of work. Such a step was patently absurd, as I admitted.

So the top beat, where Plunket Greene had his great day nearly a century ago, remains oddly lifeless. The last time I was there, in September 1994, there was still very little in the way of invertebrate life, and I saw no trout. But let us keep a sense of proportion about

Chapter Five - The Way We Live Now

this. Downstream towards Hurstbourne Priors, there is a stretch from the church up to the road bridge, which the previous summer - 1993 - had been in a parlous condition. Lack of flow over successive summers and winters had left the gravel bed choked by a carpet of silt. The emerald ranunculus had been invaded by the dread blanketweed, and - despite the continued presence of the trout - there was a darkness, a lifelessness about it. But what a transformation a year of decent rainfall had wrought. The silt had been washed away, the blanketweed repulsed, the gravel shone again. Despite all its vicissitudes, a doctor would have pronounced the Bourne to be in a pretty chipper state.

6. A Ragbag, Medley, or Pot-pourri

On Bridges

The fisherman who is kept from his fishing requires an occasional glimpse of water if he is not to become peevish and dispirited. The odd sighting of sunlight on a gleaming surface, preferably accompanied by a weeping willow or two, provides balm for the soul oppressed by the daily grind. That is why we anglers treasure bridges.

A thousand times, passing back and forth along the M4 near Reading, I have felt a surge of irritation and frustration. It afflicts me at the same spot, where the motorway crosses the Loddon, the Berkshire river on which - a few miles downstream - I learned my fishing as a lad. The bridge is an ugly thing, but that is to be expected. Its unforgiveable offence is that its discoloured grey slabs of concrete forbid any view of the water below. I know the river is there, but I am denied its healing influence. That bridge is a thoroughly ill-natured object.

The Far From Compleat Angler

Towards London, the same motorway crosses the Thames. Aesthetically speaking, this bridge is equally bankrupt. But it has one, immense, saving grace. It is edged by railings which permit a brief but sustained sight of our greatest river. There are boats, islands, jetties, trees, waterfowl. Heading to or away from the vile metropolis, I am cheered by it.

There is another Thames bridge that I love dearly, although it is a good many years since I stood on it, rod in hand. It is a long, elegant, three-arched affair in warm red brick, which curves over one part of the river at Sonning. Just upstream of it, on the right bank, stands a massive chestnut tree, with branches trailing to the water. A great bed of underwater cabbages extends from the foot of the bridge to those branches. This green jungle was the haunt of pike.

We used to stand on the narrow pavement, lean out over the water, and swing a livebait towards the chestnut. When the pike were on the feed, it was unusual for the float to travel more than a few feet before shooting under. Often we could see the pike dash from cover to seize the bait. Then it was a matter of dragging the beast across to the other side, where it could be netted from the towpath. They fought like fury, but rarely weighed more than five pounds or so, although once - fishing with a deadbait from the downstream side of the bridge - I hooked one which sailed with irresistible force up under the middle arch, and broke me in the shadows.

There were several other bridges at Sonning which used to occupy our attention, although none matched the red brick one in gracefulness. My eldest brother, fishing from the footbridge, hooked the legendary monster pike of the area, which had a reputation for devouring ducks, snapping at swans and the like. It rolled over and snapped his line as if it had been thread. Just upstream from the footbridge was the mill, with another bridge. As I have mentioned before, this was the scene of my substantial fishing baptism, and many were the murky dawns which found us lined up along the iron parapet, waiting for the chub and barbel to show an interest. Where the millstream met the main river, below this bridge, a swirling eddy was created which, in autumn, was another fine spot for pike. We would drift herrings around it, suspended under old-fashioned pike bungs shaped like turnips. On one occasion, my brother Matthew

Chapter Six - A Ragbag, Medley, or Pot-pourri

got his herring entangled in a bramble on the near bank, and went downstream to free it, leaving his rod and new Ambidex fixed spool reel propped up on the bridge. Having retrieved the bait, he lobbed it back into the current, whereupon it toppled his rod and reel over the edge, and into the water.

My favourite bridge view of all is on my favourite trout river of all, the Eden, beside the village of Langwathby. The road from Langwathby to Penrith used to cross the river by a beautiful, humped red sandstone bridge. This survived for three hundred years or so, until it was washed away by a mighty flood about thirty years ago, and replaced by a dismal steel and concrete structure. But it remains a wonderful vantage point from which to survey a great breadth of water, assess river height and colour, and scan for swooping swifts and rising trout.

Fishing beneath bridges, particularly low bridges, is an awkward business. It is tricky to propel the fly to the right spot, and more so to tell what is happening in the gloom. I remember spending half an afternoon on a big fish which was feeding noisily in the darkness under a tiny brick bridge on a Kennet sidestream. Eventually, after much cursing, I managed to shoot the fly well up into the tunnel, struck when I heard a gulp, and pulled out a hideous hook-jawed horror of three-and-a-half pounds which gave scarcely a kick in protest.

In contrast, there was a bridge on a surging mountain stream in Slovakia, whose functional nastiness was mitigated by the snowy peaks of the High Tatras in the distance beyond. Wading up from below, I came across a pocket of trout under each arch, picking off the hatching olives with cheerful abandon in the shadows. I emerged the other side with a brace and a half of fat half-pounders, which brought a mighty grin to the normally mournful features of my friend Slavo, the local vet.

I can see other bridges now: one in Transylvania which framed the setting sun and the rises of a cluster of good grayling; half a dozen sturdy stone ones in Ireland, standing invitations to stop and peer; another in Ireland, beside Ashford Castle, on which Miheal Ryan stood smoking a cigarette and drinking Guinness, before turning to pick up his net and fetch the boat, because he had seen the salmon

The Far From Compleat Angler

rise to my fly; a wooden footbridge at Wargrave, with the feet of the postman sounding on it as we sat in the boat below where the barbel lurked.

A bridge is a test. No true fisherman can pass one without lingering, or at least turning for that cheering glimpse. I have in mind the denouement of a detective story. My detective hero, a piscatorial Morse, is with the chief suspect. The villain's hitherto unbreakable alibi depends in some way - the details are a trifle sketchy - on him passing himself off as a passionate angler. With our hero beside him, the murderer drives over a supremely seductive bridge, with a glittering trout stream below. But he looks neither right nor left. Our man, having marked down a two-pounder rising by the willows on the left, grabs the scoundrel with the cry: 'Impostor!' Well, I think it has possibilities.

The Character of Fish

I met a man in Cracow a few years ago who was, in a quiet way, the maddest angler I've ever encountered. Dissatisfied with merely outwitting trout, he wanted to know what it was like to be a trout. To this end, he would swim on his back, underwater, in the icy Dunajec - which flows down from the Tatras - looking up at the surface to observe the food trout eat. He told me he'd sampled some mayflies and found them disappointingly tasteless. The extent - if any - to which Andrzej achieved the desired identification was obscure. But, without going to similar extremes, I do sometimes find myself speculating on the character of fishes, and of the society they comprise. I am not talking here of macho fish, muscled monsters of the deep like mako, marlin, broadbill tuna, sawfish. For them - fish to shatter a man's strength and forge his spirit in fire - you must search the oceans.

The freshwater world is different, smaller in scale, more orderly, its citizens generally law-abiding and aware of their place in the hierarchy. Take the tench, for instance: to Walton, it was the physician, curing the ailments of other fish with the balm contained

Chapter Six - A Ragbag, Medley, or Pot-pourri

in its slime. Of course this is tosh. Neither is the tench an elemental force of the deep. Rather, it is a lovely, golden-olive, smooth-scaled bottom-feeder; a quiet, peaceable inhabitant of placid canals and dark, reed-fringed ponds.

But ruminating anthropomorphically, I could indeed see the tench as a GP in a country practice: solid, respected, a source of sound advice and well-tested prescriptions. He is sensible enough, but in terms of brainpower must yield to the carp, whose supremacy as a repository of wisdom is undisputed. The carp is large, ponderous, with great, mailed flanks, a vast, rubbery mouth, and a mighty tail. He, too, is a fish of still waters, old moats, monastery ponds and the like. His authority and reputation for sagacity spring from his size, and the difficulty anglers traditionally experience in catching him. I see him as the senior partner in a long-established law firm - a fair and moral influence, but sharp-witted as well; and much admired in the community for his work on local charities and as chairman of the school governors.

The carp rubs along nicely with the tench, for philosophically they have much in common. But he has a powerful prejudice against his nearest rival in terms of size - the pike. The pike is a dangerous, troublesome element in society: a savage, greedy, unscrupulous predator, immune to civilising forces. For his part, the pike fears the carp for his superior learning, and despises him for eating worms and grubs when there are so much more substantial meals around. The pike is a ruthless and dynamic self-made businessman - a property tycoon, perhaps, or hungry asset-stripper. I admire him for his dash, but I think the carp would make the more reliable friend.

I would be happy, too, to make a friend of the chub. I like chub - most anglers do. He could be a customs man, an electrician, even a hack. It would not really matter. The thing about the chub is that he is a family man, can take a joke, is keen on rugby and cricket, always stands his round in the pub. And I am fond of perch. They are handsome fellows, with their black stripes across olive sides, and red fins. They bristle with pugnacity and commonsense - would make good police officers, backbench MPs of the no-compromise tendency, teachers of the old school.

The Far From Compleat Angler

The roach, on the other hand, is fastidious and delicate - in publishing, I should say, or playing woodwind in a symphony orchestra. Bream are slab-sided and devoid of imagination, given to making dull speeches at dull council meetings. Eels are slimy and sinister: offering loans to the gullible at murderous rates of interest. In the main, the coarse fish are professional types. The gilded nobility, of course, is drawn from the salmonidae, with the salmon as monarch, the trout in its finery as prince and princess, and the grayling as topdrawer aristocracy.

But how, you may wonder, might I see myself, were I to be catapulted into the water sphere? I should like to think that I combined the wisdom of the carp with the athletic glory of the salmon, the natty elegance of the chalkstream trout with the hidden menace of the pike, the explosive power of the marlin with the........

No, no, not really. I would be content as a chub, or better still, as a barbel: big, but not bloated, handsome but not effete, strong but definitely not macho, thoughtful, even a bit moody at times, but at bottom (which is where the barbel feeds) a thoroughly decent, dependable yeoman farmer type.

Eels in High Places

Warning: there are aspects of the following narrative which some may find offensive. There is no sex, gratuitous or otherwise; and all gross and vile language has been edited out. But there are scenes which may be considered depraved. They involve, among other things, a manure heap, a container of worms, and a bucket of live eels. I fear, too, that I may incur the disgust of the purist/traditionalist - the man who splutters at one-day cricket, quivers indignantly at the idea of rugby union going professional, and believes politicians should put the interests of the country before their own. If such a man knows anything about the river Test in Hampshire, he will take a dim view of someone who, invited to fish the most celebrated trout stream in the world, arrives harbouring ambitions against eels.

Chapter Six - A Ragbag, Medley, or Pot-pourri

It is difficult to convey to a non-angler the degree of the impropriety. To arrive at a Buckingham Palace garden party wearing a tee-shirt and Bermuda shorts, to walk out at Lords with a baseball bat, to shoot at a crow on a grouse moor - this might give some idea of my offence. I could not help myself, though. I know I should have been thinking of trout as I bowled down the Test valley past villages like Bossington and Mottisfont, hallowed by dry fly men through the ages. But the eels kept intruding, and in the boot, next to the fly rod and waders, was the infamous eel tackle.

The eel gets a bad press. It is despised and reviled, relegated to the piscatorial ghetto. Its appearance is hideous. Its sliminess and convulsive muscularity make it horrible to touch. Its feeding habits are not salubrious, for it is the scavenger of the depths. It skulks in dark places, crawls along ditches at night, and travels half way round the world to mate. But I have a soft spot for them, and so does my friend Stevie. And as it was going to be a long day and a hot one, and we knew that the trout would be most unlikely to rise properly until the evening, we felt no shame to be rooting through the manure heap for nasty brandling worms.

While the others dozed in the heat of the afternoon, we, the hunters, hunted. We prowled the banks, scouring the water for the tell-tale wave of an eelish tail or the movement of a questing snout. They showed up well against the pale, chalky bottom. Then the fun began. The skill was to land a bunch of worms a foot or so above the snout, to spot the bait on the bottom, and to wait for the savour to activate the eel's foraging instincts. As often as not, the snout would eventually move up towards the worms, descend on them, and drift away. A sharp strike, a brief tussle, and the thrashing beast was on the bank. A boot was jammed on its neck while the hook was removed, and into the bucket it went.

It took us a little time to master this new art. With only one rod between us, there were inevitable arguments of a who-does-what nature. The heat and the tension rendered us somewhat overwrought. Worms were cast round rushes, bites were missed, oaths were uttered. But by the end of a gruelling session, there were half-a-dozen good eels in the bucket, and the talk was of fillets on the barbecue.

Stevie, an expert in such matters, described the technique of skinning the creatures. Nails came into it, and pliers, but I shall spare you the grislier details.

I would, however, like to commend the attitude taken by our hosts. They were initially uncomprehending. Requests for a garden fork and directions to the manure heap were received with bemusement. But when they knew we were happy, they were happy too, which made them the best sort of hosts. The children - of whom there were a number - found live eels much more entertaining than dead trout. The offer of a fiver to the first who dared place a naked foot in the eel bucket provoked a lively half-hour.

Come evening, and the lengthening of the shadows, and our minds were at last recalled to higher things, such as the noble trout. As the sun declined, taking the glare off the water, the river came to life. Sedges began to hatch, and the trout to chase them. Stevie, who had taken off his trousers because of the heat and was standing in the middle of the river in a pair of green-checked boxer shorts, rose and missed the same fish four times. He looked at his hook, found there wasn't one, put on a new fly, caught a chub and yelled with rage and disbelief. Soon, though, he was catching proper fish. We all were.

A glowing moon rose behind us, and between it and the molten sky in the west flowed the Test, dark and alive with feeding fish. I had a brace of spanking grayling and three trout, all of which I returned. The last trout was a violent bruiser which must been close on four pounds. By the time I had eased him back, full darkness had closed in. Thanks to Test trout, Test eels and kind friends, it had been a magical day.

Let's Hear it From the Expert

The word has a fine, satisfying resonance to it: 'He's something of an expert on...' or 'You know, she's the leading expert in her field...' Yes, it must be a grand thing to be acknowledged as an expert. But how do you set about it? It cannot be done by self proclamation. To introduce your contribution by saying: 'Actually, I'm a bit of an expert on...' is

Chapter Six - A Ragbag, Medley, or Pot-pourri

to invite derision. I know, because I've tried it. No, it has to be done by the acclamation of others. You must infiltrate their collective consciousness, blind them with your science, grasp every opportunity to impress upon them the vast reach of your knowledge. You need unshakeable self-belief and a powerful streak of arrogance - though this you must disguise with affectations of humility, otherwise your audience will merely hate you. The final ingredient - helpful but not essential - is a bare modicum of expertise.

When considering my own qualifications to be counted among the great congregation of angling experts, I must be clear-headed. I have never had an original thought about the techniques of the sport in the thirty odd years I have been at it. I depend now, and always will, on the inspirations of others. On the other hand, I should like to think that I am sufficiently quick-witted to master the art of passing off other people's bright ideas as my own. My fatal flaw is self-belief. Sooner or later, the would-be expert has to put himself to the test; to expose his expertise to public scrutiny. I have now done this. I found the experience rather humbling, and have decided to return to the ranks of the non-expert.

I had been inveigled into joining a panel of authorities to field questions from the Berkshire branch of the Salmon and Trout Association. I was a late replacement for that celebrated scourge of spies and spymasters, Chapman Pincher. With me on the platform were two undoubted thoroughbreds from the breed of true expert: Neil Patterson, a brilliant chalkstream fisher and outstanding fly dresser; and John Maitland, a member of the British fly fishing team and a renowned extractor of monster trout from Rutland Water. The first question concerned barbless hooks, and I made an ass of myself by regurgitating some theory I had half-read in an American magazine that morning. Then a lady asked the panel if it considered the colour of a fly line to be a matter of importance. 'Tom,' the chairman said to me, 'any thoughts on that one?'

Well, my own fly line was once white and is now grey and cracked with age and abuse. What concerns me, however, is not its colour, but its habit of sinking when it should be floating. I told the questioner that I used whatever line I happened to have until I could use it no more, then bought the cheapest possible replacement. I could tell from her expression that this was not the expert's reply.

Someone else wondered if the panel had a particular tactic for those glaring summer days when not a fish will rise. I suggested going home, or going to sleep under a hedge. Neil Patterson proposed using a bluebottle fly. I could tell which answer impressed, and it was not mine. So it went on. Did the panel regard a salmon fly tied on a treble hook superior to a double? The matter had never crossed my mind. Why did so many right-handed anglers hold their rods in their left hands? I could not remember which hand I did use. Someone asked if fish could hear. I said they surely could - but did they dream? At least that got a laugh.

Afterwards everyone, from the chairman down, was most kind. But I felt naked, and I know now that I am not cut out to be an expert. I don't even want to be one. When you think about it, what is the synonym for expert? Know-all, which isn't half so pleasing. No, let me be an anonymous, amateurish mediocrity any day.

Lies, Damned Lies and Fishermen's Tales

My text is a paragraph from the *Daily Telegraph*: 'A monster mirror carp weighing 20lb was hooked out of the River Waveney in Norfolk yesterday. The angler claimed that the successful bait was a pork pie'.

In not much more than two dozen words, the writer achieves a compression of ignorance and prejudice which borders on the miraculous. Unhappily, it is a combination all too typical of the way in which the uninformed view the angler and his sport. Let me deal first with the 'monster mirror carp'. It is nothing of the sort. It is a fine specimen and larger by far than any I have ever caught. But a glance at the angling press will show that, each week, half a dozen bigger mirror carp are recorded - fish above 30lb and even 40lb. We proceed to the inelegant compound verb 'hooked out'. This is a ludicrous solecism. One might as well have Nick Faldo 'putting off' in the Open. Fish are hooked. They are then caught, or they escape.

Chapter Six - A Ragbag, Medley, or Pot-pourri

It is at the start of the second sentence that we arrive at the truly pernicious part of the text: 'The angler claimed that...' I would submit that this is an open invitation to the reader - an incitement, even - to get ready to disbelieve. It is a signal: 'Pay attention, improbable assertion approaching'. The warning is amply justified by the final seven words ...' the successful bait was a pork pie'. This is patently absurd. The carp has a fair-sized mouth and a healthy appetite, but it could no more swallow an entire pork pie than I could a dead alligator. The effect of this nonsense - whether intended or not - is to provoke a hoot of derision, and that monstrous slur: 'Typical fisherman's tale'.

That, of course, means fisherman's lie. How the myth about the angler's shaky grasp on reality entered the public consciousness, I do not know. But it is a constant component of the image, along with green umbrellas, illimitable and idiotic patience, imperviousness to foul weather, maggots in the fridge, and a few others.

There is a droll anecdote to illustrate the canard, told by the writer Patrick Chalmers. He was fishing a Thames weirpool and hooked one of the big trout that lurk in those turbulent places. He saw the fish clearly before it broke away. A friend appeared and asked for a visual impression of the fish's size. Chalmers held up his hands, two feet or so apart. A few months later he was surprised - and initially pleased - to come across a picture in a London magazine of himself beside the weirpool, hands apart. He admired the elegance of the scene, and congratulated himself on the modesty of his estimate of the trout's proportions. Then he saw the caption: 'The Liar'.

I have met out-and-out liars among the angling fraternity. I recall a man with a bald head and staring eyes, from whom I used to buy books. He would bombard me with highly coloured accounts of the great fish he had outwitted. One day he told me of a lake and stream in Surrey, from which he claimed to have caught seven trout of more than seven pounds each. This, I think, was a falsehood.

However, in general the fisherman's vices are more often those of exaggeration, omission and unwitting distortion rather than of outright intent to deceive. For example, there is the mysterious way in which fish which were nearly, but not quite captured, grow in size over the years with the retelling of the account of their escape. The great pike which my eldest brother hooked from the footbridge at Sonning was one such. At the time its weight was estimated as 25 pounds. The last I heard it was 40 and still rising.

It is only natural that the fish which get away should be bigger than the ones which don't; partly because it makes some sense that they should; and partly because it is healing to the wounded spirit to believe that the trout confounded us because it was bigger, stronger and more cunning than any other in the river - rather than because we made a hash of things. In the same way, it is merely human to blame our failures on outside agencies - mainly the weather - rather than on ourselves; to see the triumphs of other anglers as being due to luck, privilege, or inside knowledge unfairly acquired, and our own as the just reward for virtue and skill.

I would not deny that anglers tend to be - shall we say? - relaxed in their regard for the literal truth. But it is unfair to interpret this behaviour as evidence of congenital weakness of character. Rather, let us see it as an imaginative response to the glory of the sport. I present the fisherman, not as fibber, but as artist.

The Fashion Page

A dubious acquaintance of mine, when asked why he habitually wears his jersey tucked into the trousers, replied: 'It makes me feel together'. So it is with the angler. The catching of fish is much, but not all. The angler must be equipped and attired in a manner to make him or her feel 'together'. I concede that I am no fashion icon myself, but I hope my advice may be of use.

The subject of tackle is too vast to be embraced in detail here, so I shall confine myself to one guiding principle. Having arrived at some idea of what you need and how much you may safely spend, you must find a proper fishing tackle shop - one where you may test the merchandise and be wisely advised. Sadly, such places are thin on the ground.

The proper fishing tackle shop may sell guns and country clothing as well, but not much else. Premises displaying baseball bats, windsurfing boards and snooker cues should be avoided.

Chapter Six - A Ragbag, Medley, or Pot-pourri

Preferably, there will be a stuffed fish or two, staring down from on high. It is reassuring to spot photographs of customers with great fish stuck on the wall. The proprietor and his assistants will be people of great tact and sensitivity. They will know when to advise, and when to be silent; when to ask the customer how his annual fishing holiday has gone, and when to refrain; when to tell of their own achievements (in order to encourage), and when to conceal them (to avoid exciting envy). They must be able to tell when to recommend a leap into the unknown, and when to yield to intractable prejudice. They must, above all, avoid the impression of impatience; for if they are unaware that buying a new rod is more than a commercial transaction, they are useless.

Appearance is a more controversial issue. My own has aroused its fair share of mockery over the years; actually, rather more than its fair share. I therefore offer my opinions with some diffidence. But let us start at the top. The hat. I bought my longest surviving one in Ireland. At that time it had a label inside proclaiming it to be the Blarney Walking Hat. The label has long gone, as has the shape, which was flat. The lining is torn, where the dog got hold of it. It does not keep out the rain, does not protect the eyes. Indeed it performs no identifiable function whatever - except that when I have it on, I catch more fish than when I don't.

So, the flat cap of subdued hue may be regarded as a safe bet. Some favour wide-brimmed tweed affairs, or bush hats, or even sun hats. It does not matter too much, as long as it does not channel rain down the back of your neck; and - a much more important proviso - it is not festooned with flies. Flies belong in boxes, which belong in bags or pockets.

The shirt should be nondescript. One of those country checks will do very well. T-shirts, in particular white T-shirts, will not do at all. These days almost no one - bar ghillies and rich people on snooty Scottish salmon rivers - wears a tie. The tweed jacket, which was once *de rigeur*, has gone the same way. But the jacket question is a tricky one. A great many anglers wear, or carry, dark green waxed cotton jackets. These are all very well, as long as they are old and worn and peppered with holes and tears. The disadvantage is that, being old and worn and full of holes, they do not keep out the rain - in my experience, even when thoroughly rewaxed. On the other hand, fishing in the rain should be avoided anyway. I have two waxed jackets, one lined and one unlined. Neither is waterproof. The unlined is more useful, in that it can be kept in a bag until required, and can be worn inside chest waders.

We come now to the waistcoat controversy. Now, there are sound men who cannot abide them. Murmurs of 'non-U' and 'naff' are heard. I was one of the anti school, until I got one. I admit that it looks awful. But aesthetic deficiencies are, in my view, outweighed by the inexhaustible usefulness of the thing. The fly fisherman can keep almost everything he needs in its pockets, leaving his bag for his rolled up jacket and (we may hope) his fish.

Trousers are of little moment, since they are mostly invisible underneath the jacket and inside the waders. Plus fours are fine for the traditionalist; moleskins equally good. Jeans are unacceptable. As for the waders, these are usually made of green rubber, and always leak. They are very hot for walking distances in, but not as hot - I believe - as neoprene, which is hugely expensive and the colour of dung.

A final word about the overall impression to be aimed at. Apart from the waders - which are likely to be less leaky if reasonably new - everything else should have a well-used, even timeless air about it. This applies to tackle, too. An old brass and bamboo net is excellent. A cane rod with ancient aluminium reel will achieve a most positive effect, assuming you know what to do with them. You may even prefer a wickerwork creel to the usual canvas bag. Remember: the last thing you want anyone to think is that you have only just taken up the sport.

On the Box

Television coverage of the one-sided world chess championship between Nigel Short and Gary Kasparov extended to 75 hours, which was doubtless pleasing to Britain's extremely small band of chess enthusiasts. For the rest of us, I suspect that the spectacle of two

Chapter Six - A Ragbag, Medley, or Pot-pourri

immensely brainy men thinking and then moving their pieces, and assorted lesser brainboxes trying to divine what they were thinking about and why they moved their pieces where they did, was not very interesting. But it set me pondering on television's scurvy treatment of the country's most popular participatory sport, fishing.

On the whole, this reflects a general prejudice: an absurd picture of a man sitting under a green umbrella beside a murky canal staring through the rain at a motionless float. I fear there are few anglers to be found in the councils of the programme-makers. Whatever the bias at work, I doubt if the total of hours given to angling since television was invented would greatly exceed the time devoted to Kasparov's heavy menace and Short's pink gums and pebbly spectacles.

There are obvious factors inhibiting fishing from rivalling, say, darts or wrestling as television spectacles. It is true that for long periods not very much happens; and that when it does, the excitement lies more in the heart of the fisherman than in the event itself. In addition, the very presence of a heavy-footed cameraman waving his lens about is inimical to the catching of fish.

But it can be done. Many years ago the BBC screened a first-rate series called *An Angler's Corner*, in which the incomparable Bernard Venables chewed his pipe, tugged his beard and paraded his wisdom and skill. Jack Hargreaves made umpteen decent, unpretentious films for Southern TV. More recently Jack Charlton and John Wilson have made series which - whatever reservations one might have about the antics of the chief performers - have at least given an idea of what fishing is like. And I confess that I have warmed considerably towards the Channel 4 programme, *Screaming Reels,* and its engaging presenter, Nick Fisher.

None of these, however, remotely approached the series which ran on BBC 2 a couple of years ago, *A Passion For Angling.* For beauty, truth, excitement and eloquence, this stands alone. What the film-maker Hugh Miles did was to recruit two of Britain's finest fishermen, Bob James and Chris Yates, and to allow them to follow their noses - while he, camera in hand, crept along behind. Yates is probably the best writer on fishing in the land, and James is his chum. Together, they were given the time and the space to present a coherent

The Far From Compleat Angler

philosophy of fishing, and to display, with commendable modesty, their astonishing accomplishments as anglers.

Of course, there were disadvantages to this highly personal, ruminative, intentionally poetic approach. As you sit beside a reedy lake watching the sun begin to suck off the dawn mist, your mind is liable to be suffused with sub-Wordsworthian images. Putting them into words which are neither syrupy nor pretentious is tricky; and having them articulated by Bernard Cribbins sometimes proved a risk too far. The music - all sighing strings and mellow chirruping woodwind - reinforced this slightly precious impression of the waterside idyll, established in the first place by Hugh Miles' miraculous camerawork. Nor, in the first programme, was I at all enraptured by the starring role given to the lad, Pete, complete with his bamboo and string and squashed tweed hat.

But these were minor cavils, compared with the marvels. The second adventure in particular - on Redmire Pool, legendary home of monstrous carp - was simply tremendous. Here, our heroes shed their self-consciousness as they contemplated the stately giants of this fabled water. The moment at which Yates' second big fish opened its rubbery lips to engulf the floating dog biscuit was almost unbearably thrilling. And the sight of the intrepid duo leaping from the upper branches of a tree up to their waists in mud and water to do battle with another leviathan eclipsed anything a paunchy darts demon or pasty-faced snooker prodigy might conjure.

I know perfectly well that this represented a highly selective, and romanticised tithe of the whole truth. The boredom, the occasional wretchedness, the rages, the heartbreak, the absurdity were either absent, or sentimentalised. But what television can do, at its best, is to give an authentic, intense taste of a reality; and that is what these programmes did. The best test is whether they would make a fisherman wish to fish. Within an hour of watching the impossibly angelic urchin Pete catch his 9lb barbel from the Hampshire Avon, I was seated beside my own favourite barbel swim, on the Kennet. I was maddened by midges, missed a succession of good bites, and in the end caught - not a barbel - but a tench of four pounds. That is real fishing.

Chapter Six - A Ragbag, Medley, or Pot-pourri

No, Robert, it's not Like That

A River Runs Through It is Hollywood's loving embrace of fly fishing, the one with the poster showing an angler with old-fashioned hat standing on a rock in a glittering river, with his line irradiated above his head by sunlight bursting through trees. Very evocative. Ever since Robert Redford brought his intensely sincere and reverential treatment of Norman MacLean's piscatorial novella to London, people who have never before exhibited the smallest interest in my obsession have been asking me: 'Is fly fishing really like that?'

In considering my reply, I have remembered the scoffing, the sneering, the moralistic spoutings, the ignorance and bigotry which I have had to endure from the non-believers over the years. I have grown acutely aware that, while golf, gardening, cycling, aerobics, tennis, computer games and a host of other pointless activities are comprehensible to the metropolitan mind, fishing is not. It is regarded as an aberration. So I have been moved to sarcasm. Yes, of course, I say - come Saturday I shall be heading north-west from London on the M40 for the Big Blackfoot, where I shall pull on my old-world battered felt hat, take my hickory rod in my hand, nod to my similarly accoutred ne'er-do-well younger brother and sour-faced dad (taciturn, as befits a minister, but all heart), wade into the swift, limpid stream and within five minutes or so have a couple of wild, fighting two-pounders on the bank.

But it is immature to indulge one's spleen. Instead, I try to forget the injuries I have suffered in defending my sport, and the fact that it took a screen god to stir an interest in these backward souls. I say forcibly: it is nothing like that. There are no rivers like the Big Blackfoot, no trout like those trout. No, you do not feel a deep spiritual oneness with Nature as the water presses against your thighs. No, the sun does not shaft through the bankside foliage in beams that pulse with insect life. Fishing is hard work, uncomfortable, often boring. It rains a lot. The wind always blows in the wrong direction. You get into tangles. There are brief periods of action during which, as often as not, everything goes wrong and you want to shoot yourself.

The Far From Compleat Angler

For some reason they find the Robert Redford version more congenial than the truth according to Fort. There are murmurs of 'old curmudgeon... miserable git... dog in the manger', and some even more abusive. These people will not be persuaded of the gulf between Arcadian Montana circa 1920 and overcrowded polluted Britain in the 1990s. And in a way, yes, they are right about my attitude. A friend who runs a tackle shop expressed the hope that the film might inspire here, as it has in the US, an explosion of interest in fly fishing. But while I sympathise with his desire to drum up more trade, I do not share his hopes. There are already more than enough anglers for our overstressed waters to accommodate. The last thing we want is an influx of hillbilly impostors asking directions to the Home Counties equivalent of the Big Blackfoot.

If I sound a trifle irritable, it is because I found *A River Runs Through It* a trifle irritating. It is moderately enjoyable, nice to look at, half an hour too long, overloaded with metaphorical and metaphysical baggage, and takes itself and fishing far too seriously. But it did set me thinking about my own formative years. At the film's heart are the relationships between the two brothers who learn to fish together, and between them and their father, who teaches them. Although my father did not fish, two of my elder brothers did (one still does), and I learned with them.

In the mythic world of Montana, the brothers grow up together, fishing; grow apart, and do not fish; come together, and go fishing. Only when standing together in the riffles of the Big Blackfoot can they forge again the bond between them. The symbolism is weighty indeed. If there was any such spirituality in the bond between my brothers and myself, it must have been buried very deep. We went fishing together. We suffered together. We swore at each other. We laughed together. Yes, I still like to go fishing with the brother who still fishes. But I doubt if there is enough depth or current in the river of our relationship to encourage the camera to linger.

Amid all the sun-drenched fantasy of the film, there was one moment of truth which struck an answering chord in me. It comes when the elder brother, Norman, having caught one good fish, hooks another. Grinning in a superior fashion, he looks across at brother Paul; who sends back across the water a grim, desperate smile,

Chapter Six - A Ragbag, Medley, or Pot-pourri

suffused with rage and envy. I recall such a moment when my brother looked at me like that. I need say no more than that I had just caught a salmon, and he had not, and that he wished very much that he had. And there have been other times when he has returned from a distant pool with an insufferable expression on his face and a catch of trout which has made me queasy with jealousy. The moral, I'm afraid, is that the more ignoble the emotion, the more real it is. The rest is just Hollywood.

Curiouser and Curiouser

I am offering a prize. Two bottles of champagne, or a day's fishing on the Kennet, will go to anyone able to furnish credible evidence of having caught, by fair angling means, a specimen of *Salvethymus Svetovidovi*, otherwise known as Svetovidov's long-finned char. This is undoubtedly the most challenging angling contest ever devised; and I am quietly confident the prize will go unclaimed. For there are certain obstacles to the pursuit of this creature which, in fairness to the more adventurous readers of this book, I should mention.

For one thing, the fish is unique to one lake in the entire world. The lake is called El'gygytgyn, and is situated in central Chutoka. Quite where Chutoka is, I am not so sure. Somewhere in eastern Siberia, possibly. Wherever it is, Lake El'gygytgyn is unlikely to figure on the tourist agenda. According to my information - garnered from a translation of a learned Russian treatise - it is frozen solid for all but two months of the year. The climate is described as extremely harsh and the fauna as extremely sparse, which I think must be another way of saying that it is a God-forsaken, wind-whipped, snowbound, ice-encrusted hellhole of a place.

Assume, however, that the intrepid angler actually manages to find Lake El'gygytgyn during its ice-free summer. The problems are only just beginning, for the quarry still has to be caught using a rod, reel and line. The long-finned char prefers to swim at a depth of 150 feet or more. In addition, it is a demersal planktivore, which means that it takes its nourishment in the form of minute particles of

The Far From Compleat Angler

life which are beyond man's ingenuity to imitate. So, even if a means were devised to sink a bait or spinner into the fish's deep, dark world, the chances of a long-finned char responding would be remoter than Chutoka itself. I did say it was a challenge.

I have not been to Lake El'gygytgyn myself, nor would anything induce me to do so. But I can claim to be one of the few fishermen in England - quite possibly the only one - to have seen Svetovidov's longfinned char in the flesh. I can exclusively report that they are very small, very dark, with a very few tiny spots, and long fins. The only interesting thing about them, apart from their habitat, is that they are the first new species of salmonid to be identified in recent times. For this, the persevering Anatoly Nikolayevich Svetovidov, who first trawled one from El'gygytgyn's frigid depths, will be honoured by ichthyologists, if not by anglers.

I saw and indeed touched this rare creature in the basement of the Natural History Museum, whence it had just arrived in a bottle of preserving alcohol from Russia. I had gone to the museum at the kind invitation of the senior scientific officer, Gordon Howes, to inquire into the habits of the giant European catfish, and the legends associated with this mysterious and disgusting freshwater monster. From tales of catfish, great writhing horrors weighing up to seven hundred pounds, I had progressed to the mightiest fish of them all, the sturgeon; and had inspected an ancient photograph of a specimen hauled by rope from the Russian Dnieper, with fourteen men standing behind it, which weighed three thousand three hundred pounds, and produced more than a quarter of a ton of caviar.

I found it difficult not to be sidetracked when surrounded by the world's greatest collection of preserved fish, three-quarters of a million of them, some dating back three hundred years and more. Soon I was peering over Gordon Howes' shoulder into the dusty cabinets on whose shelves the fishes of the world gleam in their multitudes, heads down or standing on their tails in their jars of fluid. I asked him about the Goliath Tigerfish. I had caught the ordinary tigerfish on the Zambesi and Lake Kariba, and had heard tales of a gigantic cousin, of unparalleled ferocity, to be found somewhere in the dark heart of Africa. Had he heard of it? Mr Howes smiled gently. Not only had he heard of it, but he had it. He produced a jar the size of

Chapter Six - A Ragbag, Medley, or Pot-pourri

a coalskuttle in which a vast fish was suspended, jaws agape, vicious teeth glinting. I was at once fired with visions of tangling with the beast in some unexplored tributary of the Upper Congo (I have since been cured by reading of the hell which Paul Boote and Jeremy Wade experienced on the same trail, and recorded in *Somewhere Down The Crazy River*).

Among other river predators Howes showed me was an Amazonian fish which made the piranha look no more threatening than Charlie Bubbles, our lethargic goldfish. He scooped it from its bottle to display its oral weaponry. From its lower jaw rose two fangs so long that Nature had provided holes through the top of its snout to accommodate them. This was Hydrolocus, the wolf-fish, a creature of nightmares.

We went to Howes' office, where I glimpsed a half-dissected cod under a microscope. On another table was a minute butterfly fish from Indonesia, which had been presented to the museum by Mungo Park. Before giving me a friendly, fishy handshake, Gordon Howes presented me with a scientific paper arguing that the rainbow trout had been wrongly classified. I reeled out into the spring sunshine, exhilarated by the unusual experience of acquiring learning.

The Premier Pastime

Everyone needs a hobby, a consuming but frivolous means of escape from work, career, decorating the house, staring lugubriously at the bank statement and all the other inescapable but uninspiring aspects of life. Without such a release, we become dull and stale. This applies as much to politicians as anyone else. One of the more dispiriting characteristics of the breed is how hard they all work, and how little interest they seem to have in anything else. If the health and happiness of the nation increased in proportion to the hours devoted by ministers to their papers, we would now live in Nirvana. But we do not, so the whole approach is obviously flawed.

I am aware that the Prime Minister loves poring over the cricket averages and cheering on Chelsea football club. But that is

The Far From Compleat Angler

insufficient, and far too passive. He should beware the example of his hobby-less predecessor, who would have done well to take up ballooning or clay pigeon shooting. At least Edward Heath had his sailing and tinkling at the piano, while Harold Wilson had golf as well as his famous affection for Huddersfield Town.

Actually, I hope Major does not take up golf. Too many of our prime ministers have professed a fondness for this worthy but uninteresting game - among them Asquith, Bonar Law and Ramsay MacDonald. In any event, I believe the dicky state of his knees would preclude it. This handicap is a shame, for walking is a respectable pastime for a PM. Baldwin combined it with what the Dictionary of National Biography calls 'an affection for the atmosphere and simple fare of old country inns'.

Somehow, I cannot see Major emulating Palmerston, who loved horse-racing and killing animals in equal measure. Lord Aberdeen's passion - otter-hunting - would hardly be acceptable today. Pitt the Younger drank port, and Canning wrote poetry - neither of which seems quite in character for the present premier. Balfour listed motoring as his recreation, but no one in his right mind could motor for pleasure in this age.

It is a disturbing fact that only two of our prime ministers were serious fishermen: Neville Chamberlain and Sir Alec Douglas-Home. I fancy that MacMillan may have dabbled a bit, for I have seen a photograph of him in tweeds and flat cap, rod in hand, beside a famous Irish salmon river. But shooting birds was definitely more in his line. The fact that Chamberlain had a six pound Test trout to his credit suggests that he was no mean performer. There is a touching account in a book by John Rennie of a weekend on the Test, at which Chamberlain was a guest. The PM fished all day, caught the biggest trout, drank several glasses of port and 'in his enthusiasm reminded me much of a schoolboy on a weekend holiday'. It was May 1939; war, resignation and death were just around the corner.

The champion prime ministerial angler was Lord Home of the Hirsel. In his volume of sporting memoirs, *Border Reflections*, this most modest of demon fishermen hardly bothers to mention the capture of salmon up to 38lb, and sea trout to 16lb. He allows himself no more than one minor boast: an account of how, having left all his

Chapter Six - A Ragbag, Medley, or Pot-pourri

baits at home, he carved a lure from a piece of driftwood and caught six salmon with it. He is a trout man too - 'so give me a light trout rod, and the dry fly, and a stream which rises clear through moor or meadow, and I ask no more of the day'. Now, that is the prime minister for me!

So, it is clear that Major should take up fishing. He might find wading rivers after salmon and trout a bit arduous, given the state of his legs. But he could sit comfortably in a boat, or beside a lake; and since he would be able to command access to the best waters, he would surely catch something, if the detectives kept their heads down. Above all, the agonies and ecstasies of fishing would provide him with a fresh and comforting sense of proportion about the cares of his great office.

The Littlest Fish

We all know how highly Jeremy Fisher esteemed the minnow, although it is typical of the little fish's treatment over the ages - the way it has been, in the jargon, marginalised - that the frog's interest should have been culinary rather than sporting. Walton, too, dwells greedily on the minnow's table qualities, suggesting that it be fried in egg yolk, with the flowers of cowslip and primrose, and a little tansy - 'a dainty dish of meat', he calls it.

But at least Walton's mind was not entirely on his plate, for he hit the mark with this tribute to the minnow: 'In hot weather he makes excellent sport for young Anglers, or boys, or women that love that recreation'. On Coniston Water this summer, the weather was hot; and while women that love that recreation were in short supply, there were plenty of boys, and a middle-aged Angler or two. And the minnows played their part.

There was a companionable shoal resident in the limpid water around the landing stage outside our boathouse. No disturbance from swimming, stone-throwing, or boat-launching would drive them away; although they would vanish in a trice on the odd occasions when a marauding perch or pike hove to in search of a snack.

The Far From Compleat Angler

During our fortnight, I made something of a study of minnow fishing. The traditional minnow net as sold in souvenir shops and general stores is virtually useless - partly because of the maddening ease with which the wire frame becomes detached from the bamboo handle, and partly because, however swift the swoop, most of the fish are swifter, and only the smallest and most foolish are left gasping in the mesh. A minnow trap is much better. A large fizzy drink bottle should be used, with the top third cut off and jammed into the bottom to make a funnel. Baited with bread, and lobbed out on the end of a rope, it proved highly alluring to medium-sized minnows.

The big ones, though - by which I mean minnows of three inches or so - are wary of such crude artifices as the subaqueous lemonade bottle. A rod, line and hook are needed for these leviathans. Some authorities recommend bread as bait. But my experience is that, more often than not, the bread ends up in the minnow's mouth and the hook somewhere else. A maggot is to be preferred. Although minnows of every size will attack it, only a big one can get it into its mouth. You must lower it carefully into the shoal, keep it off the bottom, and be vigilant. The little ones will fling themselves at it, causing it to shoot hither and thither. But after a time it disappears inside the mouth of one of the fat fellows. A gentle raising of the rod tip - restrain the tendency of excitable children to jerk it skywards - and it should be ready for the bucket.

I concede that there is something a little ludicrous about the cry of 'What a corker!' greeting the capture of a fish the length of the little finger. But our minnow fishing did - as they say - provide hours of fun for young and old alike. The children progressed rapidly from hamfistedness to deftness, and the yells of despair gave way to: 'A minnow, a minnow, I have him by the nose'. But having accumulated your store of them, what next? My copy of *Fishes of the British Isles* speaks of a banquet given by William of Wyckham for Richard the Second at which seven gallons of minnows - costing eleven shillings and eight pence - were wolfed down. Notwithstanding that example, we did not eat them. We had a higher purpose. We used them as bait.

There is a reedy bay across the lake from the house we were renting, with cool, dark depths frequented by pike and the odd perch. Most days we rowed across there to float fish with our minnows. It

Chapter Six - A Ragbag, Medley, or Pot-pourri

was exceedingly pleasant to sit in the boat watching the cork floats bobbing on the ripples. Every so often, one would begin to jerk about, or, even more thrillingly, disappear without warning. These pike fought like demons, surging irresistibly along the bottom before rising to shake their heads and lash their tails on the surface.

The best was nine pounds, and it was delicious cooked with capers and spinach, and subsequently as fishcakes. In view of the weather - fourteen rainless days, most of them of unbroken sunshine - it was almost miraculous that we should have had such sport. It was thanks to the minnows that we did. One afternoon, standing in the shallows after swimming across the lake, I watched a shoal of them around my feet. They were feeding on the minute titbits I had stirred up from the stones, and I could feel them nibbling at my toes in a most friendly fashion. I like minnows.

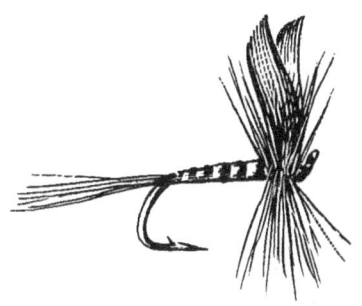

7. Cold Feet in Poland

In the summer of 1990 I went on a three month trip around eastern Europe. I took my battered Peugeot 205, crammed it with essential fishing gear, and a great quantity of emergency supplies - tent, drugs, bandages and the like - as well as two boxes of books, almost all of which I could safely have left at home; took the ferry from Harwich to Hamburg; drove across Germany; spent my first night in Poland fearing starvation and robbery at a wretched border hotel; drove south along the edge of the Upper Silesian Industrial District, avoiding towns as appalling to look as they were impossible to pronounce: Strzemicszyce, Sosnowiec, Zabrze; arriving on a gorgeous summer evening in Cracow, where Leszek Trojanowski, a dentist, was waiting for me at his house in Ziaji Street, a five minute walk from the city's ancient and celebrated university.

Leszek was the son of the oldest friend of my friend Adam. Adam himself had fled to England during the war, married Pamela, a childhood friend of my father, and had lived in London for many years, regarding himself as more English than the English, but to

The Far From Compleat Angler

everyone else unmistakeably, and unalterably Polish. I had fished with him for many years, and he had told me tales of the rivers of his Polish youth: principally of the salmon and seatrout of the Dunajec, which flows north out of the Tatras, the mountains which form part of the Carpathian chain, and which divide southern Poland from Slovakia. Together, we had planned a journey there. But when the time came, with the sudden annihilation of the Communist tyrannies, it was too late for Adam. He was too old, and he lived his own return through me, by instructing Leszek to look after me.

Hardly had I arrived in Cracow than we had left it, racing south towards the mountains. A month before there had been five feet of snow on the slopes around the village of Polrzecki, where Leszek had a weekend home (he attributed his prosperity to the eternal truth that, toothache being toothache, communists and capitalists were equally willing to reward the man who could make the hurt go away). Now the meadows were of the most intense green, brushed with the colours of wild flowers. The hilltops were thickly wooded. The fields were divided into thin strips according to the medieval pattern, and worked by hand. In recent years, the village had become a refuge for the well-to-do from the city, and the gaps between the old wooden houses and barns had been filled with chalets like Leszek's, steep-hipped against the snowfalls, with balconies and neat gardens, and strong fences to keep out intruders.

The Dunajec was my first Polish river, and it was an uncomfortable baptism. Accustomed to the unhurried meanderings of the chalkstreams of southern England, I was unsettled by the elemental strength of this torrent rushing from its source among the snowbound Carpathians towards its confluence with the Vistula in the lowlands beyond Cracow. Although the weather was blissful, the last stride into summer had only just been taken, and the water of the Dunajec was icy, its colour the steely, milky grey-blue of liquefied snow.

On the far side rose the steep slopes of the Gorce national park, blanketed in beech and larch. Against the blue of the sky, a pair of falcons wheeled; while swifts dipped at the water's edge. Leszek cut

Chapter Seven - Cold Feet in Poland

a tough stick of ash, whipped a loop of twine to it, and gave it to me as a wading staff. 'Is too early for swimming,' he said with an unnerving grin. The power of the river pulled at my legs as I waded out, and the studded holes of my waders shifted over smooth boulders. There was no sign of life at or beneath the surface, but as I had come all this way to fish, I began to do so. The effort was wasted, for as soon as the line and flies hit the water, they were wrenched away by the current. If there were any trout in the vicinity, which seemed improbable, they would have had to display uncommon determination and agility to hook themselves.

As is often the case, the far bank looked more promising, and I thought I would make my way across. The depth was no more than four or five feet, and I was wearing chest waders. Leszek shook his head as I edged out. A vivid picture burst into my mind, of legs in green rubber pointing at the sky, kicking impotently with me underneath, all sweeping downstream into the distance. Crablike, I returned the way I had come. By now, I had made the first significant angling discovery of the trip, that these waders leaked. I sat on the bank in the sunshine, pulled the wretched things off, and thawed. Leszek appeared with two miserable trout, which he had killed even though they were well below the size limit. He said the water was too cold, and the bigger fish were not yet awake. I agreed.

The writer Tony Pawson had kindly provided me with a succession of angling contacts in eastern Europe, and a few days after my chilly debut on the Dunajec, I headed east to find the first of them. Jurek Kowalski was a doctor, and the captain of Poland's highly successful flyfishing team. He lived in Krosno, a town about two-thirds of the way between Cracow and what was then Poland's border with the Soviet Union. I collected him, and together we headed further east, to the San, which was Jurek's river. He had contributed a short section to Tony Pawson's book about flyfishing around the world. His words held out an irresistible promise to the fisherman, that of pursuing familiar species in an unknown setting.

A three-pound brown trout from the Kennet is a fine thing. But to catch a specimen in an Andean torrent, in an Appalachian brook,

The Far From Compleat Angler

in wind-blasted Tierra Del Fuego or the sun-toasted Rift Valley of Kenya, in the foothills of the Karakorams or the Snowy Mountains of New South Wales or the Arctic tundra, or in any of the other far-flung lands where trout and grayling thrive - that, I considered, must be something else. In the safe territory of my mind, I had been there. I had wandered Lebanon's Bekaa Valley, and the tributaries of the Oxus. I had picked my way along the treeless estuaries of the Falklands where the huge seatrout run. I had climbed the ridges of the Caucasus, rod in hand, and watched the sun sink behind Ethiopia's Bale Mountains, and seen the same sun hang night and day over Lapland's sixty thousand lakes. But in the prosaic physical sense, I had never broken away, until now.

Jurek and I crossed the San at Sanok. The river here was wider than the Thames and more powerful, though shallower, the brown boulders of its bottom clearly visible from above. But the water at Sanok was polluted, and we pressed on upstream, to a place called Lacski. The river here was very broad, perhaps 150 yards; twice as wide as the Dunajec, but without that river's wildness. The surface was smooth, except where ruffled by a big boulder. The far bank was thick with willow and alder, the shadows of the trees darkening the water.

The technique developed by Jurek and his friends for the San and the Dunajec involved the use of two heavy nymphs, fished on a very short line in a way that allowed the flies to drift down to the fish at the speed of the current. It was simple when Jurek employed it, but I could make nothing of it. I tried to imitate him, crouching over the water with rod held high, watching the cast for any check or deviation. But after a time, I reverted to the English method. I put on a little dry fly, a whisp of brown against the shifting greens and blues and blacks of the surface film. Three times it disappeared in a minute sip, and each time I missed the fish.

The sun declined behind us, turning the trails of cloud amber. The blue of the sky darkened, and the air became utterly still. Flies began to hatch everywhere, and across the river rings appeared, losing themselves in ripples, as the fish fed. Swifts came in their hundreds, wheeling and banking, dipping their beaks to pick off the insects. Jurek loomed in the dusk. He said he had caught a few small ones,

Chapter Seven - Cold Feet in Poland

nothing worth keeping. As we drove off downstream, myriads of flies swirled above the warm road, spattering against the windscreen like rain. The beams of the headlights pulsed with the multitudes of particles of airborne life. We had to stop, to scrape the layer of corpses from the glass. The night air murmured with secret vitality.

The San rises in a valley near the Uzok pass, in the Ukraine, and for its first fifty miles forms the border with Poland. It then breaks north, through the wild and lovely region known as the Bieszczady. A few miles above the town of Lesko, it is trapped in its valley by two dams. The bigger of the two reservoirs, at Solina, cools the water and traps most of the silt brought down from the mountains by storms and snowmelt. The river which leaves the dams is comparatively pure, its condition ideal for trout and grayling.

At dawn the next day Jurek and I were on the water immediately below the second dam. The dew was heavy on the grass, and the halflight was filled with the deep sound of the turbines and the roar of escaping water. The cloudless sky was growing paler as we tackled up. But the sun was hidden below the line formed by the tops of the beeches and oaks on the far bank, and the river was black. It was also extremely cold, and flowing with a power which made wading precarious.

I used my nine-and-a-half foot rod with a sinking line, to get the big black fly down. The fish were still lying deep. On the second or third cast I felt a sharp twitch, and the resistance of my first Polish trout. By now there was sufficient light for me to admire the red and black spots speckling its olive sides. There was a familiarity in its beauty and slippery coldness which comforted me. But it was only a little fish, and I put it back. I caught another, and then a third, big enough to kill, but too lovely to warrant it. Then a much bigger fish took with a thump at the limit of my casting range. The rod bucked, and I staggered, losing my footing for a second. Everything went slack, and when I reeled in I found the hook had snapped. I shouted English curses, and retreated to the bank to smoke a cigarette and contemplate the international character of dismay.

The Far From Compleat Angler

At about ten o'clock the sun blazed over the trees. Where its rays struck the water, the fish would not take. As it rose, the band in shadow narrowed. At last the entire surface was bathed in light, and we stopped fishing.

The weather blighted my fishing on the San. Day after day, the sun was fiercely hot and piercingly brilliant; nor was summer sufficiently advanced for a reliable evening rise to develop. One morning we began at 4.15, which was a complete failure. We tried at dusk, and were caught by a storm which rolled down from the mountains without any warning. We returned to the stretch below the dam. By now my waders were rotting at a number of strategic points, and I shuddered as the water invaded. For the first half hour or so I expected a fish at every cast. Gradually, though, the motion of wrist and elbow became automatic; the sun rose, and I accepted defeat. I lay down on the bank, pulled off the treacherous leggings, and slept in the sun until awakened by the thunder of my own snoring.

In between these more or less unproductive sessions, Jurek showed me the beauties of the Bieszczady, a landscape of densely wooded hills, meadows thick with wild flowers and broken by streams, dotted with simple wooden farmhouses. This is one of the last refuges of the European bison, and had been rigorously preserved as hunting grounds for the apparatchiks from Warsaw. Tito had come here to shoot a bison, while the Polish Prime Minister of the time had had to content himself with a bear. These days, we were told, the party men no longer came. They were too busy passing themselves off as good capitalist democrats. Foreign currency was now the only acceptable barter for the lives of these creatures. A Swiss businessman had flown in by helicopter a few months before, armed with a battery of rifles and a licence entitling him to kill an immobile, grazing bison. The Swiss had shot the beast, then taken it back to Zurich in his aircraft.

The towns of the Bieszczady were few and far between, which was as well, for they were dismal places. I went with Jurek to Sanok to buy postcards. The town was notorious as the location for the

Chapter Seven - Cold Feet in Poland

factory where they made the Autosan bus. 'Here,' Jurek told me, 'they make buses, the worst buses in Poland, the worst buses in the world.' They presented striking images of industrial backwardness, blackened with accretions of carbon, panting and rattling up gentle inclines enclosed in a haze of exhaust, scarcely able to summon the acceleration to overtake the horsedrawn carts which, symbolically speaking, they closely resembled.

Sanok was slumbrous and dirty. There were no postcards illustrating the beauties of the Bieszczady. Instead they showed either municipal buildings or unnaturally brilliant flowers: fevered roses and jaundiced primroses. A little way downstream from the bridge over the river a man was fishing from a wheelchair. He was in the water with his shrivelled legs stretched out in front of him, the water gurgling between the spokes of the wheels. The evening sun was still warm, and there were children swimming not far from him, shouting and splashing. But he, intent on his rod, did not seem to mind them.

A little dispirited by the listlessness which imbued the town, we went to fish just above Lesko. It was a popular stretch, and there were at least a dozen fishermen out in the water. But the river here was immensely broad, subdivided into a multiplicity of smaller streams. I waded out, sending forth ripples to disturb the golden sheen of the surface. In mid-river the water was near the top of my waders, but ahead I could see submerged boulders, with a tempting curl of water beyond; so I tiptoed forward, and found a sanctuary of firm silt between the rocks.

Jurek was a hundred yards or so upstream, poised like a heron as his heavy nymphs searched beneath the far bank. The sun was off the water, and there was a trickle of light olives into the riffle in front of me. As the insects struggled in the surface film, the trout picked them off from below, and the swifts from above. Using a tiny Ginger Quill, I caught fish after fish. They were as small as they were eager; nothing much above half a pound. After an hour, the hatch faltered, dying away altogether as the shadows lengthened and the temperature fell. The blasted waders were once again full of water, and I began to shiver uncontrollably. I edged down from my refuge, took a few steps and went into a hole; then splashed back to the bank. Above, the stars were showing themselves, and the night air was alive with the unnerving flight of bats.

I drove Jurek to Skoczow, a small town in the western Carpathians. A flyfishing competition was being held there, at which he was due to name the team which would travel to Wales later that year to defend the title won the previous year in Finland. Jurek told me he was intending to drop two of the members, who had defied his orders by getting drunk. In the hotel where we stayed, the arguments unleashed by this decision were audible through the thin walls long into the night. In the morning Jurek was pale and subdued, and the other fishermen kept clear of him.

He introduced me to a character whose appearance would have attracted attention anywhere, and here was as outlandish as that of a Ghanaian chief in tribal robes. He had a scrubby beard and shoulder-length hair, gathered into a pony tail. He wore a black silk vest, baggy white tracksuit trousers, and Reebok running shoes. On his head was a wide-brimmed grey felt hat with a black band. He was standing beside a Japanese jeep, itself an exotic sight among the clapped-out Fiats, Ladas and Trabants.

His name was Janusz Wanicki, and he spoke fluent, fractured English, larded with obscenity. He was an artist. I looked inquiringly at the jeep. 'No, not here. You think Polish painters drive Honda jeeps? I live in Finland. You know Finland? Strange country, mad people. But rich, so much money.' I gathered that he was employed by the Finnish government as an art conservator, and that he supplemented an already considerable income by painting portraits of public figures. 'I paint every bastard in government. They pay good for these pictures, because the bloody Finns can't paint.'

Jurek was anxious to escape the fury of recrimination that his team selection had provoked, so Janusz drove him and me to the village of Wisla, close to the border with Czechoslovakia. The village gives its name to Poland's greatest river, which we know as the Vistula. Here, in these hills, it was an infant, a baby of tiny pools, miniature pebbly runs and smooth glides. Janusz and I fished, while

Chapter Seven - Cold Feet in Poland

Jurek watched and wandered. We caught a great many little trout, but nothing big. It was a delicious pleasure, though, to be in boots, free of the leaky waders, on a stream where a flick of the wrist would deliver the fly as far as I could want it to go.

I bade a fond farewell to Jurek, who had to return to his work in Krosno. It had been decided that Janusz would take me in hand, which was as well, since the country was now in the grip of an acute petrol shortage, which an affluent Pole was better able to circumvent than I would have been. We drove in the jeep to a village called Lopusna, on the Upper Dunajec. There we met Andrzej Fox, a teacher from Cracow and another name on Tony Pawson's contact list. Andrzej had been forced to queue for thirteen hours to obtain enough fuel to get his geriatric Fiat out of Cracow. He took Janusz and me to a holiday centre which the local Fishing Association had use of. We shared a room which was half-filled by a colossal Soviet-made television, as big as a fridge, whose colours were those of nightmares. Downstairs was a spacious restaurant, which opened only to serve us a breakfast of cold sausage, hard cheese and stale bread, accompanied by a tureen containing hot, diluted milk and noodles.

Next to this sepulchral establishment was a fish hatchery, where trout and grayling were reared for stocking in the Dunajec and other rivers. In one dark tank were a dozen huchen - in Latin, *hucho hucho*, known in England as the Danubian salmon, even though they are not true salmon and almost extinct in the Danube. Since pollution and dam building blocked the runs of Atlantic salmon into the Vistula and Dunajec, efforts had been made to introduce this distant cousin; even though it is, for the angler, a somewhat unrewarding creature, since it almost never rises to a fly, will take a bait or spinner with reluctance, and then only in the depths of winter. Its body is similar to that of the salmon, but its squat, flattened head gives it a menacing aspect.

The stream which supplied the hatchery ran between a wooden church and an 18th century manor house to join the Dunajec in the centre of the village. The stretch of the river downstream from Lopusna had nothing of the ferocity which had so alarmed me when fishing with Leszek. Here it was no more than energetic, as it pressed its way between high, tree-topped banks down a succession of long, stony runs and surging pools, which might have been designed for

The Far From Compleat Angler

salmon to rest or run. But the migrant species had long departed; only the trout and grayling remained, and they were far from easy to catch as the tropical weather persisted.

Andrzej was conspicuously impoverished, and in poor health. He spoke little English, and that with immense effort, usually abandoning sentences midway with sad gestures of impotence. But there were words and phrases in English which he pronounced with confidence; not that anyone but an angler would have understood them. Little Chap, Wickham's Fancy, Greenwell's Glory, Teal and Silver, Partridge and Orange - when Andrzej articulated the names of these flies, his face would light up with the pleasure his fluency gave him. In his view, these creations of feather, fur, silk and tinsel represented Great Britain's principal contribution to world civilisation. He was filled with reverence for the traditions of the Hampshire chalkstreams and the lochs and rivers of Scotland. To him the influential English writers - Halford, Skues, Grey of Falloden and the rest - were spiritual leaders. His head was filled with fishing, its history, its mythology, its morality.

He had an old Hardy salmon reel. It had a cracked drum, and there were no salmon, but he took it everywhere. He loved to slip it from its bag and display it to a fellow enthusiast, as if he were a high priest in the ancient religion of the fishermen of England. He also had an old Hardy catalogue, with coloured plates illustrating flies, and innumerable testimonials lauding the efficacy of the company's products in remote corners of the Empire. This catalogue was Andrzej's bible. Within its foxed pages a system of belief had been codified, to whose secrets he had been made privy, and of whose primacy he was jealously proud.

This fanaticism caused some tension between him and Janusz. Janusz's attitude to his homeland and its people was characteristic of the exile, combining contempt with an overpowering, nostalgic passion. In fishing he was, like me, an amateur; whereas Andrzej was an expert. Andrzej regarded himself as the master, and Janusz as his wayward pupil; and he sustained this apprehension of their relationship with steely determination. As we travelled around in the jeep, there came from Andrzej a flow of words as constant as the current of the Dunajec. Janusz would stare out of the window in silent

Chapter Seven - Cold Feet in Poland

exasperation, occasionally barking interruptions, uttering derisive laughs, or drowning Andrzej with rock music from the cassette player. Less often he would attempt to discuss an issue with Andrzej. I would ask Janusz what it was, and he would light another cigarette and jerk his head in the older man's direction: 'Fishing, fishing, always f...... fishing'.

Andrzej should have been a first-rate bore, but he was nothing of the sort. His innocence disarmed us, and there was a freshness to his enthusiasm which was infectious. He knew every yard of the Dunajec and its tributaries, and every square yard of the countryside. He was able to show us places which, on our own, we would never have found. He would direct Janusz down a track leading from a country road into a dark barrier of fir trees. We would bounce along between the pines and spruces, until, with magical suddenness, a stream would appear before us and Janusz would stop and jump down, crying out with the excitement of the discovery.

The loveliest river was the Bialka, whose source was Morskie Oko, the Eye of the Sea, one of a cluster of glacial lakes trapped beneath granite cliffs in the High Tatras. Tumbling through a forest from this icy pool, the Bialka threaded its way towards the Dunajec, with no more than a scattering of hamlets along its banks. Its water was marvellously pure, its crystallinity given a greenish tinge by the weed clinging to the stony bed. Much of the time it was broken into two or three streams, broken by banks of dazzling white stones.

It was full of grayling and trout, eager seizers of a fly. On our first visit, we split up. I went downstream, intending to fish up. The sun was shining, but it was not as hot as before, and black clouds were manoeuvring across the sky to give notice of a change in the weather. I took a path which curved this way and that through the pines, with the murmur of the river to my right. Then I cut across and found myself at the bottom of an irresistible pool.

At its head was a stunted bush against whose roots the water washed as it broke away from the main stream over a bank of stones, to sweep against a miniature limestone cliff before straightening, slowing, and deepening. I knelt on the stones, and cast up towards the bush. I could not see my Gold-Ribbed Hare's Ear in the white water, but spotted it as it emerged. Then there was a wink of silver beneath

The Far From Compleat Angler

the surface, and it was gone. I felt the terror of the grayling in its twisting rush for freedom, but I swung it into the slack water at my feet and slid it across the stones to my hand. I removed the hook from the soft membrane of its mouth, and held it upright for a moment, until it darted back to its place in the pool.

I worked my way upstream, sampling all the varieties of water that this exquisite stream provided. The fish were not big, and many of them I missed, unprepared for the speed of their dash at the fly. The fishing absorbed all my concentration, and I was hardly aware of the passing of time until, suddenly, I realised I was hungry. I looked around me. The river's course and the configuration of the trees seemed familiar; then unfamiliar. I took one path, then another, came back to the river, took other paths. On three occasions I came upon a family having a picnic on a grassy bank, each time from a different direction. The sun had disappeared, thunder rolled, rain dropped from a leaden sky. I trotted hither and thither in the panic of being lost; then came upon Janusz and Andrzej, eating bread and sausage and drinking beer. Andrzej was looking pleased with himself. He had caught a score of small fish, and one big grayling.

The next day we were in the mountain resort of Zakopane, and it continued to rain. The town was dank and grubby, the mountains cloaked in cloud. Up and down the main street wandered squads of holidaymakers in boots and anoraks, emanating boredom. Wet horses munched in their nosebags, motionless in the shafts of their cabs, embroidered headdresses hanging limply over their ears. Behind them the drivers, old men with rheumy eyes and cheeks mottled with broken veins, sat smoking in silence, their round black hats tilted back, their white woollen trousers smeared with ash. No one hired a cab. No one bought anything at the craft stalls. No one did anything much, except to dodge for cover when the rain came down harder.

We were there to met a Polish fishing legend, the world fly fishing champion, Wladislaw Trzebunia-Nebes. He was a man of Zakopane and the Dunajec, a Highlander and proud of it. Janusz had acted as the Polish team's guide in Finland, and had become friendly with Trzebunia. The champion himself had secured a position as angler-in-residence at a salmon fishing lodge run by a German in

Chapter Seven - Cold Feet in Poland

Norway. There he earned enough in three months to live a life of ease in Zakopane the rest of the year.

Together, we all set off to fish the Dunajec above Lopusna. Trzebunia was the master of the short-line nymphing technique, and to watch him fish was an education. He waded swiftly down the stream, working his flies through the pockets behind each foam-topped rock. He cast every few seconds, whipping the flies from below to flick them across, holding his rod high as they came down. He would be still for no more than a moment, before striding on to the next rock. He was marvellously sure-footed, and utterly absorbed in the business of the moment to the exclusion of all else.

I watched him for a time, then wandered upstream, looking for less turbulent water. I passed Andrzej, precariously balanced in midstream, and paused to photograph him as he landed a grayling of respectable size. Janusz had waded to the other side, ignoring the fact that the river here marked the border, and that he was on Slovak soil. I came to a quieter stretch, where a meadow bright with buttercups and celandines sloped gently down to the water. For a time I tried to pursue the Trzebunia method. But I tired of the resulting tangles, and took up a spare rod I had brought, and fished with a dry fly. There was a hatch of dark olives, sufficient to arouse appetites. I caught a chub, then two nice grayling of over a pound each. Returning downstream I met Janusz, who told me that Trzebunia was approaching the twenty mark.

Further down, I was accosted by a rickety, unshaven old man with a wandering left eye, who smelled strongly of drink. Unable to communicate with me, he approached Trzebunia, who was wading to the bank. A tremendous row flared instantly between them. Janusz appeared, and told me the import of the ancient's complaint was that I should not have been using two rods. Trzebunia's response was to accuse him of gross discourtesy to a most distinguished English guest. Every so often one or other of the two protagonists in the argument would walk a few steps away, as if the matter had been settled. Then rage would be fanned into life again, the two heads would come together, and the insults would fly.

Janusz was helpless with laughter. Eventually he said: 'The old man is drunk. Wladislaw is calling him a dickhead. He ask Wladislaw

The Far From Compleat Angler

who is the dickhead, it is him. You see him hitting his chest. He say he have medals, Wladislaw have no medals. Wladislaw saying they are dickhead medals. That old man is as drunk as four arseholes.' At last hostilities were suspended. The old man looked exhausted. He insisted on shaking hands with me before making his way slowly back to the bar.

That evening I said goodbye to Andrzej. I gave him a book about English flies. He presented me with a collection of his own flies, including one with a stiff, iron-grey hackle which was to prove deadly in Bohemia, Slovakia and Romania, becoming a talisman until I lost it in a branch beside a Transylvanian brook. The parting between him and Janusz was affectionate. On the way back to Cracow, Janusz said: 'Andrzej is mad. He wishes he is a fish. Maybe he thinks he is a fish. But I like him OK, except he makes me want to get drunk like hell.'

8. Trials and Small Triumphs in Bohemia and Slovakia

In those days, of course, it was still Czechoslovakia. But they were an ill-assorted couple, Bohemia and Slovakia, with Moravia mediating between them. The Bohemians, in spite of the associations of the name, belong to central Europe, are comfortable with Germans and Austrians, and regarded the Slovakians as idle, feckless, drunken, disorganised, and backward. The Slovakians, ever mindful of their distance from the capital and seat of power, Prague, saw the people of the west as Teutonic, imperialistic, materialistic, and dull. A communist tyranny of convenience manacled them together, but never eroded the suspicion between them; a suspicion which hardened into open hostility after the crushing of Dubcek's Prague Spring in 1968, for it was at the invitation of the Slovakian Communist Party that the Russian tanks came.

My first port of call was an appalling town called Litvinov, which lies to the north of Prague, not far from the border with what was then

The Far From Compleat Angler

East Germany. My contact there was a man called Tomas Kroupa, who worked in a lowly capacity at the neighbouring petrochemical complex, a vast, smoke-shrouded, stinking hell-on-earth which stretched away into the apparently infinite distance beneath the balcony of his flat in Lenin Street. Tomas's passions were his family, his work, his garden and fishing. He had contributed a number of highly technical articles on pike fishing to a Czechoslovak magazine. I had brought him an English video on pike fishing. He watched it with intense concentration, although - despite the fact that he spoke excellent English - he could make little of the commentary, which was delivered in a thick Birmingham accent. Tomas asked me innumerable questions about pike fishing, almost none of which I could answer. He seemed disappointed that I had heard of none of the great figures of the English pike fishing scene, who were familiar titans to him.

The morning after my arrival, Tomas and I left on what was to be a week's fishing. He was disconcertingly ill-informed about the programme. I found that a combination of poverty, fatherhood and lack of transport had prevented him from doing any fishing for the previous two years; and that he knew almost nothing about fly fishing, which was what we were supposed to be doing. He said he had enlisted a guide, Stanislaw Skryas, a fellow contributor to the fishing magazine. Tomas had met him but once, but had unquestioning faith in his status as an expert, with immense experience of Bohemian trout streams and matchless knowledge of the best methods and times.

But before collecting Stanislaw, there was the matter of my licence. Tomas was filled with apprehension on this subject. He had never heard of an Englishman coming to his country to fish. It might well be that none had ever done so. He was unimpressed that I had had no difficulty in Poland. The Poles, he implied, were a thoroughly ill-disciplined lot. In his country regulation was everything. We drove to Karlovy Vary, which used to be German and known as Carlsbad. It was a famous spa town, and its stuccoed hotels and pompous colonnaded bath-houses still breathed an imperial, Teutonic self-regard. We went to the offices of the proverbially inefficient national tourist authority Cedok. On hearing Tomas' humble inquiry about fishing licences, the doughy face of the matron behind the counter

Chapter Eight - In Bohemia and Slovakia

resolved itself into an expression of desperation. It seemed that on that very day Cedok had indeed assumed the responsibility of issuing licences from the local angling association. Regrettably, the responsibility had not been accompanied by the necessary forms. Tomas nodded heavily, and offered no protest.

We proceeded to another vile urban sprawl, Sokolov, where we found Stanislaw Skryas. He had been a policeman, and was now earning a precarious living as a glassblower. He had long lank black hair, a drooping moustache, and smoked incessantly. Together, we all went to the Cedok office in Sokolov, where an exchange identical in its essentials to that in Karlovy Vary took place. We were advised to try at Cheb, another twenty-five miles to the west.

On the way there, I expressed surprise at the obstacles we were meeting. Tomas and Standa (the abbreviation for Stansilaw) expressed surprise at my surprise. Maybe in the West the wish to have a licence and the ability to pay for it were easily translated into the obtention of it. But here a different culture prevailed. I suggested that I should fish without a licence, and plead ignorance if caught. They were appalled.

'It is against the law', said Tomas sternly.
'Yes, but this is fishing'.
'And don't you have laws for fishing in England?'
'Yes, but...'
'And don't you follow the laws?'
'Of course. Most of the time, anyway'.
'Here fishermen obey the laws. In Slovakia maybe is different. In England, too, maybe. But here...'

The Cedok matron in Cheb had the new forms, and told me that I was the first foreign applicant. She produced an enormous folder, and assembled a heap of papers and carbons. The form was in German and its completion was a lengthy business, as each of its numerous sections had to be translated by the matron into Czech for the benefit of Tomas, and by him into English, my responses making the return journey. The requirements and conditions were exacting. I must at all times carry the licence, a net, a pair of scissors, and other equipment necessary to land and dispose of fish, including a tape measure to show if it were big enough to kill. I must furnish the authorities

The Far From Compleat Angler

with a written record of where I had fished, and for how long, and of what I had caught. In return, I was permitted to fish on two days in any week, only on rivers designated for trout and grayling, in just one of the eleven districts into which Bohemia was divided for the administrations of angling. The cost was sixty eight dollars. In Poland I had paid the equivalent of two, to fish wherever I liked for a fortnight.

The next morning we headed south, and came to a town called Tachov, in the extreme west of Bohemia. Standa directed me to stop near a bridge. Tomas said something to him, and he nodded at the brown stream flowing sluggishly past a transport yard in which a few rusted buses stood, looking exceedingly folorn.

'He says we fish here', Tomas said. 'Standa says he has caught big grayling here'.

'Here? It doesn't look very...' I did not want to seem unappreciative of my first Bohemian trout stream. We got out of the car. The water was dark and lifeless, its surface broken - not by feeding fish - but by the spokes of bicycle wheels and the rims of abandoned petrol drums. 'I will tell Standa we don't like to fish here?' Tomas asked. I agreed. Our guide shrugged his shoulders, and lit another cigarette.

We left Tachov and followed the course of the river, the Mze, to the east. The sky began to lighten, the grey becoming pale blue. The road took us into rolling countryside, with immense fields. We came to a village of whitewashed, red-roofed cottages. A track led to the right, through head-high maize, to a dilapidated bridge, where we stopped. We assembled our tackle, and Tomas and Standa marched ahead of me across a lush meadow to the river. They searched up and down the bank, pausing now and then to study the map which was attached to their licences. Finally they agreed that this was indeed a place where we might legitimately fish. They took out pens and began to write in their licences. Tomas explained that they were recording the date, time, place and intended quarry.

'You must also write these things', he said in schoolmasterly fashion.

'I've left my licence in the car. I'll fill it in when we've finished'.

Tomas was scandalised. 'That is not possible. The regulations say you must write before fishing. Here, I show you.' He waved pages of

Chapter Eight - In Bohemia and Slovakia

instructions at me. Resentfully I trudged back to the car to fetch the document.

My irritation did not last long, though. It was chased away by the beauty of the day and of the little river. Here, it had thrown off the grubby passivity imposed on it by the town. It twisted its way between willows and alders in a succession of stony runs and slow pools. The sunshine was filtered through the canopy of leaves, and the stream sparkled with the mingled light and shade. Butterflies and bees shimmered and hummed above the meadow grass. On the water, olives were hatching, to be seized by the grayling and the swifts which dashed beneath the trailing branches.

It was not difficult fishing. One after another, the grayling came to the net, dorsal fins bristling. They were of respectable size, up to three quarters of a pound, but there was no point in keeping them. At the head of one pool were two slabs of stone, between which the water forced its way with unusual urgency. The banks were steep and tangled with vegetation, and the casting tricky. I caught a couple of little ones at the bottom of the pool, but I could see the bigger ones were in the lee of the far boulder, where a floating fly was instantly whisked past them. I put on a big leaded mayfly nymph, and dropped it just below the face of the boulder. There was a violent tug. I struck with equal violence and the fish plunged, snapping the cast. I was convinced I had discovered the secret, and was tying on another nymph as quickly as I could when Standa appeared and stood on the boulder. All the fish in the pool stopped rising at once.

The improvement in his stock resulting from this delightful morning's fishing was short-lived. In the early evening we arrived in Susice, which stands on the River Otava near the border with Austria. Standa said we must go at once to a stretch of the river where, a couple of years before, he had caught large numbers of large grayling. We drove out of town, took a track off the main road, and bounced along it for several miles, repeatedly thumping the exhaust pipe on the ridge down the middle. Standa urged me onwards, exuding confidence, until a fallen lime tree blocked our way. To our right, beyond a tangled undergrowth, was a broad, swift river. On the other side, cloaked in white dust, was a cement factory standing beside a limestone quarry, operating at full throttle. Standa went downstream,

The Far From Compleat Angler

returning some time later with a tale of a huge trout lost at the net. I went upstream, in a vain attempt to escape from the dust. I flogged away gloomily, listening to limestone being excavated and crushed into powder, and caught nothing.

Standa said he had remembered that the best fishing was not, after all, next to the cement factory, but a little way upstream from Susice. We drove up and down the road while he alternated blank stares at passing landmarks with disbelieving scrutiny of the map, the while blowing out his cheeks and muttering in mystification. After a time, Tomas and I - tantalised by glimpses of a golden stream through the trees - tired of this familiar performance. I drove into a field, on the other side of which the Otava flowed swift and clear between beeches and willows.

I began to fish a run where the current spilled over rocks against the bank where roots showed dimly in shadow. It was full of fish, gloriously spotted wild trout which rose eagerly. I worked my way downstream, absorbed in the fishing, the only distraction being the passing through of a succession of kayaks propelled by beefy, jolly Bohemians. I hooked a muscular female paddler on my backcast, prompting a screech of shock. She manouevred to the bank, where I detached the nymph from her lifejacket, stammering apologies.

Eventually I came across tents and cabins, scattered among the pine trees. Tomas appeared, looking pleased with himself. Was this not a beautiful river, he asked, smiling. It turned out that this was the very place for which Standa had been looking. It seemed odd to me that he should have been unable to locate a campsite extending down a mile or more of river bank. But Tomas was right: it *was* beautiful on this river flowing through the wooded Sumava mountains, with the sun blazing down. So we rented a couple of cabins, and fished.

The weather remained magnificent. Each night the temperature dropped below freezing. Each morning revealed a sky of the most intense blue above the spiky tops of the pine trees, with the river flashing silver and gold in the sunlight. The only drawback was the democratic nature of the fishing. Many of the campers were there to

Chapter Eight - In Bohemia and Slovakia

fish, and there were no rules or understandings governing proximity. To catch a trout and be seen doing so was to find, within seconds, another angler splashing into the water a few yards away. If I cried a protesting 'Oi', which I did a few times, it was heard as 'Ahoy', the universal Bohemian greeting, and met with a wave and a smile.

On our last day I set off upstream in search of solitude. I passed through a hamlet, with a church half-hidden among beech trees. Following the river upstream, I came to a bridge with a dark, deep pool beneath. Fish were feeding hard, but some vagary of the current or light seemed to deter them from taking the fly. I made my way downstream through a grove of limes, to a bend where a beech dipped its branches into a curl of water. I waded across the river a little way above, and edged down until I was on a gravel bank at the head of the pool. There, standing in the sunshine with the crystal water tugging at my legs, I smoked a cigarette and scanned the surface where it was shaded by the branches. Trout were feeding in the manner of children at a birthday party. Large brown flies were hatching in profusion. Some were being devoured just below the surface, as they struggled to rid themselves of their nymphal cases. Others fluttered frenziedly, trapped in the surface film, until a gulp engulfed them, sending waves bouncing against the far bank.

The fly was some kind of daytime sedge, unfamiliar to me. I searched through the boxes in the pockets of my waistcoat. In one I found three enormous fluffy brown objects. I could not remember where, or why I had bought them, but they looked about right. By now the fish had abandoned all caution. Time and again my huge fly sailed into the pool and was seized. They were not big fish, but they were plump, in prime condition, and fought with muscular wildness. I had no reason to kill them, so I held each so I could gaze at the black and red spots, the golden sides, the blood-red gills, before twisting out the fly and letting it dash away.

That evening I stood on the wooden bridge which crossed the Otava in the middle of the campsite. I smoked, and watched a man casting below me in the gathering darkness. I had had enough, knowing I could not achieve again the exquisite pleasure of my morning. As the sun declined, a colossal cloud of sedges began an upstream flight, towards and then past me. It extended as far as I could see downstream, a host reaching from the surface of the water to the tops of the trees. As the cloud met the sunlight, the insects were lit, like flakes of gold, a million million of them, never falling.

Returning to the north, Standa suggested stopping to fish a tributary of the Mze, the Kosovy Potok. He said he had enjoyed fast and furious sport with grayling on a stretch he could remember clearly. He led us down a forest path, in our waders. Occasionally we had glimpses of an overgrown, murky stream. Several times Tomas asked if we were close to our destination. But Standa insisted we must press on. He had just remembered, he said, that this angling nirvana was immediately above the Kosovy Potok's junction with the Mze, and not on this river at all. It could not, he said, be more than half a kilometre further.

Thigh waders with metal-studded soles are not the ideal footwear for a forced march. Several kilometres later, with the sun hot and the flies increasingly noisome, Tomas and I rebelled. As we set off back the way we had come, Standa relapsed into sullen silence. 'Standa does not know this place, I think', Tomas said. 'Like most other places', I replied sourly. ' I want to ask a question, Tom. Every place we fish, Standa always says he has hooked the biggest fish, but always it is gone. But when I am with him, he catches same as me. Only when I cannot see him, then he hooks big fish. Do you believe these big fish?'

'No', I said savagely.

'I think you are right. He is... ' Tomas paused, concentrated. Then he smiled. 'He is inventing big fish, I think'.

In the few hours left to us, we went back to where we had fished on the first day of our excursion. The sun was still shining, and the grayling were still rising. The difference was that Tomas, who had struggled then, this time led the way. I spent some time watching him. His technique was ungainly, but he was in tune with the water and the fish. Every few minutes he gave a cry of excitement as the lift of his wrist met living resistance. His smile as he splashed to the bank was

Chapter Eight - In Bohemia and Slovakia

wide. 'This fishing I like very much', he said. 'This river I like very much. These graylings also I like very much'.

I met Pavel Janicek outside a block of flats in the vast industrial centre of Ostrava, in northern Moravia. He regarded himself as an honorary Slovakian, although this hideous city had been his birthplace and was his home. Pavel had high cheekbones, a typical Slavic moustache, and a mighty stomach. I greeted him in English. He responded in German. I told him, in English, that I could not speak German. He replied, in German, that he could not speak English. This was a blow. Pavel, like Jurek Kowalski, had contributed to Tony Pawson's book. As this was in English, I had assumed that he would be able to speak it. It was now clear to me that if we did not communicate in German, we would not communicate at all.

We went east, along the southern flanks of the Carpathians. As we travelled, the cobwebbed recesses of my memory began to yield a nugget or two. Nouns emerged, singly, and Pavel was encouraged. Pronouns surfaced, hovered, and attached themselves to verbs. Primitive grammatical structures took shape. Pavel roared encouragement and clapped me on the back. I should not exaggerate the abundance of this linguistic blooming. We could understand each other in fishing matters, and the simpler aspects of life - the weather, food, beer and so on. Attempts to embrace more complex issues usually foundered. There was a strong temptation falsely to claim understanding. I would nod forcefully at whatever Pavel was saying, and reply: 'Ich verstehe'. He would look pleased and surprised, and continue. Eventually we reach a point at which something more than an affirmative was required of me. He would understand that I had understood nothing, and back to the beginning we would go.

It was hard work, but better than silence. The hours slipped by as we crossed the valley of the flood-swollen Vah, reached Poprad and the river of the same name, and followed it north until we came to the small, dusty town of Podolinec. Pavel directed me to a house where I paid the equivalent of two pounds for a licence. We were given vodka, and the wife of the man who issued the licences produced a

The Far From Compleat Angler

plate of fried trout and potatoes. Another fisherman appeared, called Slavo Truska, who led us to a mountain stream a mile of two from the town. Upstream, framed in the fiery trails of cloud left by the dying sun, were the snowy spears of the High Tatras. With my first cast I caught a grayling, then a little trout. I waded further, and got a bootfull of snow-cold water for my troubles.

We drove to a campsite on the banks of the Poprad, where Pavel's fishing friends were waiting for him in the restaurant. My Bohemian companions, Tomas and Standa, were both teetotallers, and with them I had become somewhat furtive and guilty about my fondness for a drink. Here in Slovakia there were no such inhibitions, and I woke up the following morning with the first true hangover of my trip. Outside, the river was a milky yellow colour, from rain and melting snow.

The Poprad, alone among the rivers of Slovakia, flows north. The others, the Vah, the Hornad, the Hron, all search for a way south and eventually their waters join those of the Danube. But the Poprad is a contrary spirit. Here, at Podolinec, it flows north-east, before curving down, then collecting itself to thrust north-west through the Carpathians to join the Dunajec in Poland. It is reputed to be a fine trout and grayling river, and Pavel was full of tales of great days with the fly. But he had the fisherman's equivalent to tennis elbow, and couldn't cast, and the water was unfishable. So, on that first morning, I was entrusted to the care of our acquaintance of the previous evening, Slavo, who was a vet. He came with his brother, Stano, who worked in a factory.

They took me back to the stream near Podolinec, which they identified at the Biela. Its source was but a few miles from that of the Polish Bialka, and its character was strikingly similar. The water had the same clarity, so pure that it gave the illusion of having no secrets. It seemed that every boulder and lesser stone was visible, picked out by a brilliant sun. We moved upstream, with the mountains facing us, dazzlingly white, their peaks sharp against the sky, touched by feathers of cloud. We rose a fish here and there, and did best in the shadows under the road bridge, where a steady trickle of olives was being intercepted in purposeful fashion. I lost a good grayling by striking too hard, then caught a fat trout which prompted

Chapter Eight - In Bohemia and Slovakia

a broad smile from Stana as he thumped it over the head and slid it into his pocket.

We fished until mid-afternoon, by which time we were too thirsty to continue. Driving back to the camp, I did not spare a glance for the peaks behind me; which was, with hindsight, a shame, for I was not to see them again. The next day the weather broke. Pavel and his chums had to return to Ostrava - 'Mann must arbeiten', he said sadly, shrugging his vast shoulders with regret at the necessity of abandoning a river for the factory. But first he wanted to organise my fishing for the rest of my stay, so we drove through a chilly morning to Spisska Stara Ves, which is on the Slovakian side of the Dunajec. There, at seven o'clock, he awoke the secretary of the angling club, the verandah of whose house was studded with the preserved heads of hundreds of trout, grayling, pike and huchen. I was the first Englishman who had ever sought permission to fish, and the occasion was toasted with plum brandy.

Back in the bar beside the Poprad we began drinking in earnest, continuing until late afternoon, when Pavel and company departed. By then the rain had set in, beating on the roof of the cabin which my friend had arranged for me to occupy. I slept, awoke feeling stale and dejected. I walked by the river, which was dirtier than ever. The rain had stopped and the atmosphere was heavy with moisture. The ranks of pine trees on each side of the valley were dark in the misty half-light. A buzzard flapped effortlessly across the water into the trees.

The accessible reach of the Dunajec was upstream from the 14th century monastery at Cerveny Klastor. Below the monastery was the start of the Dunajec gorge, whose entrance was guarded on the Polish side by the tooth-like crags of the Tre Korune, the Three Crowns. To get to the river from my base on the Poprad, I had to drive across a miniature range of mountains knows as the Spisska Magura. It was the grass-cutting season, and the women were out in the fields with their scythes. Rising and falling with the slopes were spiky prongs of wood, over which the grass was hung to dry, before being stored to feed the animals through the winter. The air was sweet with the smell of the grass, and alive with the sweep of scythes and the cries and songs of the cutters.

The landscape was rich and varied, as was the mix of peoples. There were Slovaks and Hungarians here; Ukrainians and Poles;

The Far From Compleat Angler

Germans and Ruthenians. Until the war there had been a number of German-speaking villages here, survivors from a colonisation hundreds of years old. Hitler's conquests inspired their people, whose passion for the fatherland was all the fiercer for their separation from it. A vicious cycle of partisan attack and Gestapo reprisal developed, fed by collaboration, treachery and hatred. And at the end all the ethnic Germans were slaughtered or expelled; apart from those in one tiny village by the Poprad, which had never subscribed to doctrines of Aryan supremacy. I strayed into it, and an old lady responded to my 'Guten Tag' with a smile of delight and a flood of gutterals.

The Dunajec seemed oddly familiar. After studying the map, I realised I was standing opposite the spot where, a few weeks and a few thousand miles before, I had fished with Janusz, Andrzej and Wladislaw Trzebunia-Nebies. I left my car, crossed a meadow, and took a path through a thicket, disturbing a deer on my way. I came to a broad, even stretch of water. Below, it broke over a gravel bar, gathering its force in two deep streams; one pushing against the far, Polish side; the other running down the near, Slovak side. In Poland, an old woman was driving her cattle through the long grass, hopping along the bank to whack her stick against their flanks, her cries of abuse and encouragement carrying across the water.

The sun broke through the cloud, lighting the sky and bringing a glow to the pale rock summits of the Tre Korune. I was alone in the water. I worked my way downstream, catching grayling here and there, losing others. Reaching the gravel bar, I fished the near stream. Almost every cast brought a sharp snatch at the flies, but for some reason I could not hook them. The water below me was fierce and broken, and I did not relish wading it in the dusk. I made my way back to the car, stumbling on another deer which leaped away in terror.

9. Nothing, and Something Ugly, in Hungary

There is one word in the notoriously intractable Hungarian language that I can pronounce with confidence. It aptly summarises the results of the majority of my fishing exertions there, and at one stage threatened to become their epitaph. The word is 'semmi'. It means 'nothing'.

I first became acquainted with it at a small, featureless lake near the town of Pilisvorosvar, north of Budapest. I had been taken there by a man called Attila Hunyadi, who had a bright red, squashed, memorably ugly face, and spectacles so powerful that, from certain angles, they made his eyeballs seem the size of melons. He was an employee of the Hungarian Fishing Association, which owned this murky stretch of water, and the guesthouse beside it in which I stayed. For I had - much to my dismay - fallen into the grip of a state bureaucracy; was, indeed, the 'distinguished guest' of the Association, a representative, in some ill-defined way, of my country.

The Far From Compleat Angler

My letter of invitation, on headed notepaper, exhorted me to deploy 'your professional skill' in pursuit of the specialities of Hungary; and a programme, specifying dates and localities, had been drawn up to enable me to do so.

This lake was the first venue, and a less encouraging start could hardly have been imagined. Mr Hunyadi beat me about the shoulders, thrust into my hands copies of articles he had written for the Fishing Association's magazine, and waved at me photographs of himself clasping fat carp and catfish to his massive chest. He unleashed a torrent of instructions at me, which confounded the lady translator who had accompanied him. 'He is saying how many fish there are in the lake, and all the different kinds. I don't know their names in English. And how many fishermen come here, and how many fish they are permitted to catch'. There were, indeed, anglers all around the lake, excepting the section immediately in front of the guesthouse and the dam to its left, which were out of bounds. Their cars were parked immediately behind them. Some were sleeping, with radios playing pop music next to their ears. Mr Hunyadi gestured to the unoccupied ground in front of the guesthouse. 'This is reserved for you', the translator explained. She and Mr Hunyadi then left.

I walked down to the muddy water. Half a dozen frogs leaped at my coming, plopping into the water. There were no other signs of life. The manager of the guesthouse gave me a stiff rod with a fixed spool reel. He impaled several grains of sweetcorn on the hook, and above it attached a metal contraption like a sofa spring, shaped like a hand grenade. Into this he packed a stiff paste of pounded maize, moulding it until it enclosed the spring. Under his direction, I hurled the projectile out towards the middle of the lake, where it landed like a depth charge. I reeled in until I could feel the weight at the other end. Then I propped the rod against a boulder, and sat down.

Nothing happened, except that the sun rose higher into the sky, and the frogs made a clamour in the reeds. After an hour or so, I reeled in. The sweetcorn was still on the hook, and blobs of paste were stuck to the spring. I had had enough, so I strolled around the lake. Each time I approached a bed of reeds, I could hear the plopping

Chapter Nine - Hungary

of the frogs. Towards the end of my walk I saw someone catch a fish, a silver bream of about six ounces. Several colleagues gathered to congratulate the successful fisherman as he unhooked it and thrust it into a tiny keepnet. I could see two other fish of similar size in the net, bellies up.

After two days of this futility, I drove to another Fishing Association guesthouse, beside a much bigger lake, Velence, which is about forty miles south-west of Budapest. It was full of Germans and Austrians, who came because it was close and cheap. I was befriended on arrival by a cultured Viennese, Peter Bock, whose fluent English rescued me from a morass of misunderstanding into which my exiguous German was rapidly leading me. He maintained a certain reserve with the Germans, who were united in their obsessive passions for fishing and football, and contempt for the Hungarians. On my first afternoon, a tremendous storm burst, sending the Hungarian workmen who were supposed to be re-tiling the roof of the guesthouse into headlong flight. The stripped area of roof was left exposed, and the water poured into the room below, bringing the ceiling down, drenching the furniture, and causing the cork tiles on the floor to rise like great wet bubbles.

The manageress of the establishment was armed with a mop, which she was using to dab at the puddles, and to arrange an assortment of buckets and bowls so that they stood beneath the cascades. The Germans surveyed this ruinous scene for a moment; then hilarity burst from them like steam from a piston. They shouted with laughter, leaning against each other as the tears ran down their faces. Had it never rained before in Hungary, they asked each other. Had they never heard of plastic sheeting? What a country! What a people! What a system!

The endurance of these Germans was amazing. They would sit in their boats for twelve or fourteen hours day, catching next to nothing. Peter and I also spent a good many hours on the water. I caught nothing at all. He had one zander of three pounds, on a livebait. They all agreed that the fishing was deteriorating fast, because of pollution. The lake was also grossly overfished, with twenty or so boats out every day in the bay by the guesthouse, and a pontoon which was permanently lined with Hungarian anglers.

The Far From Compleat Angler

By the time I got to Lake Balaton, I was saying 'semmi' with great confidence. Balaton is the great inland sea, seventy miles or so long, which the guidebooks dutifully refer to as the Hungarian Riviera. Once, it must have been a paradise. I remembered a chapter from BB's *Confessions of a Carp Fisher*, recounting the experiences of the Balaton fisherman, Michael Varga, who plied these waters when they were pure, and the hills and sandy shores around were uncorrupted. Michael had taken the writer to witness the spawning of the carp in the Tapolca brook. They had waited in Michael's boat, beneath the castle at Szligliget, until the procession of the carp began; thousand upon thousand of them, 'a living chain', making their pilgrimage to mate in the pools among the waving reeds.

Now the Tapolca brook, the reeds, the pools had long since disappeared under the spread of concrete and tarmac. The lake had been engorged by the beast of tourism, reduced to a playground for the visitors from across the border: a colonising force demanding German beer, German food, parts for German cars, German newspapers and magazines, and a servant-race speaking German.

I stayed at a camp on the western side of the Tihany peninsula, whose bluffs thrust out into Balaton's milky waters about a third of the way along the northern shore. It was full of German fishermen and their families. There was a shed in which a German couple were preparing for their journey home. They were standing over a stone slab, knives in hand, gutting carp and thrusting them into plastic bags.

The Hungarian manager of the camp invited me to accompany him and his friends on a nocturnal expedition after zander, which were once immensely prolific before pollution, severe eutrophication, predatory commercial netting and exploitation by anglers did their work. Dusk was falling as the motor boat surged away from the little harbour in the reeds. We were heading for one of the deeper parts of the lake, where the dwindling population of zander had taken refuge. The fall of darkness began to restore to the lake a degree of the mystery and grandeur of which it had been robbed. The tacky resorts lining the whole of the southern shore, and most of the northern, faded into invisibility. Brilliant stars dusted the sky above, and a breeze blew, slapping water against the sides of the boat.

Chapter Nine - Hungary

Somewhere in the middle we anchored. The wind had stiffened, setting up a swell which rocked the boat unsettlingly. I was given a rod strong enough to subdue a hammerhead shark. The baits were flung into the darkness, and an oil lamp was hung, to illuminate the little plastic rings attached to the lines. Should a fish take, I was told, the ring would leap upwards. Everyone sat down and smoked. The conversation came in bursts, the silences between filled with the sounds of the lake. The lamp swayed in the wind, accompanied in a silent ballet by the plastic rings. Then one, mine, jumped decisively. I struck and felt a distant resistance. I pulled the fish in without difficulty. A silver shape splashed at the surface, and a slender zander, with bulging eyes and sharp teeth rising from a protruding lower jaw, was lifted aboard. It was unhooked, and attached, still alive, to a spring clip which was lowered over the side.

I rebaited and cast out. For a time there was a sharp sense of expectancy. We bent towards our rods, willing the fish to approach, to be hungry, to be big. But there were no more bites, and the expectancy withered. The noise of the waves against the boat became louder, and the oscillations of the lamp more violent. At midnight we headed back.

Although I had managed to break my duck at Balaton, I did not care for these opaque sheets of water; nor for the parasitic way in which they were being exploited. What I needed was running water; gravel under my feet instead of a wet seat under my bottom. I would have preferred proper mountains too, instead of these tame slopes which the Hungarians called mountains, with their weekend cabins, fenced gardens, neat vineyards. I needed a trout stream, on which I might redeem my bogus reputation for professional expertise.

Unfortunately, Hungary - for all the blessings of its climate, food, culture and so on - is deficient in the matter of trout. Indeed, there was - so my letter from the Hungarian Fishing Association informed me - but one trout stream in the entire country. It was called the Viszlo, and it flowed into Balaton. It was the pride of Rajnai Arpad, the Association's local secretary; a man who loved singing as much

The Far From Compleat Angler

as fishing, and was about to leave with the Veszprem choral society for a tour of Finland.

We drove out of Tapolca, through rolling grasslands where groups of soldiers were lolling around on roadsides, or marching lethargically across country. Rajnai told me this had been a favoured area for joint exercises with the Russians, until the abrupt and unmourned departure of the Red Army a year before. Beyond the artillery ranges, we came to a valley with gently shelving sides, and I began to feel the excitement of a new river. Rajnai said there were great trout to be caught in the Viszlo, fish of up to five kilos. Although he was somewhat vague about methods, I had visions of a classic chalkstream. I forgot the hours spent in boats and on bankside, the protesting ache of buttocks, the trickling of rainwater down neck and back, the maggots and tins of rancid sweetcorn, all the sitting and watching and waiting for nothing, 'semmi'. I jumped from the car, and reached for my fly rod.

Doubt surfaced when I saw Rajnai holding a telescopic rod which extended to no more than four feet. I gestured uncertainly at my rod. He smiled uncertainly back. I realised that, although we were evidently about to fish, I could see no water. Facing us was a wall of vegetation, fifteen or twenty feet high. Rajnai disappeared into this thicket, and I followed, trying to steer my rod between the nettles which reached to my nose, and the branches which flicked at my head. I could hear Rajnai ahead, beating a path. Then I stumbled upon him. Beyond was the stream. It appeared from the foot of a barrier of trees and bushes to the right, dropping over a miniature fall into a channel no more than a yard wide, before widening into a pool the size of the average third bedroom in an Edwardian semi-detached house.

Below where we stood, the banks closed together. The branches of the willows, beeches, alders and other assorted trees and shrubs interlocked to form the roof of a tunnel into which the stream disappeared. The water was unnervingly clear, as transparent as the celebrated apricot brandy of Kecsemet. The bed was of fine gravel, above which trailed strands of intensely green weed, seething with freshwater shrimp and snails. I could see no sign whatever of fish.

Chapter Nine - Hungary

Rajnai urged me to begin operations. I slipped as quietly as I could into the water. It was extraordinarily deep, and my head was level with Rajnai's feet. The trees left no more than a small, ragged circle of sky over my head, and I felt mild claustrophobia. To my relief, Rajnai bade me good luck, and vanished into the undergrowth. I found that by positioning myself on the far side of the pool, and keeping the rod horizontal, I could flick a nymph upstream. But it was inconceivable that any trout - assuming they existed - would have held their ground in the face of my invasion. For the sake of appearances, I cast a few times, then lost the fly in a willow branch. I floundered to dry land, concluding correctly, after five minutes on Hungary's only trout stream, that I would catch nothing.

After a decent interval I fought my way downstream in search of my host. It was mid-afternoon and extremely hot. In one of the gaps in the wall of trees, I found Rajnai. I watched him propel a spinner into the shadows, and wind energetically until the lure reappeared. He asked me how I had done. I wiped the sweat from my face and replied 'semmi'. I gestured helplessly at the trees and my rod, and he nodded sympathetically. He said he had hooked a trout and lost it.

In the evening, after Rajnai had departed for a singing rehearsal, I explored further afield. A mile or two downstream, the water was open enough to be fished with a fly. But I could find nothing to fish for. There was no hatch of fly, and no movement beneath the surface, apart from the idle waving of the weed. I did not know what to make of Rajnai's accounts of great trophies. He was a kind, genial man; but also an employee of the state, with a livelihood to protect in precarious times.

The little river was doomed anyway. Its water came from deep underground, and reached the surface as a result of being pumped out of the shafts at the huge bauxite mine near Tapolca. No one wanted the bauxite any more, and the decision had been taken to close the mine from which the Viszlo derived its chill, pellucid water. By the following year, it would cease to flow. After my futile efforts, I was able to take a detached view of this loss. I had had more than enough of western Hungary; of bauxite mines, Fishing Association lodges, German fish slayers, restaurants reverberating with disco music, suburbanised hillsides, state officials economical with the truth,

The Far From Compleat Angler

places which had once been beautiful and were now defiled. Relief, if there were to be any, must lie to the east.

The great Hungarian river is not the Danube, which belongs to all of central Europe, but the Tisza. It is the liquid spine of the Alfold, the Great Plain which fills the whole of the east of the country. These are the limitless flatlands where the tragic destiny of the Magyar - the moustachioed, teak-brown, dark-eyed, black-hatted horseman - was played out to the strains of the gipsy's lament and the stamping csardas. The mythology of the harsh, passionate life of the plains was embraced hungrily by poets and painters. Needless to say, the reality has been thoroughly trampled in the march of the 20th century.

The Tisza rises in Moldavia and joins the Danube near Belgrade. Its gradient is extraordinarily gentle, and in times past its course was distinguished by immense meanderings. In early spring, the melting of snow in the Carpathians to the north and east would send yellow floods boiling down river; and overnight vast areas of low-lying land would be inundated. A journey between Budapest and the important livestock markets at Debrecen in the east might be interrupted for weeks, until the waters abated and the ferry crossing points reappeared.

Settlements were scattered and isolated. People tended to stay where they were, or paddle about in flat-bottomed boats. The winters were hard almost beyond belief; in the worst of them, great packs of starving, green-eyed wolves came down from the snowbound mountains, ranging across the ice to harry humans and livestock alike. But there were compensations. The silt spread by the floods made the fields marvellously fertile. And the waters of the Tisza teemed with sturgeon, carp, pike, catfish and lesser species, in quantities so vast that when the flood waters receded, the land was left covered in a gasping, flapping harvest, to be fed to people and animals, and dug into the ground as fertilizer.

A hundred and fifty years or so ago, the taming of the Tisza began: a vast project to raise and straighten banks, to build flood defences, to put a stop to unruly behaviour. In the process, the

Chapter Nine - Hungary

romance of the Great Plain has been thoroughly destroyed. In place of the wilderness of grass and salt marsh, where the herds of sheep and cattle wandered and the dust storms roared, are now spread square mile upon square mile of maize, sunflowers, orchards, and goose farms. The low, whitewashed tanyas, where the cowboys would rest beneath the spreading acacias, are now weekend homes for the well-to-do of Budapest, or hotels offering riding holidays. The cowboys perform tricks on horseback, and are paid by the state.

The landscape, shorn of its remoteness and harshness, is boring. But the river, though domesticated, retains more than a vestige of its grandeur. I approached it from Budapest in the company of Tamas Hajas, a voluble, restless specimen of Hungary's new breed of entrepreneur. Hajas worked as an agent for a big German company, selling fishing and hunting gear and arranging trips for clients. He loathed the Fishing Association, and characterised all its staff and deeds as Stalinist; and was heartily loathed in return.

Hajas ran a fishing camp at a little town called Kiskore. It was reached by a rough road which ran beside a lagoon. We raced past clusters of wooden holiday chalets, restaurants, discos and meagrely equipped amusement parks. There were hundreds of boats moored or dragged onto the banks. The lagoon narrowed, its far side defined by a thick belt of trees. The water was a soapy green colour, its surface stirred by the occasional hot breath of wind. We stopped in a cloud of dust, to be greeted by a grimy individual with matted black hair and many days' growth of beard. He ushered us onto his boat, and we roared across the lagoon towards the trees. A reed bed appeared, and a channel through it. Hajas cut the engine, and paddled the boat through the reeds. On the far side was a wide expanse of yellowish water, moving with massive serenity from right to left. This was the Tisza.

The camp was on one of a string of islands which separated the moving river from a basin constructed to take excess water in time of flood. It consisted of seven or eight tents scattered under the trees. The biggest tent was the kitchen, whose frame was hung with salamis, smoked sausages and cheeses. We sat and drank beer and palinka, the colourless and powerful spirit of these parts. Eventually Hajas departed for Budapest, leaving me in the charge of the grubby boatman, whose name was Csaba. I went to sleep, exhausted by drinking and the heat.

I awoke to witness a familiar, but unexpected phenomenon. Above the water, large, pale insects were lifting themselves into clumsy flight. At first there were only a few of them, circling and zigzagging. But gradually the numbers increased, until the air quivered with them. In the quiet eddies by the bank, objects like small twigs were surfacing, and breaking open as their inhabitants struggled to free themselves. This was the mayfly, which I was used to seeing on the Kennet, and which I associated with the gross gluttony of trout.

Here, though, on this Hungarian river of determined bottom feeders, there was no such feasting. Swifts, swallows and wagtails skimmed back and forth, helping themselves delicately. But there were no gulps from below. After a time the water was speckled with the insects in their millions, while the air above pulsed with multitudes. Above the yellow flag irises and marigolds along the banks hung clouds of males, rising and falling in their mating dance (it is tempting to see ecstasy and abandonment in the ceaseless movement, even though we know that this is the only means by which a creature unable to hover and with eyes on the top of his head can focus on passing females).

Csaba collected some of the flies, and I legered a cocktail of them in a hole between two willows. It seemed, and turned out to be, a fruitless exercise. The sun was sinking in a molten sky behind me, and Csaba suggested alternative sport. With a slightly shamefaced smile, he grasped a home-made spear, and we went off in the boat. He paddled us through the channel into the lagoon. At the back of the island was a bay, fringed by a thick bed of reeds. We edged into it, slowly and silently. Csaba took my Hungarian dictionary, and found the word he wanted - 'ponti', pronounced with an aspirated 'h' at the end. It meant carp. He pointed at the reeds with his paddle, and I heard a distinct kissing sound, of a fish sucking titbits. Csaba grinned wolfishly, and ran his forefinger across the point of the spear. Weary of catching 'semmi', I was content to jettison sporting ethics. I nodded enthusiastically, and we nosed towards the reeds.

The excitement did not last long. Each time we got close to the source of the kissing, it stopped. Csaba would lay down his weapon

Chapter Nine - Hungary

with a sigh and shrug his shoulders. Occasionally there was a terrific boil as our prey took flight. The spear was never thrown; perhaps it was all a show, to divert a clueless foreigner. We returned to the camp, to pick up a friend of Csaba's who had a torch sewn into the peak of his baseball cap. We then paddled back to the bay, this time armed with fishing rods. Immediately there was a tremendous crescendo of thunder, followed by a downpour of tropical violence. We fled for the island.

The next morning we fished again from the boat, and I learned a variant on 'semmi' - 'nem ehes', not hungry. After lunch the sky began to darken in the east. Clouds rolled towards us, black above the lentil yellow of the river. Csaba suggested a trip up-river. It was an absurd idea; but anything would have been better than more hours sitting in the mud on the island. There was a murmur of thunder as we left, which soon became loud, insistent and continuous. Threads of lightning sprang across the leaden sky, and the rain burst down, blotting out the banks. We sought refuge in a small inlet, where two families were camping. Between two of the tents was a fire, over which a blackened pot was hanging. In it was a dark stew which gave off a powerfully fishy smell. A bowl was filled and handed to me. The flesh of the fish was firm and slightly gelatinous, and utterly delicious. I asked what it was. 'Horrrcha', our hosts said with relish.

A boy plucked at my sleeve and I followed him along the bank, until we reached a post on which a fish's head had been stuck. There was a stick holding its jaws apart, and the open mouth was hardly smaller than the cross-section of the head. Above this cavernous opening, reminiscent of a cross-channel ferry ready for loading, protruded two feelers eight or ten inches long. Four lesser barbules hung from the lower jaw. The eyes were black, flattened against the skull, and the mouth was equipped, not with teeth, but with two bars like hardened sandpaper, designed to grind and crush. The skin on top of the creature's head was mottled green. It paled around the gills, turning beneath the jaw to a jellyfish white. The body, had it not been turned into stew, would have been long, tapering into a fleshy, muscular tail; the belly a sickly white, the top a marbled green, yellow, brown and black. In English this was a catfish; in German, a wels; in

The Far From Compleat Angler

Hungarian, harcsa; in Latin, *silurus glanis*; in whatever language, unchallengeably the most repellent freshwater fish in Europe.

It is a creature of nightmares. Its territory is the bottom, and it likes soft mud against its belly. It rests by day and feeds by night, and if its appetites are satisfied, it grows to monstrous proportions. The biggest I could track down was dragged by a yoke of oxen from the Dnieper in Russia, and was fourteen feet long, weighing seven hundred pounds. Seeing that head in the boy's hands, I longed to catch a more modest example. But the storms had turned the river ochreous, and impossible, and I left Hajas' camp fishless.

By the time I returned to the Tisza, the weather had become settled again, and the river was back to its normal summer condition. I stayed in Tiszafured, a hot, dusty little place on the north-eastern tip of the Kiskore reservoir. I was the guest of Gabor Hegedus, an employee of the Fishing Association, and his wife Marta. Gabor, like Hajas, arranged fishing for German and Austrian clients. The previous year one of them had caught a catfish of fifty-four kilos, and a photograph of him hugging this whiskery monstrosity had appeared on the cover of Germany's most popular angling magazine. Since then Gabor had been almost overwhelmed by the demand for his services.

As a teenage girl, his wife had spent a month in Telford, staying with a pen friend, and she remembered it with transcendent gratitude and happiness. Marta had retained a powerful affection for England and the English, which contrasted strikingly with her distaste for the Germans and Austrians on whom her husband's business depended. She spoke English fluently, was widely read in English literature, and was reading Arthur Ransome to her children. She was a delightful woman, and an exceedingly good cook.

Tiszafured was one of Hungary's busiest holiday resorts, and the chief recreation was fishing. There were boats everywhere on the river: tucked into reed beds, shaded beneath the willows, poking out between waterlogged branches, buzzing incessantly up and down the open water. Every gap in the trees along the banks had its resident

Chapter Nine - Hungary

angler, usually with tent, stove, washing-line and other equipment suggestive of long tenure.

Gabor was too busy with his Germans to fish with me, so I was entrusted to his boatman, Colti, who was younger and considerably cleaner than Csaba. Gabor assured me that no one on the river knew more about the ways and haunts of the harcsa. I was up at five. The sky was opal, and the sun was rising in a blaze of pink and gold over the trees. But there was enough chill in the air to leave trails of mist above the green water. We went downstream, past a post which recorded that we were 415 kilometres away from the junction with the Danube. We passed numerous anglers, crouched beside their rods, as still as herons. None reported any success.

We tied up to a big willow beside an eddy. I had expected to use something pretty substantial for bait - a dead dog, perhaps, or a haunch of wild boar. I felt faintly disappointed when Cold worked my hook through the bodies of a fat worm and a large brown burrowing insect which he kept in a jar. Under his direction, I chucked this meagre mouthful into the middle of the river, propped my rod against the side of the boat, and settled down to wait.

This, the immobile, contemplative vigil, was the leitmotiv of my fishing in Hungary. It is what the outside world is thinking of when it mocks the fisherman's patience as a species of ridiculous and pointless endurance. And I realised how sick I was of the frozen introspection, the back and leg ache, the numbness of buttocks, the thirst, hunger, bladder strain - all made more acute by the longing for something to happen and the conviction that it never would.

Then it did. I was in a trance when the rod tip was wrenched down. Colti grabbed the butt, struck, and cried 'harcsa'. Then he grinned and handed the rod to me. I felt a solid, shuddering resistance, and pictured that wide, horrible head shaking in the depths, the muscle-packed tail thrashing, searching for some root or sunken branch to twist itself around. But the tackle was strong, and I dragged it in without much trouble, until Colti leaned forward with the net and scooped it aboard. As catfish go, it was a tiddler, no more than six or seven pounds. But, small and odious though it was, it still represented my supreme angling triumph in Hungary.

The Far From Compleat Angler

The vigil was resumed. It got hotter and hotter. The frogs went to sleep, the swirls of feeding fish ceased. Occasionally there was a flash of electric blue as a kingfisher passed, and high above, the crows and the odd hawk wheeled. But on the river, a thick, slumbrous peace had descended. In the late morning we packed up, but by the evening I was back in the boat again. It was my last night in Hungary, and - according to Gabor and Colti - a perfect one for harcsa. Velvet darkness enveloped us, and fish began to feed. Through the whine of the mosquitoes and the din of the frogs came tremendous splashes and heartstopping swirls. Colti produced a curious wooden implement, with a slender fluted stem leading to a flattened, circular end. With this he gently punched the surface, producing a hollow, popping sound which - he maintained - was audible to fish up to two kilometres away. It was supposed to exercise some strange fascination which would draw them towards my worm, lying in the mud beneath the boat.

The ruse failed, as did all the others. The fish were surely 'ehes', for the noise of their predations continued to carry up and down and across the water. But we never had a bite, and gradually even Colti's optimism waned. We shared a last bottle of beer, and I smoked a final cigarette. As the boat slid across the inky water towards the landing stage, there were more menacing splashes along the banks. I heard boar grunting and crashing through the undergrowth on the far side. The night birds, owls and nightingales, were in full voice. The river gleamed in the moonlight, its current pulling at us with gentle insistence. It seemed as if its secret life was reaching a pitch of intensity just as we were leaving it.

10. Trout, Bears and other Amusements in Romania

I was nervous about Romania. If a tenth of what I had been told about the place was true, by crossing the border from Hungary I was more or less guaranteeing an early and probably violent end to my journey. Soon - possibly on this very road leading from the infinity of the plain into the foothills of the Transylvanian Carpathians - I would be attacked, robbed, murdered. According to oral testimony, this was a country whose inherently primitive people had been reduced by the insane tyrant Ceausescu to a condition of barbarousness hardly distinguishable from that of the Huns, Avars, Tartars and other bloodthirsty hordes which had swarmed this way in centuries past.

Leszek had told me that the Romanians were 'aboriginals... they eat their own children'. Jurek had solemnly informed that I would be able to pleasure myself with a twelve-year-old Romanian girl in return for a spoonful of lemonade powder; although he cautioned me that, while I did so, her father and brothers would be plotting how to

The Far From Compleat Angler

rob and kill me. This view of the country was one of the few things on which Bohemians and Slovakians agreed. Tomas Kroupa had also mentioned cannibalism, and the fact that all the rivers in Romania were poisoned. Pavel had encountered the Romanian team at the fly fishing championships. Their tackle, he said, was as primitive as they were; and they had failed to pay their hotel bills.

The warnings became more urgent in Hungary. Romania was a land of bandits, pimps, prostitutes, cheats, murderers, barbarians, madmen. Marta and Gabor Hegedus told me of the organised oppression of Hungarians living in Transylvania. I realised only later the extent to which the Hungarian perspective was coloured by the beliefs that Transylvania belonged spiritually (as it once had politically) to Hungary; and that the Romanians were an inferior race.

The road passed through a patchwork of irregularly-shaped little fields. Here, as in Slovakia, grass-cutting was in full swing. The scythes laid trails, pitchforks thrust back and forth in the sunlight, mounds of grass stood like green warts. Caravans of horsedrawn carts creaked and clattered along the road, hauling the fodder to be stored for winter. The villages reeked of poverty and neglect. They were full of people standing around; waiting for a bus, I thought. But when one came, no one got on it. It was as if they were just there to check that nothing was happening.

My destination was the city of Tirgu-Mures, where another of Tony Pawson's contacts, a man named Grigore Lungu, was supposed to be awaiting me. By early evening I had reached the outskirts, where factories spewing out noxious yellow smoke were mixed with small, grimy houses and dingy blocks of flats. I sought directions, and found myself in a forest of grey apartment blocks. Up the stairs of one was a door, with 'Lungu' on the nameplate. Inside was a muscular, powerful man, with thick, crinkly iron-grey hair, a big moustache, and a bigger nose, a wide white smile. He was watching the World Cup match between Romania and the Republic of Ireland. 'It is a good game, I think,' he said. 'We have more skill, but the Irish, they have... I don't know the word.'

'Passion,' I suggested.

'Maybe. You like beer?' I admitted I did, and he gave me one. He led me into a spacious living room, filled with solid 19th century

Chapter Ten - Romania

furniture, with a rich carpet in the Persian style. 'The carpet is made in my factory,' Grigore said. 'It is very good quality. In New York they are paying two thousand dollars for this. Now we will watch the match. Later we will talk about fishing.'

The cabin stood in an orchard of cherry trees, on which the crimson fruit was just ripening. Behind it was a thick hedge of thorn and brambles, with rolling pastures beyond. Each morning, at dawn, the longhorned cattle were led out into the fields along a lane which ran past the cabin from the village's only road. The cows had big bells tied around their loose-skinned necks. As first light stole into the valley, the clanging of the bells mixed with the sleepy, irritable admonitions of the boys and girls who stumbled up the rutted track behind their beasts.

Here, the valley was gentle, and the sides were cut into little fields, with grassy slopes above, speckled with sheep and crisscrossed with paths, which looked like stitching on green cloth. Towards the mountains, the valley narrowed. The meadows gave way to woods of hazel, oak and beech, cut by tiny streams. Further into the distance, the ridges were blanketed in forests of pine and spruce. These were the Caliman Mountains, one of the numerous sub-divisions of the Transylvanian Carpathians. They rise to the north of the river Mures, which eventually joins the Tisza at the Hungarian city of Szeged.

The village in which Grigore's holiday cabin was situated was called Bistra Muresului, after the little river, the Bistra, and the great river, the Mures. There were two hundred or so homes, mostly of wood. They were plastered in ochre, cream, olive, and peacock blue, with terracotta tiled roofs and shaded verandahs. Most had enclosed outside yards, with wooden gateways riotously carved with wild boar, deer, sunflowers, swags of leaves and bunches of grapes. Each yard had its flowerbed, and most a selection of walnut, almond and mulberry trees. By our standards, the village was primitive. Although most houses had electricity, the supply was erratic in the extreme. Some had televisions, with abysmal reception. Flushing lavatories were unknown, and water was heated on wood-burning stoves. Some

The Far From Compleat Angler

of the more prosperous residents had cars, but they were of less use than horses and carts because petrol was almost unobtainable.

They did, at least, have enough to eat - at that time, an unusual blessing in Romania. The farms produced sufficient for the families which owned them; any surplus was bartered for non-essentials like fuel and lightbulbs. They toiled endlessly, but the land was rich enough to provide. Their lives had been lightly touched by the 20th century, let alone by the dreams of the agro-industrial elysium hatched in the marbled chambers of the presidential palace in faraway Bucharest.

Grigore's cabin was built on land owned by his friend, Mr Floria, who was manager of the local logging company. He emanated a calm, peasant craftiness. He was immensely strong and fat, with a brown, jowly face, and narrow eyes, usually shaded by a wide straw hat. His movements were unhurried, his speech soft and courteous, his authority unquestioned. He was, by reputation, a keen-eyed shot and a deadly catcher of trout, although I never fished with him.

Before I could fish, Grigore had to go to Bucharest - a ten hour drive - to obtain a fishing permit for me. On the same trip, he secured government permission to privatise the company in Tirgu-Mures of which he was managing director. On his return, he reported that the arranging of his company's affairs had proved considerably more straightforward than the licence. I have this document before me now: 'Autorizatie de Pescuit Domnul TOM FORT din Anglia este autorizat sa Pescuiasca... in fondurile de pescuit mentionate in anexe din cadrul judetelor: Cluj, Hunedoara, Mure se Suceava....' and so on, a preamble stamped by the Ministerul Silviculturii to six pages listing the rivers and lakes on which I was permitted to fish for trout and grayling. There were more than a hundred in all, and I never even saw a tenth of them. It would have taken a decade to do justice to this permit, and I had no more than a few weeks. Moreover, it covered only four areas. Maramures, most of Moldavia, and much of southern Transylvania were excluded - not to mention the amazing abundance of the distant Danube delta.

The miracle was that so much of this wealth of water had not been irredeemably ruined by the industrial unheaval pursued with such manic determination by Ceausescu. There were, of course, many rivers which had been poisoned, and others which had been broken by

Chapter Ten - Romania

hydro-electric projects. But the mountain streams, in which trout and grayling had thrived since the Ice Age, had remained comparatively uncorrupted, though severely affected by poaching.

Grigore took me first to the Ilva, which ran into the Mures about fifteen miles upstream from our village. Its valley was steeper and narrower than that of the Bistra. The slopes, thick with pine and spruce, rose abruptly, confining a dark, silent cleft. The stream was tiny, a necklace of little pools connected by bubbling runs and miniature waterfalls. The water was wonderfully clear, and full of small, wild, hungry trout and grayling. But initially I was confounded by the scale. Grigore crouched and dibbled his flies in the quick water, every so often lifting his wrist sharply to bring a flashing, kicking fish to hand. But I found the method difficult to imitate; and that first evening I caught but one trout, not much longer than my middle finger, which seized one of my flies while I was looking at the others.

We returned the next day, and followed the forest road high into the mountains. It brought us out above the main belt of trees, at a height of four thousand feet or so, into hot, brilliant sunshine. Grigore's friend, Ioan, prepared a barbecue of fillets of pork and spicy sausage; while we lounged around drinking beer, watching the blue smoke rise into the blue sky, smelling the scents of pine needles, wild flowers, moss and grilling meat. Later I read, while Grigore and Ioan snored in the sun. Then, with the sun off the water, we fished again.

At first I continued to flounder. I could not believe that there were any fish worth catching in the tiny pools. I got into an enervating series of tangles, and lost the brilliantly successful fly, with stiff grey hackles, which Andrzej Fox had given me in Poland. Despair was threatening when, at last, I came on a spot suitable for my English technique.

There was a small bridge, below which the stream widened into the first substantial pool I had seen on the Ilva. The surface was marbled by competing currents, and as I peered at it, I saw it broken by the dimples of feeding fish. The sun had dropped below the line of the hills, and the water beneath the bridge appeared as molten gold. I cast up towards it, using two bushy dry flies, which twisted and darted in the current. One vanished in a little splash, but I was too

The Far From Compleat Angler

slow, and felt the fish for no more than a split second. Next cast, the same fly was taken again, and a minute later I unhooked a plump little grayling. Triumphant, I admired the rise and collapse of the outsize dorsal fin, then let it go.

The darkness deepened as we worked our way downstream. On the outskirts of a village, another bridge took the road over the river. Immediately above it was a long, slow pool, curved like a boomerang. Most of the surface was in black shadow. But on the far side, beneath a wall of rock, was a band which reflected the last of the sky's light in smooth amber. Fish were feeding enthusiastically, flinging themselves at a line of fluttering sedges drifting down from the trailing branches of a beech. I scrambled down the bank beside the bridge, to a ledge just above the water. I tied on a large, untidy Cinnamon sedge, and flicked it towards the far bank. Once, twice, fish rushed at it and missed. Shaking with excitement, I dried the fly, and cast again. I saw its whiskery outline for a second, lost it, then glimpsed it again. As it followed the curve of the pool, I sensed rather than saw the attack. I raised the rod tip and felt the plunge of the fish.

Ioan heard my cry, and came to stand on the bridge. He was joined by two villagers, who abandoned the cows they had been leading to watch the fun. The fish was thrashing back and forth a few yards away. I could not see it, but I held on until its struggles weakened. I grasped my net, and lifted the fish towards me until it broke the surface close to my feet. I scooped at it and missed. At the second attempt it slid into the mesh. I seized it, hit it over the head with a stone, and struggled up the bank with it.

By now a small crowd had gathered. With smiles, the trout was appraised. Handshakes followed, and exclamations of astonishment when I showed them the fly. It was an extraordinarily sweet moment. And the size of the trout? I will stake my reputation that it exceeded nine ounces.

Exploiting his excellent contacts in the region, Grigore had arranged for me to stay and fish at a sanctuary buried deep in the Giurgelui mountains, a place called Lapusna. It was surrounded by a fifteen foot

Chapter Ten - Romania

high fence, and was accessible through formidable gates. Within was a building as long a football pitch, in a frowning Alpine style, with verandahs and balconies, and windows tucked under steep roofs. The base was of stone, the rest of wood, blackened with tar and as sombre as the forest which stretched away in all directions.

It was the Royal Hunting Lodge, commissioned by the third of Romania's four kings, Carol II, an able, unscrupulous, vindictive despot. Here he and his friends slaughtered game; and in the glades he wandered with his voluptuous mistress, the notorious Madame Lupescu. The mountains swarm with deer, wolves, lynx, wild cat, red squirrels, ptarmigan, and bear; and it was inevitable that Ceausescu would requisition it to pursue his own demented notions of sport.

He had a staff of half a dozen or so, on station in the forest, whose task was to identify outsize bears, track them, and lure them into the sights of the dictator's rifle. There was a clearing near the Royal lodge, where the confrontation between man and beast was enacted. In the middle was a wooden shed, with an opening at one side, and a high voltage light over it. When I was there, the ground in front of the shed was covered with bones from slaughtered horses. Some still had morsels of flesh attached; there was the sweet smell of putrefaction in the air, and immense clouds of flies shimmered in the sunlight. There was a path leading into the forest, with a slender tree trunk on either side. A notch had been cut into each trunk at a height of about seven and a half feet.

Ceausescu would come when he had been assured that a big bear had become a regular visitor to the clearing. The horsemeat was the bait; the notches were to assess the dimensions of the creature as it shambled contentedly back into the forest, on its hind legs, grateful for the free meal. Ceausescu would sit in the shed, rifle resting on the window ledge, as dusk fell. The forester would alert him to the beast's coming. They would listen to the munching of horseflesh, teeth and claws at work. Then a switch would be flicked, the clearing would be flooded with light; and there, fifteen yards away, upright and blinded, would be the target: eight feet and six hundred pounds of brown bear, the remains of his last evening meal still gripped in his paws. The dictator's finger would squeeze, and there would be celebrations long into the night at the lodge, while

The Far From Compleat Angler

the corpse was being prepared for transfer to the trophy collection in Bucharest.

I did not stay in the lodge itself, which was draughty and gloomy and crammed with furniture made out of, or decorated with, antlers; but in a sturdy wooden cottage nearby, where the caretaker's wife brought food, and lit the wood-burning stove for the hot water. Just outside the compound was the stream, the Gurghui, which was comparable in size and character to the Barle in Devon, where it drops from the moor into its wooded valley below Withypool. The water ran clear, with a stony bottom which gave it a golden lustre in sunlight. Cascades had been built every few hundred yards, to create pools which were pleasant for fishing, and easily poached.

A little way downstream from the entrance to the lodge was a bridge, above which was a long, tempting pool. Grigore's friend, the Judge - who had made the arrangements - directed me to fish it. I began to do so, using a dry fly, a method with which he had no patience. He strode off, and I inspected the pool more closely. On the far side there was a line of big boulders, which pushed the current into a glide, in which the odd fish was rising. I waded up, marking a trout which took confidently, three times. I was just about to deliver my fly when the tranquillity of the evening was fractured by a terrific crashing among the pine trees on the far bank, and the appearance of a huge pair of antlers. Beneath them was a pair of large, liquid eyes, a noble head, and a massive russet body. I staggered back, and after a moment the stag bounded uphill, vanishing instantly into the blackness of the forest.

Next morning I ate boiled eggs, yoghurt, salami, sheep's cheese and wild strawberries for breakfast, and went back to the pool. At once I caught a plump, heavily spotted trout on a Hare's Ear. I knocked it on the head, wrapped it in a damp cabbage leaf, and prepared for great things. I was hailed by a fisherman I had met the previous day, a teacher from Tirgu-Mures. He spoke good English, and his wife had a big bag of cherries which I helped myself to. So I passed a pleasant forty minutes or so, before resuming fishing. I lost another trout, bigger than the first. Then there was a further interruption, from the district fishing supervisor, who - rather to my surprise - also spoke English. He explained that I should not be

Chapter Ten - Romania

fishing on my own, that he should have been guiding me. But he was clearly disinclined to press the matter, and we chatted in that pleasant way that anglers, who've never met each other before and never will again, are able.

By the time he had departed on his rounds, it was too hot to fish, and the rise had petered out. I lunched off homemade chicken soup, grilled pork and kidneys, spicy sausages, and bowls of wild mushrooms; slept; went back to the river.

I felt uneasy. I had done a great deal of talking about bears, and reading about them, and speculating about them. From that, it is but a short step to hearing them. I should say that I never actually saw a bear while I was in Romania - at least one which hadn't been stuffed, or converted into a rug. But my awareness of them was acute, and I think my fishing suffered. On the Gurghui that evening - the bear's preferred time for a snack - I heard plenty. Instead of concentrating on the water, I found myself peering into the twilit forest, listening for heavy breathing and the snapping of twigs beneath questing paws, expecting a glimpse of a hairy form.

The forest is sometimes described as silent, but it is surprising how many different sounds there are, if you are listening for them; and how they work on the imagination. In the mud beside one pool I found a pair of round, deep footprints. I am no naturalist, but I know there are not many forest beasts in the habit of walking around on their back legs. I heard, or thought I heard, something moving purposefully through the undergrowth. A power over which I had no control sent me into flight, an undignified exit pursued by (imagined) bear.

The beekeepers of Brosteni were at work in a broad meadow beside the river. Around their hives trembled clouds of bees, their murmur drowned by the noise of the water. There were three of them, in grubby white coats, with trousers tucked into leather boots. Grigore drove up to them, greeted them, introduced me. It was a sticky encounter. I was given spoonfuls of pure honey, flecked with fragments of wax, legs and wings; then pieces of dripping comb, then honey flavoured

The Far From Compleat Angler

with mint, strawberry, violet, blackberry. I had coffee sweetened with honey, mineral water with honey, brandy with honey. They gave me curd cheese with honey, then more cheese, this time with bilberry jam. We exchanged syrupy handshakes, and they pressed us to take a big jar of honey with comb to add to our other provisions. As we left them, I asked Grigore if he had paid them anything. He looked at me, and said: 'There is nothing to pay. These are friendly people. They like to give.'

We were in Moldavia, the north-eastern province which stretches up to what was then the Soviet border. The weather had at last broken, and had become raw and wet. The Bistrita River, near Brosteni, was hugely swollen, a torrent of cafe-au-lait. In the town itself, an official of the forestry ministry gave us permission to stay in a guesthouse beside the Neagra, a tributary of the Bistrita. The official said, casually, that there were bears everywhere up the valley. The fishing, he reported, could be excellent.

The Neagra ran chocolate-coloured through a broad valley. The lower slopes were covered by lush woods of oak, ash and hornbeam; with the hilltops washed by waves of the familiar, darker green of the conifers. We came at length to a village high in the valley. Our friend in Brosteni had told us that, three weeks before, a woman here had been attacked by a female bear as she went into the woods to round up cattle. The woman's ear had been ripped off, her body slashed open, and she was expected to die in hospital. It was that sort of place, on the edge of the world; where people cut wood, hunted game, kept animals, grew grass, cultivated a few meagre crops. There were few men to be seen, and the women were toiling at the grass-cutting.

Ceausescu had come here, too, to shoot bears. But the guesthouse where he stayed had been badly neglected. It was damp, the lavatory did not work, and there was no hot water. We retreated to the river, which in normal circumstances would have been one to gladden the heart. It snaked down the valley in a string of little pools and runs. Each bend enclosed an enticing curl of water, which washed against the roots of a willow or alder. Despite the colour, we came upon a flat stretch where fish were rising. They were very small indeed, but they gave us an hour of fun, before one of the storms which had been

Chapter Ten - Romania

chasing each other around the hills paused long enough to bring down curtains of rain and send us back to the cabin.

We made a melancholy meal in the darkness, while the windows rattled in the gale and the rain pounded on the metal roof. I went to my damp bed, and listened on my radio to the World Cup semi-final between England and West Germany. The match seemed endless (Germany won on penalties after extra time) and I wavered between sleep and patriotic consciousness as the commentary - punctuated by startling bursts of electrical interference - droned on. I felt a little sad at England's defeat; much sadder at the damage done to fishing prospects.

But next morning the Neagra was just fishable. Watched throughout by a pair of buzzards which wheeled and glided above our heads, mewing incessantly, we caught fish after fish: trout, and grayling like silver ingots. They were all small, but it was enough to give a tantalising taste of what might have been. In a letter many months later, Grigore described an autumn trip back to the same river. 'I fished some wonderful trouts,' he recorded.

Grigore had arranged one more excursion for me, to the southern Carpathians. My companion was to be a manager at his company, a Hungarian called Istvan Horvath. He had a stringy, undernourished appearance, with lank black hair, sad dark eyes, and a shaggy moustache whose ends he was for ever twisting and tugging. He smoked incessantly, spoke French about as well as me, and - being a Hungarian in Romania - throbbed with resentment against those he regarded as his oppressors.

This was Istvan's principal passion. His secondary one was more sympathetic, though occasionally tiresome. It was for the high peaks of the Retezat Mountains to the south of Tirgu-Mures. This is the last colossal upheaval of the Carpathian chain, extending from the Iron Gates in the west to Siret in the east. This massif is two hundred miles long, a formidable barrier hemming in the north of the Danube plain, and facing down the fierce, rugged mountains of Bulgaria beyond. Up to the tree line, these are characteristically Carpathian hills, sheeted

The Far From Compleat Angler

in forest and split by valleys enclosing tumbling streams. But above rise lines of sharp, bare schists bound by looping ridges. There are meadows spotted with huge stones, behind which - in the brief period when the snows are gone - burst forth orchids and saxifrages. And in the shallow bowls between the outcrops are the lakes, like sapphires in the sunshine, like granite under cloud.

The expedition had an unpromising start. It was dark and teeming with rain when I arrived at Istvan's flat. He had already warned me of the dangers of being in the mountains in bad weather, and I was looking forward to the trip being cancelled. But he was ready, with a rucksack nearly as tall as himself.

'Pas de probleme,' he replied airily when I asked him for the third time whether it was safe to go. 'Ici, il pleut. Mais en Retezat, qui sait?' He smiled reassuringly. 'Nous verrons.' He picked up his rucksack, gasping with the effort. It seemed excessive for the two days we planned to be away. The explanation appeared - Istvan's wife and daughter. Would I mind if they came too? Istvan said his wife spoke English and would be of great assistance in our conversation. He went out, and I told her - in English - what her husband had said. She registered incomprehension. At the third time of asking, she shook her head emphatically and said: 'No Engleesh.'

We set off through the pounding rain. Istvan lit a cigarette and I opened my window to let the smoke out. His wife leant forward and whispered in his ear. He asked me if I would shut the window, as she was unusually sensitive to the cold. I did so, and asked him if he would mind not smoking in the car.

As we drove south-west down the valley of the Mures, then through Alba Iulia and past Sebes, Istvan expatiated on the Hungarian question. We reached the principal river of Retezat, the Riul Mare. To the south, the mountains formed a dark massive barrier, their tops lost in cloud. We drove along the river, which was reduced to a meagre trickle. Higher up, its gorge was plugged with a vast heap of rubble, the Riul Mare dam, constructed from boulders and earth torn from the surrounding hillsides, leaving savage gashes.

Beyond the dam was a milky blue sheet of water, trapped between steep walls of loose rock. Beside it lorries roared in all directions, gears grinding. Above it was the cabana where we were to

Chapter Ten - Romania

stay. Next to this dreary building was a dungheap, occupied by two fierce-looking cocks and a pair of hideously wattled turkeys. As we pulled up, the turkeys high-stepped towards the car, scarlet dewlaps flapping. Istvan's daughter cringed in terror, and burst into tears. A dilapidated old man appeared, shooed the birds away, and greeted us with wild enthusiasm, as if we were the first humans to come his way for many a long year. The sanitary arrangements inside were squalid. We had one room, in which were two beds. Istvan said the Horvath family would occupy one; the other was for me. I looked forward to the night with foreboding.

While Mrs Horvath prepared our evening meal, Istvan and I went down to the lake. There were two or three anglers casting spinners, and Istvan - who was a fisherman in a minor way - joined them. I desultorily cast a fly where the river flowed into the lake, but nothing happened. Back at the cabana, I instantly regretted having accepted Istvan's offer to supply the provisions. Laid out on the table were a loaf of stale bread; a slab of greasy processed cheese in a cellophane pack with the words 'Denmark - Food Aid' stamped on it; a pot containing a brown slimy substance said to be pate; and a tin of pork luncheon meat from Finland, also stamped 'Food Aid'.

With the help of a sleeping pill and a couple of slugs of malt whisky, I slept peacefully. Breakfast was the same in its essentials as supper. Istvan assembled the leftovers and packed them away to serve as our lunch in the mountains. I suggested bringing one of the three bottles of beer I had been given by Grigore. 'Le alcool est mauvais dans les montagnes,' Istvan said sternly. 'Nous buvons l'eau de la rivière.' I put the bottle in my own bag.

We set off in the car, and my spirits began to revive as the dam and the lake disappeared behind us. It was a dewy, shining morning, with sunlight flooding across a brilliant sky; although ahead ominous trails of cloud were curled around the highest ridges. Gradually, the road - which was unmade - became narrower, squeezed between a soaring wall of rock on one side and a plunging gorge on the other. Istvan issued a stream of advice and encouragement, tugging at his moustache and occasionally leaning out of the window to adjust the wing mirror, in order to improve his view of our rear.

The Far From Compleat Angler

After an hour we reached the end of the road, a clearing in the trees at a height of more than five-and-a-half thousand feet. Three shepherds were there, with packhorses, on their way to tend their flocks in the high pastures for the rest of the summer. Istvan lifted his rucksack onto his shoulders, exhaling sharply with the effort. I asked him what was in it. He explained that it did not do to take the mountains lightly; one must have a tent, spare clothes, medical supplies, cooking equipment, blankets. What about maps? He looked at me scornfully and tapped his head. The map was in here. He knew these paths as well as the streets of Tirgu-Mures. He strode off into the trees. I followed, with my fishing bag over one shoulder - reassuringly heavy with beer - and my rod in one hand.

The path led down into a gulch, over a small stream, then ascended a steep slope in a series of zig-zags. To our left a much bigger stream descended in haste from the distant lakes. To begin with, I had difficulty keeping up with Istvan. But he slowed dramatically, and when we reached the first ridge, he discarded the rucksack and sank to the ground, drawing quick, shallow breaths. His face was grey and shiny with sweat.

Thereafter the way became somewhat easier, and tremendous views opened in all directions. Across the gorge, screes of bone-white boulders had spilled down, broken by grass, stunted rhododendrons and dwarf pines. Beyond, naked ridges thrust serrated edges into a cottony mist. Our side of the valley was gentler, and we met fawn-coloured, bony cattle with clanging bells at their necks. We came to the first of the lakes, Lia. There were two or three tents at the far end. Scattered across the bog grass in front of them were relics of previous visits: scorchmarks and mounds of cans and bottles. I made my way to the water's edge, made up a cast of wet flies, and began to cast. Istvan chatted to the campers for a while before joining me.

'I think we will not fish here,' he said.

'Why not?'

'They say the dam workers were here yesterday. With nets. They took away enough trout to fill this.' He patted his rucksack. 'We will go on. This mountain air is making me better. I should not smoke so much.' He lit a cigarette. 'Yes, fifty or sixty a day. It is too much.'

Chapter Ten - Romania

The next lake, Ana, was a place of fond memory for Istvan. The previous year he had caught a trout of nearly two kilos here, and he assured me that there were many others just as big. I wandered along the leeward shore, casting. Dark clouds were building up from the west, turning the colour of the water from glacial blue to slate grey. Sharp breaths of wind broke the calm, sending ripples against the rocks on the far shore. The lake looked cold and empty. I was startled, on looking behind me, to see Istvan pulling in a trout of half a pound or so.

We ate a lunch whose austerity was only partly mitigated by my beer. Istvan said that, because of the weather, it would not be safe to attempt the eight-hour round trip he had originally envisaged. I was relieved to hear it. Istvan led the way up the hill behind us. Beyond was the largest of the Retezat lakes, Bucura, glittering in a bowl below us. Above it towered the jagged heights of Mount Peleaga, rising to nearly eight thousand feet. Stretched across the distant skyline, like a sheet on a washing line, was the Bucura Saddle.

Istvan returned to Lake Ana to fish, while I lay on the soft grass, feeling the breeze against my cheek, smelling the heather, listening for the cry of the ever-present buzzards. I dozed for a while; was awoken by the tinny tinkle of a radio which reached me from a caravan crossing the saddle a good ten miles away. I made my way downhill, and found Istvan already on the move. He gestured at the pass leading from Ana to the next lake in the chain. A mist was leaking through it, spreading across the screes. Istvan said something about hailstones like eggs, and hurried off. We kept comfortably ahead of the mist, Istvan almost trotting as the gravitational pull of the rucksack propelled him downhill. A few moments after we had reached the car, the storm burst around us.

That evening I fished the Riul Mare above the dam lake. It was rough and rocky, its water amazingly clear. I caught one trout, which was about three inches long. Istvan's trout made a welcome variation to our evening meal, as the bread was now too stale to cut, and the Finnish luncheon meat smelled like decomposed reindeer. The remainder of our provisions took their final bow next morning, after which I returned to the Riul Mare, and then followed a tributary which flowed in from the west.

The Far From Compleat Angler

Although I had my rod, my chief motive was to escape from Istvan. I strode up into an enchanted valley. The crests of the hills were covered in spruce and pine, and the grass which swept down to the stream was spotted with grub-like sheep. I turned a corner and was faced by an immense vista. On left and right, escarpments plunged into the valley, each bluer and less distinct as they stretched away into the distance. Blocking the furthest end was a mass of green, rising to a summit which was invisible in the thin grey cloud. I swung my binoculars across this forest, and saw a silver gleam, the cataract by which the river issued from the mountainside.

I came upon a clump of wild strawberries, and half-filled my cap with them. I ate them beside the stream, and watched a peregrine falcon circle with gripping, inconceivable slowness. After a time I felt strong enough to face Istvan again.

11. SOUTH OF THE DANUBE: INTERLUDES IN BULGARIA AND CROATIA

My angling quest in Bulgaria was not, I must confess, an unqualified success. It began badly, proceeded indifferently, and ended in premature anticlimax. Along the way, though, there were diverting glimpses of the possibilities which a more resourceful visitor might care to exploit.

My introduction to the country was an eight hour wait at the absurdly named Bridge of Friendship, which spans the Danube between Romania and Bulgaria, and an early morning embrace from the many tentacled monster created by the Bulgarian authorities to separate foreigners from their precious currency. On arrival in Sofia, I hunted down the offices of the Bulgarian Fishing Association (the somnolent tourist office in London had been unaware of the existence of such an organisation, and unable to establish whether there were any fish in Bulgaria).

Within a few hours, secretary Arsov and translator Poliakov had commandeered a minivan and a driver, and we were bouncing up the road into the Rila Mountains, and the famous monastery hidden deep

The Far From Compleat Angler

within. Beneath its soaring walls, and the lines of tourist coaches, flowed the Rilska river, and in a shaded spot beside its crystal waters we found the Local Expert.

Every angler is familiar with the Local Expert. He knows the places other men do not know, and uses flies no one else has thought of. When we think we have done well, he has done better. When we have caught nothing, he always has a brace or two. He was made to irritate us, and to humble us. If we listen to him - and, more often than not, he is happy to share at least a few of his secrets - we will learn a thing or two. Unfortunately, my communication with this choice example of the species was necessarily restricted by the absence of a common language. But he sat me down, plied me with salty goat's milk cheese and apricot brandy, displayed a pair of eight inch trout he had caught that morning, tied me a fly of bizarre appearance from a clump of wild boar's hair, then grasped his bamboo with string tied to the end (no nonsense here about reels), and bade me follow.

It was easier to understand the instruction than to observe it. He bounded up-river from boulder to boulder like a chamois, pausing here and there to dibble his fly in a tiny pool. I was hard pressed to match his pace; indeed, keeping him in sight rapidly replaced fishing as my first priority, since I was anxious not to become lost in this wild region, where bears were likely to outnumber humans. On the rare occasion I had leisure to fish a pool, I found the trout would dash at the hairy fly but would not take hold. The Local Expert, when I managed to catch up with him, gesticulated at the sun blazing overhead. We agreed that it was in the wrong place and likely to remain so. So we retraced our steps, and the Local Expert - who must have been seventy at least - asked secretary Arsov how old I was. I fear my red face, gasping and wheezing, slipping and sliding, had been noted; and had not impressed.

That night we stayed at a trout farm run by the Fishing Association. It lay in a grassy, wooded bowl fringed by the pale, bare ridges of the Rila, Pirin and Rhodope mountains. Bright and early on the morrow I was taken to the stream which supplied the trout farm, and urged to start fishing. If secretary Arsov had a fault, it was that he was somewhat sparing with his advice, which - combined with the Bulgarian habit of shaking the head to signify assent and nodding it for the negative - left me a little hazy as to what I should be doing.

Chapter Eleven - Bulgaria and Croatia

The stream was very small and the water very clear. With the removal of several thousand trees, it would have made a delightful piece of dry fly fishing. As it was, all I could do was to catapult my flies through the infrequent gaps in the forest, and hope for the best. In one of these spots, an eager little fellow impaled himself. He was a rainbow, evidently from the farm; but a Bulgarian trout nonetheless, and my only one. For that was the sum of it. We visited some lakes in the Rhodopes, in one of which someone was reputed to have caught a 25-pound trout, using fish eggs as bait. But the sun was broiling again and any fish were out of sight, so drinking beer in the shade and surveying the spectacular scenery seemed a better bet than flogging the unforgiving water.

I had intended to take off on my own to explore some other streams of which I had had good reports from secretary Arsov. But a vital element was lacking: petrol. There was none to be had, and in the end I had to flee to the border with no more than a few fluid ounces left in my tank. It was particularly annoying, as I had had an invitation to stay in one of the monks' cells in the monastery at Rila, with the prospect of another sortie to the river below. I had entertained visions of showing the Local Expert a thing or two; perhaps even of presenting the Abbot (if there were one) with a plate of trout for his breakfast. But it was not to be.

By this stage of my journey I had become increasingly prey to homesickness, and was beginning to run short of money. I decided that I would bypass the celebrated trout and grayling fishing of Slovenia, ignore my invitation to explore the dubious potential of the Harz Mountains in East Germany, and get back to England. But there was one river of which I had read in Tony Pawson's book, and which I was determined not to miss: the Gacka.

This amazing piece of water bursts from the ground at the foot of a hill about eighty miles or so south of Zagreb. From its birth it is a fully fledged river, extremely deep, extremely clear, and (when I fished it) extremely full of whacking great fish. It runs for a mere ten miles or so into a lake, and the cream of the water was in the hands of the celebrated Gacka Hotel, where I arrived in the middle of another burning afternoon. Having been booked in by a memorably insolent receptionist, I made acquaintance with a most courteous,

The Far From Compleat Angler

French-speaking professor of philosophy from Zagreb University. He showed me the river, which he had fished for thirty years, and told me that I must use a nymph, 'au fond', down deep.

The water was stocked with rainbow trout of a pound or so, which grew at tremendous speed on the lavish feeding. Five and six pounders were reasonably common, but these were no simple-minded stockies, as I found during my all-too-brief stay. That evening, bemoaning my lack of weighted nymphs and my ignorance of how I would fish them even if I had any, I noticed the blue-winged olives were hatching. I dashed off to my car, grabbed the box with my remaining stock of Orange Quills in it, dashed back and immediately caught a fish of a pound-and-a-half. Cheered by the prospect of great slaughter, I continued; but found the trout irritatingly choosy. Two big fish surged at the Orange Quill in the dusk, but each time, growing increasingly distraught, I struck far too quickly.

The next evening, my last, I returned to the same stretch, and again the BWOs began to hatch. I lost my last decent Orange Quill with a wild cast into a tree, then lost my head as big trout feasted around me. I tried fly after fly, olives and sedges and fancy patterns; but in the slow, clear water, the fish were not to be deceived. Finally, when it was almost completely dark, I hooked one. He jumped twice, heavy splashes, surged through a weedbed. I conceded line, and he barrelled downstream, and broke me. It was over in the time it has taken me to describe it, and I beat the water with my rod and cursed in infantile fashion.

Back at the hotel I met the philosophy professor, looking far from philosophical. He had, he told me, hooked the biggest trout of his life. He had fought it for an eternity, beaten it, brought it close enough to the net to measure its vast size; and the hook had come away. 'How big?' I asked him. 'Five kilos, I think,' he replied brokenly.

Not long ago, I read that the Gacka Hotel had been destroyed in the civil war. The very notion of a fishing hotel in such a place seems absurd, from a different world. But the river must still be there, and maybe some of the trout. Even at this distance, I can feel the sadness of the professor from Zagreb University; and his hope that, one day, the madness will end and the fishermen will return.

12. Brazilian Gold

Seen from above, the great river wound in easy curves through the dull green of the forest - like an anaconda, I thought, wishing vainly that a more startling metaphor would come to mind. It was terracotta in colour, thick with red earth washed down by the rains a thousand miles to the east. The aircraft wheeled, and the river burst into foam over the fabled Falls of Iguacu. Several Germans, bristling with cameras, rushed to the windows to obtain views. My own was blotted out by a backside in green stretch pants.

'Alas, poor Niagara,' Mrs Roosevelt sighed when she saw the Iguacu Falls, conceding that the North American wonder had to take second place to the South American. And they are an astounding sight, curving in a tumultuous bow from the Brazilian to the Argentine banks of the River Iguacu. There are almost three hundred cataracts, stretching across a distance in excess of two miles, broken by islands and outcrops. The grandest, part obscured by the plumes of spray drifting skywards to form an

The Far From Compleat Angler

ever-present cloud, is on the inside of the great bend, tight against the Brazilian shore.

There is little love between Argentina and Brazil; and the Argentines have built a nasty, squat, modernist intruder of a hotel on their side, an expression of resentment against Brazil's title to the best of the Falls. Brazil's elegant answer is the Hotel das Cataratas, a splendid confection in pink and white, which looks like a wedding cake dropped accidentally into the sombre green of the forest. We were there for five days, my friend P and I; not to fish the Iguacu itself, which was just as well in view of its condition, but to explore the much vaster Parana river, into which the Iguacu debouches some fifteen miles below the falls.

I had been conscious of this, the second river of Brazil after the Amazon, for many years. I had bought a book, long out of print, which was called *The Golden River*. It was a stirring account by the great J.W. Hills and a man called Dunbar of a journey up the Parana, which rises in central Brazil, forms part of the border between that country and Paraguay, cuts down through Argentina, and eventually - after two thousand miles - joins the Uruguay in the estuary of the River Plate. A while later I found another book, *The Dorado*, by Hills and G.W. Harrisson - 'the greatest of dorado fishermen', as he is called in the preface. This is a much more specialised volume, which incorporates much of the fishing material from *The Golden River*.

These two books lingered in my mind. They dated from a long departed era, when the appetite of the upper-class, moneyed Englishman drove him to wander the world in search of new challenges, new quarries. Across the Empire, the English shot, hunted and fished for their recreation, in their characteristically thorough and determined style. Where possible, motivated by that sentimental nostalgia for the land they had left behind, they would duplicate the sport of boyhood: hence the import of trout to the streams of Kashmir, Ceylon, South Africa and Kenya.

The Spanish and Portuguese had beaten them to the conquest of South America. But eventually the English arrived, opening mines, harvesting coffee, helping themselves to precious stones

Chapter Twelve - Brazilian Gold

and metals. The fishermen among these hardy wealth-seekers who found themselves by the great rivers of southern Brazil encountered a fish which reminded them of Scotland. In Portuguese, it is the 'dourado'; in Spanish, the 'dorado'. With that typical disdain for local usage, the English called it the Golden Salmon. Of course it is no sort of salmon. But the 'golden' is right, for as it bursts through the surface, twisting and leaping, it glows a deep, buttery yellow, like an ingot in sunlight. And it is a magnificent creature, its fins, tummy and head burnished with that gold, its broad flanks spotted with black, its wide predator's mouth bristling with teeth. What doubtless reminded those pioneers of *salmo salar* was its fight. It has the same muscular vigour and indomitable will to seek freedom which, allied to the power of the rivers in which it lives, make it a good deal harder to subdue.

As I say, the pictures painted by Hills and his companions stayed with me, and occasionally I used to wonder whether the fish that had thrilled them was still to be found. Then I read that two Englishmen were offering dourado fishing, and one February I forsook dreary England for the comforts of the Hotel das Cataratas, and found myself beside the Parana. The shock was considerable, and I was silent as I looked across to Paraguay on the far bank, half a mile or so away. Between me and a country about which I knew almost nothing beyond the reputation of General Stroessner extended a brown, surging flood, marbled with competing currents, boiling with terrifying whirlpools.

Had someone told me that its volume exceeded that of all the rivers of Britain put together - or of Europe - I should not have been surprised, for in places the Parana plunges to a depth of six hundred feet, and the water travels at the speed of a charging buffalo. It is impossible to convey the overpowering impression that this irresistible force of nature made on me. I was nervous, and a small, insistent voice in my head told me: 'You can't fish in that.' But fish we did, if you could call it that.

The base for our operations was the whimsically named late (Yacht) Club das Cataratas. In idle moments, of which there were many, we discussed with our host, Edward Rodbourne,

The Far From Compleat Angler

the prospects for staging the inaugural Iate Club regatta, a prospect complicated by the certainty that any 'iate' launched into the Parana would be washed up in Argentina before a jib could be raised above a bowsprit. The Iate Club was one of the more prestigious amenities of a town called Foz do Iguacu. In Hills' time it had been no more than a sun-drenched, slumbrous frontier post. In those days the Parana was rendered impassable a few miles upstream by the Falls of Guayru, an even more intimidating obstacle than the Falls of Iguacu. But Guayru had been tamed, replaced by the biggest dam in the world, Ituapu, a towering, repellent five mile long wall of concrete which harnessed the power of the river, providing electricity for the whole of Paraguay and a sizeable chunk of Brazil.

Fifty thousand men came to build Ituapu, and Foz was turned into a boom town. Across the water is the Paraguayan town of Cuidad Presidente Stroessner, a place of casinos and tax-free shops, and the bridge between the two was permanently clogged with traffic. Visitors poured into Foz to see the falls and the dam, and to enjoy the attractions of the town itself. Chief among these was sex at a modest price. Foz was studded with clubs with names like Sex Appeal, comprising dance-floors infested with meagrely dressed young girls, and knocking shop facilities accessible through discreet side doors. 'They'd be most offended if you thought they were whores,' Edward explained. 'They call themselves programme girls. Many men come here and marry them. They make very good wives.'

More congenial by far were the restaurants: some with glistening barbecued meats carved from skewers onto your plate; others where you dipped into an earthenware pot bubbling with prawns, squid and mussels cooked in coconut milk; and with everything that superb drink of Brazil, caiparinha - cane spirit poured over crushed ice, with sliced lemon and sugar.

All this was very fine, and compensated richly for the disappointing quality of the fishing. It is a sad fact that, in fishing as in life, reality and dreams rarely coincide. Nourished by Hills' writing, my imagination had conjured a gripping scenario. He had

Chapter Twelve - Brazilian Gold

caught his fish spinning with silver and copper spoons, and great fish they were, forty pounds and more. This is how I had seen myself, flexing my spinning rod to send my lure flying into the racing stream, then the savage take, and the battle; or even going further than Hills, to show that they would take a fly.

But, alas, the river was fifteen feet above normal, and dirty. Much worse, the Iguacu was truly filthy, and the water below the junction a little way down from Foz was completely out of order. In addition, the style espoused by Hills and other English adventurers had conspicuously failed to take root. The Brazilians and Argentinians who came to Foz knew nothing of spinning. They and the local boatmen practised a method which was uninspiring, to say the least. It involved impaling on the hook a live fish called a morenita - which is like a cross between an eel and an outsize garden slug - with a large weight above. This was hurled upstream from the boat, which then zoomed downstream with the current. Sometimes we reached the end of a drift without anything happening. Sometimes we had a bite. Very occasionally we caught a fish. But most of the time we got hooked up on the rocks.

Ah, the rocks, the rocks. What a multitude we struck into, and failed to land. P would stand at one end of the boat, red-faced under a vile green baseball cap. I would be at the other end, in a rather natty straw hat and daft long shorts, exposed flesh shiny with sun cream. I would smirk as P's rod bent into a boulder again, and he began cursing; then curse myself as I felt the unyielding weight of the Parana bottom. Between us were Edward, and our boatman Jorge, grinning at our antics.

Jorge was a dark-skinned humorist, with a dazzling set of teeth which one of his grateful clients - a dentist - had sent him by post. He had a bullet somewhere in his head, one of several legacies of a lawless youth. He handled the speed boat with a marvellously insouciant care, and in his company I gradually lost my nervousness of the Parana, though never my awe.

Of the two of us who had come from England, I was supposed to be the expert. P - who in his profession has something of a reputation as a fierce and combative interrogator and mangler of public

The Far From Compleat Angler

figures - made great play of my supposed standing. He himself, he avowed (with some justice) was a bungler as a fisherman; but I, with my battery of rods and multiplicity of theories, would show these locals a thing or two. I tried my hardest to explode this slur of expertise, by displaying thorough and constant incompetence. And I fancy I succeeded pretty well, for it took no more than a day for Jorge to abandon his attitude of respect, and replace it with one of genial contempt.

Our performance was, on the whole, pathetic. But we did catch some fish. P caught a piranha, which looked rather like him, and an even more evil-looking object called a mother-in-law fish. We had a few small dourado, and I hooked one decent one which took the bait with such violence that my multiplier reel over-ran and jammed. The fish got off, and everyone - apart from me - had a good laugh at the expert's discomfiture. Another day Edward, taking time off from schadenfreude, managed to land a tremendous 28 pounder which was roasted whole, and eaten to the accompaniment of many caiparinhas and much rejoicing.

It was all great fun, but the thought kept nagging at me, that we should not be fishing with these horrible, slimy morenitas, but spinning. I did try, but it seemed hopeless. The spoons and lures I had brought from England were invisible two inches beneath the surface, and were dragged across and down at such speed as to make any take inconceivable.

Then, on our last day, we had a maddeningly tantalising glimpse of what might have been. We had been trailing our morenitas around in futile fashion, while the sun rose high above us. Heat-blasted, we were heading for the sanctuary of the Iate Club when Jorge spotted dourado slashing at fry near the shore. I rigged up a spinning rod as he edged the boat in towards them. I cast a big copper spoon into the run, and hooked a fish at once, and it plunged and got off. I hooked another, then another, and each threw the hooks. I remembered Hills' instruction, to use no more than a single hook and keep it razor-sharp, to have any hope of penetrating the bone of a dourado's mouth; and I swore at myself for having

Chapter Twelve - Brazilian Gold

trebles, unsharpened. I cast again, and as the spoon swung round there was a terrific golden boil at it. My Hardy rod bent like a horse-shoe and the line, new 20-pound breaking strain Stren, parted as if it had been thread.

The trip was a curious experience, the town of Foz a curious place, shabby, glitzy, tacky, unappealing. Opposite it, on the Paraguayan shore, extended a succession of extravagant villas, the refuges - so we were told - of drug barons, arms dealers, and crooks of every shade. Once downstream, the sub-tropical rainforest closed in on the water, stretching away on either side into immeasurable distances. It was a forbidding sight, this rearing barrier of bamboo and palm, and tangled trees with pale trunks, like bones.

One afternoon we beached on the Paraguayan shore, well downstream from the junction between the Iguacu and the Parana. We followed a path through the trees, led by Edward, brandishing a metal hook with which he promised to fend off any of the numerous venomous snakes with which the forest abounded. We saw none, nor any of the jaguars, pumas, tapirs or wild boar reputed to lurk in the shadows. Eventually we came to a clearing above the river, in which mouldered a strange institute of learning.

It had been the home of Moyses Santiago Bertoni, a one-time Swiss anarchist who had fled to South America and devoted the greater part of a lifetime of awesome industry to studying the people, the customs, the creatures and the plants of Paraguay. Here, stuffed on sagging shelves, was the residue of his library, seven thousand mildewed volumes left out of forty thousand. He had written more than five hundred himself, all typed on a primitive machine given him by Theodore Roosevelt, and printed on his own press. There were other relics: his top hat, false teeth, visiting cards, and - outside - the trees he had planted, and the graves of Bertoni himself and his family.

The sun was dying when we returned to the boat. As we made our way upriver to Foz, Jorge related tales of things strange and inexplicable. He told us of the woman who had given birth to a monkey; and another who had conceived a creature half-human and half-toad; and of a foreman at the dam who had resigned because his wife had had an affair with their mastiff, and produced puppies. He spoke without his usual smile, and it was not until we had left the black, frowning forest behind, and the lights of the town appeared, that we were able to laugh again.

13. SOMETIMES A SALMON

Until last January I had not caught a salmon in Scotland, nor a salmon of twenty pounds. The day I filled both these gaps in my education was horribly wet and cold, and apart from the fish, the experience was not one on which I look with particular pride or pleasure. I was sitting in a boat on the Kinnaird beat of the Tay, observing a technique which the Tay men call harling. It involves working back and forth across the water, with baits trailing out behind, and is exceedingly boring. The fish took the ghillie's Kynoch Killer, I played it, and he netted it. It gave a tremendous fight, and was a wonderful fish in its silver and lilac sheen. But I hardly felt that it was mine, nor that it deserved to die in such a way. If I ever catch another salmon in Scotland, I want it to be on the fly.

The closest I have come to that was one November morning, and it was not that close. The trip was to have been a glorious conclusion to the game fishing season, a piscatorial equivalent of the blaze of triumph with which a romantic symphony ends. We were going to the Borders, to do battle with the fish which forge their way up the Tweed

The Far From Compleat Angler

as autumn begins to think of giving way to winter. This is bonanza time on the Tweed; given decent, but not excessive rainfall, failure should be a remote prospect.

You will notice that I say 'on the Tweed'. We, I regret to say, were not on it. Near it, yes; connected with it, yes; but on it, no. And herein lay the flaw in my symphonic structure, for our fishing was on the Teviot, which runs into the Tweed at Kelso forming that famous spot for fish slaying, the Junction Pool. Now the Teviot is a very pleasant stream, running through pleasant countryside. But the problem - that backend anyway - was that the salmon preferred the Tweed. When they arrived at the Junction, most of them decided against turning left towards the beat where my companions and I were plying our rods.

This explained why our fishing was to be had at modest cost, while the prime beats of the Tweed were reserved for a well-connected elite prepared to pay five hundred pounds or so a day for their fun. But although the fish in the Teviot were not numerous, there were some, and they could be caught. I know this because I saw it happen, even if - and this is the whimper with which my symphony perforce ended - it did not happen to any of us. This failure was painful, and gave rise to emotions that did me little credit. When I looked upstream from the spot where I was flogging away to see a fisherman (a local, I was sure, with unfair local knowledge) tailing a fresh-run ten pounder, I experienced a surge of shameful envy. When I heard of the great catches on the Junction Pool - a hundred salmon and more in a few days - that envy became something close to detestation.

This is a very bad thing for a fisherman to confess. We are brothers and sisters of the angle, and should rejoice in the joy of our fellows. It is a sad reflection of the corrupt age in which we live that it should be a good deal easier to practise all that virtue when you yourself have a salmon on the bank. My only consolation was that I did come closest. At ten o'clock on the last of our three days, I was fishing down an attractive, ripply run in the middle of our beat. The water had fallen, and I was using a floating line with a small Comet. As the line came curling round by the roots of an alder, it stopped. There was a heave, a furious eruption on the surface, and then - nothing. That was it: the climax that wasn't, the salmon that rose and was not caught.

Chapter Thirteen - Sometimes a Salmon

The main lesson was obvious. Of the five of us, none was intimately acquainted with the water, and none was a truly expert salmon angler. Nor did we fish as hard as we should have; the warmth, toasted sandwiches and beer of the local pubs proving a potent counter-attraction. With more experience, more skill and more effort we might well have had a fish or two. With more money, we might have been on the Tweed, and would certainly have scored.

My failure on the Spey was more complete, for I never even rose a fish. This time, money did not come into it, for I was on what is known in the industry as a freebie. The idea, as the slim and smartly suited PR lady explained at the airport, was to gather together a group of key journos, take them fishing, and introduce them to the range of malt whiskies which the sponsors, United Distillers, produced. 'Key journos, eh!' I said to myself. The expression was revolting, but the notion of being considered one was undeniably soothing to the ego. I had, in the past, taken a dim view of these outings arranged by public relations people. But I now realised that I confused high moral principle with envy. What was wrong with freebies was not that they were immoral, but that I was not on them.

This philosophical sea-change began to dawn on me as the aeroplane skimmed through the skies towards Inverness. The sea sparkled to my right, while on the other side the late snows of the Cairngorms glistened in the sun, and I was able to count a score of rivers and streams threading their way down heather-brown valleys. By the time I was sitting in a spacious chalet by the river, spooning date pudding and fudge sauce down my throat, and sipping my Gewurtztraminer, I was thoroughly converted to the new thinking. How else, I reflected - as I held up my plate for seconds of the heavenly suet - how else would I ever get to fish on Scotland's most famous salmon river, and thereby inform others about what it was like?

The Spey is, as the football managers are inclined to say, a bit special. It flows through superlative Highland scenery, and is magnificently proportioned for salmon fishing, a succession of

The Far From Compleat Angler

pools and runs with hardly a duff yard of water in its entire length. Since I could never hope to afford the fortune it costs to fish there, I was clearly under a strong moral obligation to grab this chance. I was also curious about the ghillies, the fellows in tweeds who are supposed to tell you where to fish, how to fish, and what to do when you have a fish on; and in between to pour forth a stream of wisdom on matters appertaining to fish. The first one I met measured his advice with some care. After he had rowed me across the river, I asked him where I should fish. Wherever you like, was his wise response. How far downstream should I go, I inquired. As far as you like, he replied, gesturing economically in the direction of the North Sea. With that, he hopped back into his boat and said he would pick me up at five.

Canny soul that he was, he had probably and correctly concluded that my chances of catching anything, and his chances of securing the sort of tip to which he was accustomed, were negligible. I knew next to nothing about the business on which I was engaged, and the conditions - piercingly brilliant sunshine and a stiff easterly wind - were not helpful. I did, however, learn something, for I prevailed upon one of the genuinely key journos present - the writer and salmon expert Crawford Little - to teach me the rudiments of Spey casting.

I doubt if I was one of Mr Little's aptest pupils. But I think I was just beginning to get the hang of whirling the rod around and propelling out the vital loop when the ghillie of few words reappeared to tell us that it was time for him to go home, and for us to retire to Tulchan Lodge for the malt tasting. Whoever had devised this jaunt, we reflected as we entered the resplendent lodge, was showing an acute appreciation of the angler/journalist's needs.

As it happens, I am not much of a whisky man; or, rather, I wasn't until I started working my way through the Classic Malts. Under the instruction of United Distillers' chief blender, we moved in an orderly fashion through a series of rich, fine brews until we arrived at an amazingly potent treasure from the Lagavulin distillery on Islay. Then, in somewhat less orderly fashion, I retraced my steps. By the end of a long and delightful evening, I would have been hard pressed

Chapter Thirteen - Sometimes a Salmon

to tell a classic malt from my grandmother's elderflower wine. They were all utterly shhplendid.

A troubled night was followed by a breakfast of paracetamol, bolstered - after an interval for recovery - by scrambled eggs and bacon from silver salvers. With the curtains of my bedroom drawn, I was half persuaded that I might be fit to return to the river. Outside, I was not so sure, for the sunshine was blindingly and disablingly brilliant, and my head felt like a punchball. But my sense of duty prevailed, and I went back to deploy my new-found Speycasting skills. Unfortunately, in the absence of Mr Little, my attempts to unfurl my loop were confounded by a thoroughly mean-spirited upstream wind. The ghillie - to whom I had, by now, taken a distinct dislike - regarded me contemptuously, and eventually I was compelled to add the Spey to the considerable list of rivers which had been too much for me.

Ireland, though, has been much kinder. It gave me my first salmon on fly, and then, in its generous way, gave me a second an hour or so later, on a river for which I did not have to pay a bean. It is the Cong, a most remarkable piece of water which is born in the limestone caverns beneath the stretch of wild land which separates the great loughs of Mask and Corrib. It bursts above ground in the village of Cong itself, and runs no more than half a mile or so past Ashford Castle into Corrib. My instructor in its ways was a prodigious fisherman, Miheal Ryan of Cong, who in the year that we were there caught two hundred salmon on his own rod from that short stretch of river.

He took me down to the Castle, gave me a fly of his own tying, and bade me fish below the stone bridge. To my intense surprise, I caught a salmon, an extremely small one. Then he told me to try above the bridge, and as I fished down he watched me from the bridge, drinking a bottle of Guinness and smoking. It is a big water, but sound wading, and I soon lost the self-consciousness I had felt at first at having to cast in front of the holidaymakers swarming back and forth over the bridge and along the banks. The fly was coming round nicely in the stream, and suddenly I was aware that Miheal had

The Far From Compleat Angler

turned away from the bridge. At that moment I felt the fish that he had seen turn at the fly under the arch. He appeared in his boat, netted a lovely, small-headed seven pounder, and grinned at my explosion of thanks and joy.

After that, there was an interval of several years in my Irish salmon fishing. I remained conscious that it was there, but as a non-salmon man, I tended to find myself trout fishing, occasionally thinking that, one day, I must come with serious intent towards salmon. One September I did just that, seduced by an advertisement in a magazine boasting of mighty catches from a hotel water on the Blackwater. There was a drought, the banks were ankle-deep in discarded dyed prawns, the other fishermen were using floats, and the hotel was horrible. But the river itself made a deep impression on me - particularly the famous stretch owned by the Duke of Devonshire with that caressing name, Careysville.

The following September, one of my brothers - who lives in Italy and is no fisherman - telephoned me to say that he was tired of reading about my failures. He suggested that I was prey to that most odious of indulgences, false modesty. No one could catch as few fish as you and stick at it, was his thesis. Ergo, you do catch fish but prefer to pretend that you don't, and then parade this sackcloth and ashes humbug. My protests were brushed aside. What we want, he told me firmly, is a triumph. And happily, while I was pondering the morality of inventing something, a triumph was delivered into my lap on such a scale that it has warmed me ever since.

I cannot claim much credit for it, beyond the fact that it was my idea that we should go to Careysville. It was luck, pure luck; and all the more glorious for being so improbable. The weekend before we were due to go, appalling news came from Ireland. My friend Niall, who was to join us from Dublin, reported a seven-foot flood. I tottered, consumed by a vision of a brown torrent bearing smashed trees, Kerrygold cows and all our hopes out to sea. But then, in answer to fervent prayer, the deluge ceased. By the time we got there, the river had resumed a more disciplined way of life. 'You'll get a fish,' was the matter-of-fact prediction from cheery, round-faced Paddy Egan, the ghillie. Hope revived, to struggle with disbelief.

Chapter Thirteen - Sometimes a Salmon

My own campaign opened disastrously. I showed Paddy my spinning line and he said it was too light. I said it was all I had. He shrugged his shoulders. Second cast, I hooked a fresh-run salmon of about eight pounds, and the line broke. Oddly enough, it was the day Britain was forced to flee from the European exchange rate mechanism - a trifling matter compared with my loss, although I fancy the then Chancellor, Norman Lamont, may have felt something of the same despair that overwhelmed me. Paddy, looking rather severe, marched me off to the tackle shop in Fermoy to replace my line.

I caught nothing that first day, although I had the dubious pleasure of watching one of our party pull out three within twenty minutes. Paddy beamed at him like a teacher with his prize pupil. Since the subject is my triumph rather than anyone else's, I shall pass over those salmon, particularly as they inspired in their captor a most regrettable and unworthy display of gloating. Nor shall I dwell on the twelve pounder which my fisherman brother caught below Careysville weir the next morning. My time came that afternoon, at the same spot where the gullible trio had given themselves up the previous day. First I had an eleven pounder, then an eight pounder. It was my turn to bask in the sunshine of Paddy's approval.

Thus far, all the fish had been caught spinning, on the distressingly but aptly named Flying Condom. Now spinning is all very well, but flyfishing is better; apart from which, no one would wish to acknowledge owing all his success to an airborne birth control device. So the next morning, with the water nicely fined down, I went to a gorgeous pool at the bottom of the fishery, which they call Corrineen. The sun was shining, a soft breeze rustled the yellowing leaves, and - halfway down - a fish took. I was transfixed with amazement and did nothing. It hooked itself, and I landed it, and though it was only six pounds, it was fresh and lovely and made me a happy man.

In fact, the whole trip had the blissful quality of the best dreams. The house was like the best sort of country house hotel, without the inconvenience of having any other guests in it. We played snooker incredibly badly beneath the antlers of some monstrous, extinct Irish elk, and one of our number went to sleep under the table. We sank

The Far From Compleat Angler

into deep armchairs in front of scented wood fires, and studied the leatherbound records of the great salmon-catching days of old. We were waited on at table by a luscious girl who told us how she would swim at night in the river, with the eels playing around her limbs. They asked what we liked to eat, and on learning that we would not turn up our noses at lobster, served five of them for dinner, fresh that morning from the market in Cork. We ate like men possessed, and I can still savour the smell of the hot crab pie which preceded the apple crumble which they gave us for lunch in the cricket pavilion which served as Careysville's fishing hut.

Best of all, there were salmon. We had nineteen of them in three-and-a-half days, about two-thirds from Careysville and the remainder from another stretch of the Blackwater, towards Mallow. Measured against the Ponoi of the Kola peninsula, or the Junction Pool on the Tweed, or the Ridge Pool on the Moy, it might not sound like much. But for us, modest achievers in angling matters, it was a triumph, which remains of blessed memory.

14. Morality and Other Matters

A Barbarian Speaks

Thus far, fishing has been largely exempt from the hostile clamour raised against those who take their pleasure in the pursuit and killing of God's creatures; partly, because fish are cold and wet, and do not arouse the same emotional response; partly, because the socially variegated nature of fishing means it cannot provoke the same species of class hatred as hunting and shooting; and partly because the new Labour party rightly sees no political benefit in persecuting it. But fishing has its enemies, and we would do well to keep an eye on them. There is an organisation called the Campaign for the Abolition of Angling, which is allied to the Hunt Saboteurs Association, and which occasionally stages minor events designed to promote the rights of fish.

Our inclination may be to exhale dismissively, and carry on regardless. But in the current climate, I doubt if we can afford to classify our opponents as lunatics and cranks, and determine to go

The Far From Compleat Angler

about enjoying our sport in peace. Those who would deprive the angler of his passion may not succeed, but nor will they go away. Quite properly, fishermen are shy of engaging in moral debate, but this is an argument which must be joined.

There is one central, inescapable, uncomfortable fact common to hunting, shooting, and fishing: they involve causing terror, injury and death to innocent creatures. Those who love these sports need to grapple honestly and carefully with the ethical questions arising from them. For the hunting fraternity to preach about the need to control the fox population is hooey. It is the most inefficient method of killing foxes imaginable. The reason they do it is that it is tremendous fun dressing up and riding around the countryside chasing a fox, and the fun outweighs the suffering of the fox. I would not seek to deny them this pleasure; but I would like to see them being a little more open about their motives. Those who shoot are, in general, more frank about why they do it. The problem with shooting's public image derives from its invasion by gross commercial interests. The slaughter which went on a few years ago of huge flocks of hand-reared, corn-stuffed, half-witted pheasants by gun-toting City smartarses brought the sport into something approaching disrepute.

Fishing attracts less obloquy, but there is still a case to be answered. The problem is that, by the standards of the abolitionists, I can offer no defence. If I am honest with myself, I must acknowledge that I believe angling to be cruel. I cannot guess at the nature of the suffering of fish, but I am pretty sure they do suffer. However, this cruelty does not trouble me enough to make me stop. In the eyes of my enemies, this must make me a barbarian. Actually, they call us sadists, which is a little wide of the mark. Fish do not scream, they hardly bleed, and they don't even blink. Any self-respecting sadist - one whose pleasure is in the pain of another - would have to be desperate indeed to give a chub a second thought.

Of course, some fishermen do try to argue that their sport is hardly cruel at all. The essence of their case - which I find wholly unconvincing - is that fish do not feel pain. They will wave around diagrams purporting to illustrate the piscine nervous system, and tell you that a hook can be driven into the mouth and the fish dragged about at the end of your line without it feeling anything more than

Chapter Fourteen - Morality and Other Matters

mild discomfort. To me, it seems far more probable that, in the limited way dictated by limited awareness, the creature does experience pain and terror in the ordeal of being caught. The only sure way to avoid inflicting that would be to give up fishing, and that I will not do. To put it crudely, my enjoyment is more important to me than the fish's misery. However - and I accept that this may appear as mere hypocrisy - I do feel under a powerful obligation to keep that pain and terror to a minimum.

That means that if I wish to eat the fish, I should net it and whack it on the head as quickly as possibly. If I wish to return it alive (which is almost all of the time) I must treat it with as much care as possible, to give it the greatest chance of continued life. We have become much better at this than we used to be. Many river trout fishermen now use barbless hooks, so the fly can be twisted out and the fish allowed to go its own way without it being handled out of the water at all. In coarse fishing, the distressing spectacle of the keepnet stuffed with feeble, injured fish is extremely rare.

I strongly approve of the growing practise of releasing game fish alive. It is all to the good that we think about why we are fishing, analyse the old stock response about the hunter's instinct. Is a dead fish really the proper and inevitable product of the operation, and does its possession really enhance our pleasure in what we have done? In my own case, the answer is only 'yes' when I truly wish to eat the creature, or have someone in mind to give it to. Most of the time, I would prefer, for the sake of convenience as well as conservation, to see it alive rather than dead. But having said that, I also hate the intolerance of the evangelists of 'catch-and-release', their assumption of a moral superiority which easily grows into fanaticism. I would defend the angler's right to kill for the pot, just as I would defend the housewife's right to feed her family on meat if she chooses. But if fishing does have a moral edge over other field sports, it is that death is not inseparable from success. We do have the choice: to kill or liberate, and we have a duty to exercise the choice with care.

We must also do more to limit our incidental brutality, to show more tenderness. Let us improve the way we handle fish. Let us avoid using excessively light line. Let us use soft net mesh, to minimise scale damage. Let us ensure that, at all times, we carry the equipment necessary for swift unhooking. Let us never leave hooks and nylon hanging from branches, and be rigorous about removing the waste left by others.

The abolitionists make much of the suffering caused by such callous carelessness, and they are justified in doing so. What they know nothing of, naturally, is the good done by anglers. Since their case makes much of the incidental harm done by us, so mine makes much of the incidental benefit. I would argue that the health of our rivers depends on fishermen. Left to farmers, industry, the government, local authorities, water companies and environmentalists, they would be lost. Anglers fight to protect their lakes and rivers from the polluters because they care deeply and passionately about them. It is not a moral cause; they care because they fish a particular water, and they defend that water because they want to continue fishing it. Take away the fishing, and you take away the care. That gone, and we will have a land of open sewers. And where will that leave the fish?

There, put briefly, is the argument of sweet reason. Should that fail to win the day, you may consider resorting to a slap in the face with a wet fish.

Other Fish to Fry

One aspect of the great European debate which has, I think, been insufficiently touched upon is the gulf between the British perspective on the matter of fish-eating and that prevailing on the Continent. It is, I fear, too wide for treaties, summits or whole blizzards of regulations to bridge. The most cheerful Euro-compromiser would be hard-pressed to identify the possibility of a common position on it.

The division can be illustrated linguistically. In French there is a word 'friture', for fry-up of little fish. In Italian it is 'frittura'. I do not know what it is in Spanish, Portuguese or Greek, but I'm prepared to bet a pair of neoprene waders that there is one. There used to be a word in English, which was tansy. But it has fallen into disuse because we no longer fry little fish.

Chapter Fourteen - Morality and Other Matters

Let us look at the typical French fisherman. He is a figure in a beret, hunched by the Seine, a caporal stuck to his lower lip. With an immensely long pole, he flicks out an infinitesimal bait, whisks out a minute fish, and drops it into a bucket, where he cares not if it lives or dies. At the end of the day, he scoops up his harvest and sets off home, already hearing the sizzle of his captures in the olive oil.

This is not the British way. On the whole, we still kill and eat our trout and salmon without anyone making much of a fuss about it. But the lesser species - the lean, toothsome pike, the fat, soft-fleshed carp, the delicate perch and the rest - they go back. I doubt if one in one thousand British coarse anglers has eaten anything he or she has caught. The old books are full of quaint recipes for freshwater fish. But we have simply lost the habit. Instead, a puritanical aversion to killing fish has developed among coarse fishers. A man found knocking a carp or tench on the head faces violence, and expulsion from his club.

As so often, prejudice is accompanied by moral pretensions. The average British fisherman knows little of how they do things abroad. But he does know that the continental angler beats everything he catches to death, and then cooks it with strange and unnatural ingredients. The foreigner is therefore classified as a barbarous fishmonger, sunk in primitive beastliness, indifferent to the suffering of his prey and to the well-being of his environment.

The view of us from abroad is equally unflattering. To the continental, the link between quarry and table is central to the sport. He is a hunter, a provider of food. The idea of sitting for hours, enduring every kind of discomfort, only to return the catch to the element from which it has been removed at such cost is laughable. It is another species of English madness. I remember trying to explain the British philosophy to a Hungarian who had grown big by eating carp and bream. At first he thought I was playing a joke on him; but when I finally convinced him I was in earnest, I myself became the joke.

As I have said before, I like to think I can see the strengths and weaknesses in both philosophies. It is wasteful and wanton to kill everything you catch, and a depredation which waters cannot stand for long. But I also dislike the English intolerance and ignorance;

it seems to me a shame that a section of our cultural and culinary heritage should have been abandoned in such a manner. So I will continue to do my bit to bring the two sides closer together. But the lead should really come from the top. One day, perhaps, the Prime Minister will tuck into 'carpe à l'ancienne' at the Elysee; and at the return banquet offer the French president stewed eel, or barbel stuffed with sweetbreads, crayfish and artichokes. On the other hand, perhaps not.

On Carp Men

A few years ago one of Britain's foremost coarse fishermen, Kevin Maddocks, was awarded one hundred and fifty thousand pounds in libel damages against an angling newspaper which had accused him of filching fish from someone else's pond. No doubt the court was told - quite properly - that no viler calumny could be laid against someone who not only made a living out of fishing, but was also chairman of the Carp Anglers Association, an honorary office which, within the sport, conferred on Mr Maddocks an almost priestly status. It was as if Mrs Whitehouse had been charged with running a porn shop, or Sir Teddy Taylor with accepting a job at the European Commission.

For the carp is not as other fish, just as carp anglers are not as other fishers. It grows to a vast size, as much as sixty pounds, and has strength to match. In addition, legend has attributed to it intelligence and cunning on a scale which other fish can only gawp at. As a result, the pursuit of carp is not so much a recreation as a vocation - even a sacred duty. Arthur Ransome observed that the man who habitually fished for carp had a 'strange look in his eyes'. He added that he had shaken hands respectfully with the man who had caught the biggest carp in England - he looked 'as if he had been in heaven and hell and had nothing more to hope from life'.

Chapter Fourteen - Morality and Other Matters

In those days big carp - fish of twenty pounds and over - were regarded as pretty well uncatchable. One authority cautioned that the beginner should expect to fish for a thousand hours before catching his first carp. Albert Buckley's 26-pounder, caught in 1930, held the record for more than two decades. In 1952 Britain's greatest fisherman, Richard Walker, landed his record carp of 44 pounds. He wrote of the moment at which, in the twilight of a September dawn, his senses first absorbed the creature's size: 'I knew it was big, and suddenly it dawned on me that it was more than that. It was tremendous!'

Nowadays a carp of forty pounds no longer astonishes the fishing world. A handful are caught each season. But the mystique of carp fishing and the fanaticism it inspires among its devotees have, if anything, intensified. It has become a cult. The carp enthusiast does not say to his wife: 'Just off for a couple of hours fishing, dear.' He announces on Friday evening, in a quiet and exalted tone, that he will not reappear until Monday morning. And should he return from his 60-hour vigil over his electric bite alarm to find the house empty and a letter from his wife's solicitors speaking of 'an alienation of affections', he will probably shrug his shoulders - and go back to oiling his reel or preparing groundbait.

Myself, I do not have the stamina or powers of endurance required for carp fishing. Many years ago, my brothers and I used to make nocturnal forays to an overgrown moat where carp lived. They weren't very big, but they were very difficult to catch - or at least we found them so, probably because we were very noisy, clumsy inexpert carp fishermen. The last time we went there, we fished with floating crust and caught both members of the resident pair of tame Canada geese (both released unharmed, if a little flustered) - but no fish.

Those who do fish successfully for carp tend to be fantastically secretive about where they do it. Occasionally, ludicrous ploys are adopted to protect the identity of hot carp spots. There was a case some time ago of a man who, to throw his challengers off the scent, disclosed a false location for his triumphs to the angling press. The result was a stampede to some carpless hole, and a great deal of bitterness.

The Far From Compleat Angler

On renowned carp waters the big fish are cherished like Arab thoroughbreds. The initiates give them names - Fred or Lucky - and they are caught and returned to the water time and again. One might deduce from this that their reputation for sagacity may have been exaggerated; or perhaps they are brainy enough to have worked out that, in return for the minor inconvenience of being dragged to the bank every so often, they are guaranteed a lifetime's cosseting. Certainly there is no fear of sudden death. An angler who knocked one on the head and sent it to a taxidermist would invite lynching.

To the unfortunate multitude who know nothing about fishing, the carp would doubtless appear slimy, clammy, gross and useless. For my part, although I am temperamentally unfit to fish for them, I still love and admire them. I side with Walton (and I'm sure Mr Maddocks would concur): 'She is the queen of rivers, a stately, good and very subtle fish'.

Wandering Dreams

The frontiers are being pushed ever further back. The Kola peninsula is now old hat. Kamchatka is the place; or maybe Yakutia, in Siberia, where the giant sturgeon run. A Romanian friend of mine, Marius-Adrian Dumitru, was invited to St Petersburg as a guest of the city's Anglers' and Hunters' Association. 'Numberless are the rivers and lakes of the great Russian taiga', was how his description began. He found hospitality without stint: 'I was assailed with real delicatessen richly aspersed with the never-failing vodka'. He travelled to the River Vilojba, east of St Petersburg, and demonstrated to incredulous Russians how the grayling would take a fly; and from there north to Karelia, and the great lake of Ladoga, where it rained for a week.

According to Marius, Ladoga is celebrated for a species of trout called the Kumja, which grows to fifteen pounds and more. But he concentrated on another species: 'Above me thousands of

Chapter Fourteen - Morality and Other Matters

ephemerids flew incessantly and the grayling came to the surface to take my forgeries. When the setting sun lengthened the shadows of the trees over the lake, I felt a fish hang heavy on my line. It was thirty centimetres long. Then the rain came down again'.

Perversely, perhaps, I find this sort of thing much more congenial to my imagination than the thought of ten days in treeless, mosquito-infested Kola, at a camp full of Americans and English, plundering salmon from the Ponoi. I would love to wander the streams that feed Ladoga. I could be lured to the lakes of Armenia, or to mighty Baikal, or the high ridges of the Caucasus. I would be very keen to try Outer Mongolia, having come across a 65-year-old copy of *The Field*, in which there was a photograph of a Mr V. de Franck, holding a vast fish called a taimen, weighing fifty-eight pounds. I believe the taimen is a relative of the grayling; I remember a lecture at the Royal Geographical Society in which a pioneer described catching one at night on an artificial mouse. Mr de Franck calls it a grim and vicious fighter, and since he caught thirty-seven of them during his trip, I am prepared to take his word for it.

The river on which he enjoyed this sport was the Gan, whose limpid waters - he says - flow from the Hingan Mountains across the plain of the North Barga. I have been unable to locate the Gan on the map, nor the town of Kantagaitu (it means The Elks Are Here) where Mr de Franck stayed. But the Argun - into which the Gan flows - forms the border between Russia and China, so it must be on one side or the other.

As a final recommendation, Mr de Franck says: 'This territory is 100 percent safe from the Chinese brigands who infest other parts of North Manchuria and have closed many promising fishing and shooting grounds to the sportsman'. I say! What cads those brigands must have been! But what a terrific hoot it would be to tell your chums where you were off to. Imagine this at the club:

Charles! Sorry to butt in.

Think nothing of it old man. Just been dreaming about my hols. Been talking to old Trotter. Guess where he's off to?

Iceland again?

The Far From Compleat Angler

Not a bit of it. The Caucasus and Kazakhstan, then down to those mountains on the Iranian side of the Caspian, ending up somewhere in Turkey where the trout are supposed to go up to thirty pounds.

Good for old Trotter. By the way, I bumped into Stinker Tinker at Lords the other day. Told me Africa's the place. He's working his way from Morocco to the Sudan-Uganda border, then over to Ethiopia, then Tanzania and Kenya. He thought he might take in Zambia and Malawi before going after the rainbows in Natal.

Lucky devil. I must say I've always fancied a detour off the Silk Road myself. Turkey, Persia, a couple of streams in Afghanistan, a few days on the upper Oxus and in the Karakorams, finishing up with Kashmir.

Mmmm. Of course there's always the South American option. Venezuala, Ecuador, Peru, Chile, Argentina. They say Argentina has the best trout fishing in the world. Or is it Chile?

Better than New Zealand and Tasmania?

So Fanshawe says. His wife's family owns a few million acres of pampas. Or is it tundra down there? Lord knows! Anyway, there are a couple of Andes thrown in, with some fabulous rivers. The only drawback is too many Americans, Fanshawe says.

Where's he off to then?

Russia. I know, bit predictable isn't it? But he likes that bank-to-bank salmon stuff.

And what about you, Charles? You've done Labrador and Newfoundland and the States.

Well, if I were a younger man with time on my hands, I'd be sorely tempted to have a crack at Papua New Guinea, or PNG as they call it. Big rainbows in the mountains - if you can dodge the poisoned arrows. That, or Sri Lanka. Or even Lebanon. I was reading the other day about this chap who caught a six-pounder in the Bekaa Valley. But as things are, I can't see myself straying far this year. Have to stay in touch with the home front, so to speak.

Scotland again?

'Fraid so. And you?

Well, I've been making a few inquiries about this river in Outer Mongolia. But (with a sigh), it looks like Devon. As usual.

Chapter Fourteen - Morality and Other Matters

Back to Being a Boy

The response to my offer to provide supper was, I thought, short on trust and long on scepticism. Their expressions seemed to say: 'We've heard that one before. Get the chops out of the freezer'. But I was quietly confident, and eager to assume the role of the hunter.

It was an old-fashioned Lake District day. Rain poured from an implacable slate sky. The fell tops were invisible, the lower slopes streaked with silver torrents. Drainpipes gushed. Sheep, trees, and holidaymakers dripped mournfully.

At such times you can forget the elegances of flyfishing. You need worms, and plenty of them, in a box that will fit into the pocket of a sound waterproof coat. The other requirements are Wellington boots, a packet of hooks, some weights, a ten foot rod with a fixed spool reel, a bag for the fish, and a sturdy indifference to the elements.

The trout of these Lakeland becks are at the sharp end of life's struggle. Little food comes their way in the turbulent pools; what there is must be grabbed at once or lost for ever. A spate is their time of plenty, as worms, beetles, caterpillars, slugs and other assorted morsels are washed into the stream. Appetites are keen and reflexes swift. The technique is simplicity itself. The angler crouches beside the pool and lobs the weighted worm into it, seeking out the eddies and holes behind rocks. The line is held between thumb and first finger, and the reaction to the jab-jab of the bite must be instantaneous (otherwise it will be found that the worm has been nabbed, or the hook swallowed).

Once a trout has been hooked, it must be transferred from its own sphere to the terrestrial one as soon as possible. Forget about playing it, and do not encumber yourself with a net. Simply swing it out of the water over the land; then seize it, unhook it, and either kill it or put it back.

I say the technique is simple, but this is not to say that this is easy fishing. There are times when the fish will not bite at all, and others when they will bite everything except the portion of the worm containing the hook. Most vexing of all is the amazing facility of these trout for wriggling free midway through the swing from water to land. Hurling yourself on your knees and clutching with bare hands at a slimy, writhing escapee is undignified and almost invariably fruitless.

This beck fishing is also physically taxing for one accustomed to strolling along the mown banks of a southern chalkstream. It involves a great deal of scrambling over devilishly slippery rocks, and slithering up and down spongy, sodden banks of moss. Sooner or later you will slide or step into a pool deeper than your boots, and wet feet will be added to other discomforts. In such circumstances, self-control is easily lost. I remember watching my brother Matthew fishing the best pool in this particular beck. He had insisted, against all advice, on using a soft-tipped fly rod; and as a result lost each of the six trout he hooked. His rage filled the damp air, and for a time I feared that he would stamp on the offending implement.

I have had my share of such nightmares in the past. But on this excursion I was favoured with a tolerable proportion of success amid the usual blunders and failures. The beck - which runs down from the fells above Ambleside - was in perfect order, coloured by the rain but not in flood. In the first decent pool I took two nice fish, one of which was a full six ounces, a good specimen in this Lilliputian world. In the next pool I lost two, thanks to a pestilential overhanging branch which inhibited the landward swing.

Thus was the pattern of the morning established until, having forged my way up two miles of valley, I found that it wasn't morning any more. I was briefly troubled by the recollection that I had promised to be back for lunch. But I reminded myself that the chief duty of the hunter was to provide for his dependents, rather than to observe bourgeois conventions such as mealtimes.

I arrived back late in the afternoon with ten trout of edible size, having put back as many more. As it turned out, the dependents turned up their noses and preferred chops, so I shared the hunter's spoils with another brother. More than thirty years ago, when I first fished the beck, I was told by an old Ambleside angler that its trout were the sweetest-tasting in the whole of the Lake District. I was pleased to find that they had lost nothing of that quality.

Chapter Fourteen - Morality and Other Matters

A Night of Nights

Most fishing is good, unmemorable fun. Unless you have the strength of character to keep a proper diary - which I do not - the days merge into an amorphous mass, from which it is possible to extract moments and details, but which cannot ever again be separated into the constituent experiences. But there are two categories of fishing expedition which linger in the mind: the hellish, when it becomes a torment; and the miraculous, those days or nights whose blessed quality stamps them in the memory, like a seal on hot wax.

In general, it is as well that there should be a balance between the bloody and the blissful. Were there too many of the former, we should have to escape and take up something less troublesome. An excess of the latter, and we (well, I) would soon shed humility and become smug and puffed up with self-regard. It is also as well that both categories should be rare, compared with the mass of the mediocre; otherwise we would become dissatisfied with the staple diet.

I have been a little worried, because I have had two wonderful, indelible nights this summer - and no recent immersions in the Slough of Despond. I hardly dare pull on my waders, for fear of the retributive catastrophe that must, by now, be in store for me. The first was my sedge night on the Suir, and I have sung that song of triumph already. The second belonged to a little loch in Inverness-shire with a Gaelic name - a'Ghreidlein - as romantic and wild as its setting in the hills that rise between the glens of Affric and Moriston. Its instigator was a man with a twinkle about him, Kyle Laidlay of Tomich.

What you need for this loch, he told us, is a night with no wind. And even then, he cautioned, there could be no certainty, for the trout were unpredictable and contrary, and the season - mid-August - was late. But they were big, he said, up to seven pounds. And if they were in the mood...

The night of no wind arrived, and there was an excitement crackling between my friend Stevie and me as we bounced up the track leading into the hills which hid the loch. Kyle was waiting for us, as were the midges. Beneath us, the surface was glass-smooth, except for the dimples of the trout. A pale, brilliant moon lit the sky

The Far From Compleat Angler

as we clambered aboard the boat. Then a tiny breath of wind sprang from somewhere to ruffle the water, and the rises stopped.

The method was straightforward. A big, hairy sedge was cast out, twitched a couple of times, then retrieved in steady pulls to create a highly visible wake on the surface. Stevie was bubbling with expectation; I was dubious. But on my third or fourth cast there was a rush at my fly, and the rod tip curved. It was not a big fish - three quarters of a pound or so - but it was a start, and I, too, became caught up in the excitement of it.

If I close my eyes, I can re-live the experience: the darkening, receding shore; the moonbeams lighting the ripples left by the sedge; the slow push of the oars; Kyle's soft, laughing voice speculating on the vagaries of trout; and at the other end of the boat, increasing frenzy. For Stevie was into fish after fish, each splash and fight accompanied by yells and an explosive commentary on his expertise as a master-angler. He had four, the last a tremendous, bigheaded, boldspotted fellow that went well over two pounds. And all that time, although we were fishing the same water with identical flies, I had nothing.

On the stroke of midnight, soon after Stevie had announced that he was hyperventilating with the strain of it, a fish took me near the reeds in quiet, resolute fashion. It fought like a hero, belying its weight (just under one-and-a-half pounds) with the power of its runs. With it duly netted, the quiet of finality settled on the loch. The fish would rise no more that night, and, suddenly, we realised how cold it had become. Back on shore we toasted the catch, and then headed down the track, leaving a'Ghreidlein with its secrets and its fish for another night.

15. Across the Water

Whether arriving by boat or plane, whether through Dublin or Cork, whether the sun is shining, or the cliffs and green fields are masked in rain clouds, Ireland invariably uplifts my heart. I shall try not to sound mawkish as I try to explain why. Certainly, it has nothing much to do with great angling triumphs, for my ratio of success to failure there - measured in terms of hours of endeavour - is probably smaller than anywhere else. In the fishing context, it is more to do with the promise than the reality. From Meath to Mayo, from Cork to Donegal, it is a land of water. There are the great lakes - Corrib, Mask, Sheelin, Erne - which hold the great trout; and a myriad of lesser ones, all sparkling with potential. There are the great rivers - Moy, Blackwater, Slaney - still thronged with rich runs of salmon; and a thousand lesser streams, any of which possesses the potential for the catch, or the day, of an angler's lifetime.

But there is much more to it than that. Ireland is a place of escape, the accessible, approachable, welcoming refuge from the tense, noisy, enervating world of work and daily life. I do not deceive myself that

The Far From Compleat Angler

the Ireland I flee to in order to refresh my soul is the true Ireland. I know perfectly well that, beyond the idyll of countryside, lake, river, mountain, whitewashed cottages, sleepy bars, and courteous people is a land riven by division, sapped by emigration, scarred by every species of urban deprivation, squalor and corruption. But that other Ireland, where the clock seems to move a little slower, where the Guinness takes that much longer to get ready, is a true part of the diversity.

The English cherish several myths about the Irish, most of which are insulting, and some are merely absurd. A myth that the Irish themselves are fond of cultivating is that their country is a great, green wet sponge. In the saturated bog-country of the west - so the legend goes - appearances by the sun are greeted with disbelieving cries by the mildewed natives. The skies are leaden, the peat heaves and quakes, the rivers run ever full, replenished by the water driven in by the never-failing south-westerlies.

My first two trips were to the West, and both were failures. In each case the weather was to blame. During the first, the gales blasted in from the Atlantic but the rain was left behind. The second was blighted by an immoveable anti-cyclone, which gave us nine days of windless sunshine, a curse made much worse by the way in which we were congratulated on our good fortune as we roamed the land looking vainly for black clouds.

Those were the days before the Irish seatrout fishing was wrecked by the expansion in salmon farming and the consequent sea lice plague. We were all lovers of Kingsmill Moore, and those tales of the Country of the Cashla: so we went with seatrout in mind, open to possibilities of brown trout and salmon. I rose and missed a very big seatrout which burst out of a wave on a stormy little lough in the bare wastes near Maam Cross; and we caught a few small ones at Ballynahinch, and on lovely Lough Tawnyard, which glistens in the hills above Delphi. I caught one good trout above the white sand of Carra, and another on Corrib, where my brother hooked a much bigger one and lost it after getting the line caught round his leg. And I had my two salmon on the Cong River, and explored the strange landscape around the Cong Canal.

The story of the canal is a farcical one, though not that funny, given the time. It was commissioned to provide work after the

Chapter Fifteen - Across The Water

Famine, the idea being to open a navigation link from Galway in the south to Ballinrobe in the north. The canal was to be the vital connection between Corrib and Mask, across a few miles of low-lying, rock-strewn wasteland. Unfortunately, little attention was paid to the nature of the rock, which was limestone. After years of prodigious labour, the course was cut, the locks and bridges were built, and the water - well, the water just drained away through the ground, and never got from Mask to Corrib at all. It remains an extraordinary legacy of folly. At the top, the water rushes from Mask at terrific speed into a lagoon, from which it emerges at significantly slacker rate. Well above Cong village, the flow becomes a trickle, then ceases altogether. For many years, the last lock has served as a bowling alley.

The fast stretch at the top, and the lagoon, hold great trout. On one visit we met a man from Birmingham who was catching them on maggots and loading them into the freezer in his camper van; inveighing constantly against the ignorance of 'Paddy' who knew nothing about the riches on his doorstep. We tried to catch them on fly in the canal, but the speed of the water was too great. On the lagoon, they rose out of reach, heavy, purposeful swirls to sedges as the sun went down; try as we might, we could not reach them. Another evening, our friend Niall Fallon - the organiser of our expeditions - had a great battle in the outflow from Mask, and caught a superb two-and-a-half pounder which was cooked on a fire and eaten in fingers as the last light dimmed over the water.

Midway through the second trip, surrounded by shrinking rivers and glassy loughs, we abandoned the west, and drove to County Tipperary. Niall said it was time we made acquaintance with Ireland's finest trout river, the Suir. Three days I fished there, and did not rise a trout; though there was never a moment when a fish was not feeding within range. Apart from Niall, who winkled out a few, no one else did much better than me. It was, to put it mildly, an eye opener. I returned to England sobered and wiser, my appreciation of my limitations as a fly fisher significantly enhanced. And I could not get this river out of my mind.

The Far From Compleat Angler

It was some years later that I was driving with Niall, following the course of the Suir upstream from Cahir. I spotted a fine mansion standing in rolling parkland, and I asked him what it was. He said it was a place of refuge for priests to wrestle with the temptation of the demon drink. Was it full? I asked innocently. 'They say they're building an extension,' Niall replied with a laugh. Doubtless this was no more than another impious calumny against the Roman Catholic Church. But it occurred to me that, should I ever need a place of sanctuary to fight the tempter, a grand house overlooking an incomparable piece of trout water would be no bad place for it.

The Suir rises in the Devilsbit mountains north of Thurles, flows by Cashel with the Slievefelim mountains to the west, skirts the Galty mountains and the Knockmealdown mountains (what wonderful names the Irish have given to their gentle hills) before forging east towards Waterford and the sea. I have fished no more than four or five of its 115 miles, yet it continues to fascinate me more than any river I know. This is partly on account of its scale. The mature river is wide, deep and powerful; it is essential to wear chest waders to fish it properly. Even more impressive is the Suir's amazing vitality, its abundance of life, which has survived innumerable atrocious acts of pollution. It is thick with weed, bursting with insect life, teeming with trout.

It took a master angler of a bygone era, Sir Edward Grey (later Grey of Falloden) to discover the Suir's potential as a dry fly river. Grey had learned the art on the exacting waters of the Itchen at Winchester. With some justice, he thought he knew a thing or two. Yet initially he found the trout of the Suir almost uncatchable, even though at that time (around 1880) they had never seen a dry fly before. Being a master, he kept at them; and he found that if he kept low in the water, and delivered the fly lightly, without any hint of drag or showing the cast, they would take. On his best day he caught eleven, the two biggest each over two-and-three-quarter pounds. 'It was,' recorded Grey, 'the wildest and most exciting and most fascinating dry fly fishing I have ever had.'

I had been mindful of Grey's account when I first visited the Suir. I had kept at them, but - not being anything approaching a master angler - I had been treated with contempt. Since then, wherever else I had caught trout, I had remembered how the Suir had trounced me.

Chapter Fifteen - Across The Water

The humiliation lingered. Now I was back, I thought, it would be different. I am older and wiser, I told myself, whereas the trout could not have grown wiser. Ergo...

They were two wild days. On the first we were at Suir Mount, where the record Irish salmon of 57 pounds was caught a good many years ago. The water here is very big, and a furious wind howled upriver, making casting a dangerous farce. It quietened in the evening, giving the promise of a compensatory evening rise. As so often with the evening rise, the promise was illusory.

Next morning we went to Swiss Cottage, the magnificent stretch below the town of Cahir, which was then the haunt of the late Liamy Farrell. The tempest, having rested overnight, was in full voice again. It roared through the great woods of oak and beech which line the banks, churned up the surface of the water, unleashed frequent downpours of icy rain, and generally made life thoroughly unpleasant. But, as we cowered in the lea of some shuddering willows, we witnessed a marvellous sight: great clouds of olives hatching and being hurled this way and that by the gale.

The trout began feasting and we rushed forth. Casting was a soul-destroying business; the wind kept whipping the fly off the water, or lashing the cast down like a snapped hawser. Yet every now and then providence permitted a fish to be covered properly, and then it might - note the word - take. I caught two, my first trout from the Suir, and Niall had three. None was bigger than a pound, but I felt that I had done at least something to erase my shame.

A couple of hours of this buffeting was as much as we could stand. Liamy Farrell suggested that shelter might be found at Ballycarron, upstream from Cahir (hence the drive past the clerical drying-out centre). So it proved, and there was still sufficient fly hatching to keep the trout interested. I found a line of them rising in an even-flowing run between high banks, over which the wind continued to blow harmlessly. I slithered down, and attacked them in a properly level-headed way. They were not easy, but I had that necessary warmth of confidence that they could be caught. By now I had learned that the prime requisite was to keep fishing, while they kept rising. They would refuse, and refuse, and refuse again, twenty times; and then might, at the twenty-first time, take. I kept at them for two hours, until

The Far From Compleat Angler

the hatch petered out. I had two handsome three-quarter pounders, and rose half a dozen others.

I returned to England much heartened. I realised that I had been deceived by catching stocked fish from the Kennet into believing that I had become an adequate dry fly fisherman. I had now learned that one wild Suir one-pounder asked more of me than any flabby pellet-fed four-pounder. I had learned to eat of the pie of humility; but I also knew that it could be done.

Since then, I have been back as often as possible. Usually the fishing has been difficult, sometimes impossible; and that is all right with me, because I wish to be tested by the Suir, I want it to set me a standard which I will always struggle to meet. But there was one evening when the river showed another side of itself, when the fish went mad.

My first intention had been to fish for salmon on the Blackwater. Word had reached me the previous week that the grilse were running. I was there on the Monday, peering over the bridge at Mallow at a gentle, shrunken stream. Where was the water, I demanded of Frank Maher, who guards and cherishes the fishing owned by a brother of Niall's at Killavullen. And where were the salmon? His sorrowful face told me the whole wretched story of the lottery that is salmon fishing. The previous Tuesday a steady rise in the water had brought the fish up in numbers. Frank had caught six on Wednesday, seven on Thursday. By Friday the level was dropping, and the grilse had sped through. By the time Niall and I had arrived, the situation was hopeless. It was Frank's opinion - offered to the accompaniment of violent profanity - that there wasn't single salmon resident on the fishery.

We held a pow-wow. The sun was beating down, the Blackwater seemed to be evaporating before our eyes. We didn't mind long odds, but no odds at all was another matter. Within half an hour we were on our way to Cahir. Within ninety minutes we were in Alice Conba's shop up the hill from the famous Norman Castle, buying her beautifully tied flies at a furious rate, as well as a couple of permits for Swiss Cottage. By half-past eight we were tackling up beside the broad, well-loved waters. It was a perfect June evening, the first warm one of summer.

Chapter Fifteen - Across The Water

I waded across the stream, went down a couple of fields, and fished up a long, deep pool towards a ramshackle weir. The air was balmy and, as the sun sank in an amber sky, the trout began to pick at a hatch of olives. But they were as fastidious as ever, and as I neared the top of the pool I still had not managed to fool one. Then I saw a clumsy, fluttering movement at the surface, and an eager pounce from a fish. It was a sedge, and within minutes, multitudes of these unprepossessing insects were appearing all over the river, and the trout were in a frenzy.

There is nothing in trout fishing to beat the excitement of an evening sedge hatch, and it was years since I had experienced one. Something about the motion of the creature as it careers across the top in its efforts to achieve flight induces abandon in even the most refined fish. The rises are savage and slashing, and the river that night boiled as the Suir trout went on the rampage.

Normally in such circumstances, I lose my head and fall in, or mislay my flies, or become hopelessly tangled, or break my cast. I began badly this time, for as I bent to release my first trout, my box of sedges, my scissors, and my bottle of flotant slid from my waistcoat pocket into the water. The flotant and the flies bobbed off downstream, with me in pursuit, and the scissors sank. I blundered after the fugitives, put them back in the same pocket, and miraculously spotted the scissors resting three feet down on a weedbed. As I bent to retrieve them, the Gink and the sedges escaped again, and the pursuit was repeated.

Thereafter, though, I did better. I regained my calm along with my essential equipment, and Miss Conba's cul-de-canard sedges did the rest. By the time I bumped into Niall, I had had seven fish. None was vast, but they had taken like tigers and fought like demons; and all had been returned. He, always more accomplished than me, had never moved more than twenty yards, and had simply lost count of the number of trout he had caught and missed.

On the bank, witnessing our endeavours, was a curious little Cahir man. He rebuked me sternly after I had waded back across the river, telling me I could have fallen into a hole and been swept away. A friend of his, he said, had had a narrow escape a couple of night before. I asked what had happened. It seemed that this friend had borrowed the reins off my informant's horse, saying he wanted to pull

The Far From Compleat Angler

a tree out of the water. He had tied a grappling hook to one end of the rope, and the other end round his leg. Throwing the hook around the tree, he had attempted to walk it to the bank, fallen headlong, and had been 'near drownded'. Unable to see the relevance of this incident to my own case, we bid farewell to the little man and left the river, hilarious and exhilarated.

When prevented from fishing in Ireland, I would console myself by reading about fishing in Ireland. I loved Kingsmill Moore, and O'Gorman's *The Practise of Angling in Ireland*, and Frank Barker's celebration of the lakes of Clare in *An Angler's Paradise*, and Peart's *A Year of Liberty*, and a crop of other curiosities from Niall Fallon's library. We both had a great affection for Maurice Headlam's *A Holiday Fisherman* and its accounts of the Suir; and an even stronger one for another Englishman, G.D. Luard, whose enchanting volumes, *Fishing: Fact or Fantasy* and *Fishing Fortunes and Misfortunes* were published by Faber during the last War.

They are simple, innocent works of reminiscence, at the heart of which is the friendship which blossomed at Harrow between Luard and Richard Grove Annesley, whose family owned a fine estate below the Galtymore mountains. The relationship is depicted with great skill, between the shy, diffident English boy with a passion for fishing, and 'Dick' - as he is always known - the confident, energetic hero figure, surrounded by an adoring family, supremely accomplished on horseback, and no less so with a salmon rod in his hand.

Luard disguised the estate under the name Ballyhimmock; and he called the rivers they fished the Big River and the Little River. But Niall had cracked the disguise, and one September we turned our backs on a lamentably shrunken and fishless Blackwater to follow the Englishman's tracks. We came to the village, which snoozed in a valley a few miles from Mallow. I was struck by the number of pubs. There cannot have been more than sixty houses, yet I counted seven licensed premises - Maigniers, Roches, Fitzgeralds, Linehans, Browns, Garrys, and the Cosy Corner. Had our purpose been to drink ourselves into oblivion, we would have needed to go no further.

Chapter Fifteen - Across The Water

But our goal lay up the hill. Using Luard's book as our guide - it was published half a century ago and described things as they were another half century before that - we found the white-tipped spears at the main gate, and turned in to follow the long drive. As we pulled up outside the creeper-clad house, and looked down to the valley below, we reflected that time moved slowly in this part of Ireland; indeed, you could doubt that it moved at all.

To Luard, as a tongue-tied seventeen-year-old, this was a magic world. It was in 1897 that he first boarded the Irish Mail, disembarking at the little whitewashed station into the sidecar and cart for the last three miles of the journey. These were the golden pre-war years - golden, that is, for the landowning classes, whose lives of ease and privilege revolved around horses and country sports, and were sustained by the exertions of their faithful retainers. Ballyhimmock's true name is Annes Grove, and for more than 200 years it has been the family home of the Grove Annesleys. Luard's friend - whose renown in those parts was derived from his long service as master of the Duhallow Hunt - died in the 1960s. The present owner is his grandson, although most of the great estate has now gone. The Little River whose trout so delighted Luard is the Awbeg. The Big River - where the boy was initiated in matters of salmon fishing with the fly - is the Blackwater.

These are the bare facts. But there is more to Annes Grove - and to Dick - than this. In Luard's books we see him as the hearty countryman par excellence - riding tirelessly to hounds, fishing for salmon and trout with immense energy and determination, striding around the estate with his dogs at his heels, attending to the needs and complaints of his tenantry, dispensing justice. Yet he had a passion which may even have exceeded those for hunting and fishing. For Dick's legacy is one of the outstanding gardens of Ireland. Thousands of visitors are drawn each year to inspect the walled garden, the slopes leading down to the river which are thick with exotic trees and shrubs, and the mass of strange and wonderful plants along the banks of the Awbeg itself.

Niall and I were received with great kindness by Mrs Annesley. She knew something of Luard - it seemed that he had been a career civil servant, rising to become clerk to the House of Lords. In those relaxed times, it had clearly been a post which allowed him ample

The Far From Compleat Angler

time to indulge his love of sketching and prodigious enthusiasm for fishing. He had died some time in the 1950s, a few years before his friend; they had remained close, although I am not clear whether Luard had continued the visits to Ballyhimmock.

We drank our tea, inspected the stuffed fish and hunting trophies in the hall, and strolled down the winding path to the river. It snaked slowly through the vegetation, the water deliciously clear, and with an amber lustre drawn from its gravel and sand bottom. We did not fish, although I believe that the Awbeg remains a decent stream. Instead we contented ourselves with spotting the trout, which were everywhere; and nodding our respects to the ghosts from long-departed days: old Tom Lonerghan, the gillie, and Jock, the wire-haired terrier, and the two friends with their fly rods at the ready, setting forth for an evening after the big fish which cruised in the flats below the house.

I have referred already to the myth of the persistent wetness of Ireland. But I accept that there are occasions when evidence to support the myth is furnished on a scale which might lead the naive to conclude that it is no myth at all. It happened to me a couple of summers ago, and it made me more aware than usual of man's puniness in the face of the force of nature. The experience of crossing a sea to fish a river which, between one day and the next, is transformed from an orderly stream into a scaled-down version of the Ganges at the height of the monsoon season is one which provides much food for philosophising.

It was mid-June, a month which, according to the poets and other ill-informed authorities, is supposed to see the first flowering of summer. They keep oddly quiet about the chances of tempest and deluge putting in an appearance, which is why I, with heart full of childish excitement, gave not a thought to the black clouds pursuing me across the Irish Sea. I had decided on a free-and-easy week. Having no money, I would spend no money. I would follow my nose, helping myself here and there to the wealth of free (or virtually free) fishing with which the island is blessed.

That first evening, I heard something on the news about people being rescued by lifeboat from their bedroom windows in North

Chapter Fifteen - Across The Water

Wales - and foolishly allowed myself a secret smile of satisfaction that Ireland seemed to be escaping the worst of it. My first stop was Niall's house, in the quiet farming country of Meath; my intention was to fish the Deel, a tricky but first-rate little stream which winds along a couple of meadows away from his front gate. He proposed a post-dinner sortie to fish the sedge. As I stood outside, getting my tackle ready, there was a sprinkling of very large drops of rain, which landed with heavy, sinister plops on the bonnet of my car. By the time we had crossed the couple of meadows, it was raining with serious intent. By the time we had legged it back to the house, it was beating down and we were soused.

It stopped about 22 hours later. A podgy Irish weather forecaster appeared on television with that guilty look of excitement that weather forecasters have when the weather achieves unprecedented awfulness. He announced that it had been probably the wettest day since Irish records began. Unconsoled by the thought of witnessing history in the making, I splashed down to the little river and found that it was a big, angry, cocoa-coloured river. There were no drowned sheep in it yet, but it seemed only a matter of time.

We were not finished, though. Reports from the west asserted that the rains had held off, and we were soon hurtling through the floods to the deeply green and thickly wooded county of Clare, and the neat little village of Corofin. As we headed down from the Slieve Aughty hills, we left the monsoon behind. The clouds were high over Clare, and the River Fergus, which flows through Corofin, was in perfect order. It connects a famous and lovely trout lough, Inchiquin, with a string of lesser lakes, and is itself a remarkable and fascinating piece of water.

Running through limestone, it is clear, rich in weed and full of trout, some very big. I know there are very big fish in it because we met one. It rose on the far side of a gorgeous pool upstream from Corofin. There was a terrific gurgling suck as a late mayfly disappeared, followed by waves. With an immense cast I managed to land my fly somewhere near, the fish dashed at it, and it missed. There were more waves.

These waves impressed us so much that we tramped up to a distant bridge, and tramped down the other side, so that we could

The Far From Compleat Angler

attack the monster properly. First cast it rushed heart-stoppingly at my mayfly, but again did not take. It then retired somewhere else to ponder the folly of its greed, and was seen no more.

That evening the sun shone, and we had some very pleasing fishing for small trout which rose with gusto to a hatch of blue-winged olives. In the morning we returned to seek a further interview with the leviathan of the pool. But he was still in purdah, and while we waited on him, the rain reached Corofin. It had that settled air of purpose about it, suggesting an ambition to last at least a week, and it drove us away from the Fergus, vowing to return one day.

My jaunt had been intended to end with some serious salmon catching on the Blackwater, where the grilse run should have been in full swing. Indeed, when we telephoned Frank Maher on our return from Corofin, it was in full swing. He had had seventeen that week, four that day. 'What about the water, Frank? Have you not had any rain?' Niall's voice was anxious, even though he was unable to accompany me. The reply was reassuring - the river was in grand order, the rain falling as summer rain should.

That night, at Niall's house, I was able to convince myself that the trip could yet be redeemed. That night, at Mallow on the Blackwater, it was tipping down. It continued to do until I arrived, and for some time after. The river was the colour of stout with a dash of milk. The violence of Frank's language knew no bounds (for, although he catches most of the fish himself, he longs for his visitors to discover the generosity of Blackwater for themselves); and in deference to him I flogged away for a day and a half without getting a touch, then carried out a strategic withdrawal back across the Irish Sea.

In describing this debacle, I hope I have not yielded to the feelings of rage and despair that its contemplation still arouses in me. I have tried to be philosophical, stoical, manly; for self-pity is tiresome. I have analysed my misfortunes in a cool and reasoned manner, searching for the positive side. There is one, and it recalls what they used to say at school about cross-country runs, arbitrary beatings, Latin verse scansion and the like: good for the character.

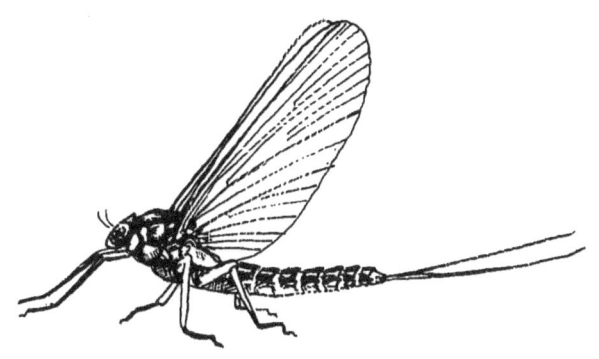

16. KENNET DAYS

I did my dry fly apprenticeship on the upper Kennet. The fishing began at Stitchcombe, and extended about two miles upstream. In those days, before it was blighted by drought and abstraction, it was an utterly gorgeous piece of water, crystalline, small in scale, packed with weed, well populated with nice stocked fish in the one- and-a-quarter to one-and-a-half pound bracket, and a smattering of wild fish. The hatches of fly were decent, but not extravagant. Olives hatched as they should from May onwards. There were black gnats and a few hawthorn. The blue winged olive would sometimes come on in the evening, as would the sedge.

The fishing was testing but rarely impossible. The wind usually blew downstream, and it took me a season or two to develop the casting skills to cope with it. I knew almost nothing about entomology when I first arrived, and I learned a necessary smattering as I went along. The Ginger Quill was ever reliable when light olives were hatching, and a black gnat would often stir a fish

The Far From Compleat Angler

where the branches of alders or willows trailed towards the water. I had some maddening times trying to imitate the BWO, and one or two triumphs among many failures with the sedge.

The great thing about the place - apart from the beauty of the winding valley, the air off the Downs, and the perfect dimensions of the water - was that you could almost always find a feeding fish. Catching it was another matter, but the stimulus to concentrated fishing was rarely wanting. I fished there for four or five years, then gave it up because I was hard up and it was a trying distance away from my home. Almost as soon as I had done so, I regretted it; although within a year or two it was already in steep decline, and only now has begun to reclaim something of its old glory. I retain the fondest memories of my days there, for I have never found any chalkstream fishing since to match it.

Two years after leaving the Savernake Flyfishers, I took a rod on a very different Kennet, at Marsh Benham, just upstream from Newbury. Here, the main river is much wider and deeper and more ponderous. Along much of it, the chalk bed is blanketed in silt. The water does not have that delicious clarity, and the bright ranunculus weed is eclipsed by coarser, less vital species of vegetation. The consolation is that there is a network of feeder streams cutting back and forth across the meadows, so that there is variety. The great drawback of Benham, as on much of the middle Kennet, is that hatches of fly - apart from the great mayfly carnival - are so poor. This deficiency is a continual theme through what I wrote while I had my rod there, and it eventually decided me to desert Berkshire for Hampshire. But, although Benham never meant as much to me as the Savernake water, I had many enjoyable and educative days there. I shall always remember it as the place where I could and should have caught really big trout - but didn't.

It irritates me that so many otherwise sensible and civilised people should be obsessed with golf. I cannot make up my mind which aspect of the game is most off-putting: the self-importance of the committee types who run it; the pettifogging rules they

Chapter Sixteen - Kennet Days

impose; the manicured artificiality of golf courses; or the inherent dullness of hitting a stationary ball and walking after it to hit it again.

I have stomped up and down a few score of fairways in my time, and have been told by those who should know that I could make something of the game. But I feel that golf and fishing are spiritually antipathetic, and that as a fisherman, I have a duty to state where I stand. However, there is one advantage that I will concede to golf, which is that you are either playing it, or you are not playing it. This may sound rather obvious, but my point is this: a man goes forth for a round of golf. He places his ball on the tee and hits it. It may land in a duckpond or a bramble thicket, but he knows that he is playing golf.

But what are we to make of the fisherman who is wearing his waders and coat, has his bag and net slung over his back, his rod in his hand - but is not casting his fly? I do not mean for a few minutes, but for hours at a time. Can he really be said to be fishing when all he is doing is stalking up and down the banks, staring at the water, and cursing the absence of visible fish life? I think not.

My season, that year, began on the last Tuesday in April. On the whole, I do not believe in April trout fishing; the first of May is the time for the off. But I had played cricket that Sunday (caught at mid-on for six, if you must know) in weather sufficiently balmy to persuade me that the trout should be on the lookout for the first titbits of the year. This opinion was not shared by the trout. Titbits there were, in the shape of hawthorns which occasionally dropped from air to water. But the trout kept their noses down while I prowled around. After a couple of hours I gave up - give it a week, I thought.

I gave it a week. By the time Sunday's match came round (given out LBW for two by an umpire who was corrupt or senile, or both) the weather had decided that it had not, after all, quite done with winter. I went to the river on the Tuesday, and began by looking at the book in the fishing hut in which members are obliged to record their catches. Now, the theory behind looking at the book is sound. If others are catching fish, it should give you

The Far From Compleat Angler

confidence that you will do the same. If, on the other hand, they are not catching anything, you are reassured that you can do no worse. So much for the theory. I found that they had been catching fish, and big ones - three of over four pounds, and one six pounder. They had all, I noted resentfully, been taken the previous Friday and Saturday before the change in the weather. Then, it had been warm and sunny, with a soft breeze from the south-west. Now, the wind was coming from the north, and the river had a steely, unfriendly look to it.

    I reminded myself that those who write about fishing must fish to have something to write about; then set off. The morning was entirely barren, as I could not find a feeding fish anywhere. My mood was not improved by an encounter with another member, who agreed that there had been no sort of hatch, before confessing, with a smirk, that he had managed a brace, one just over four pounds and the other just under. I asked him what fly he had been using, and he produced something which looked like the business end of a garden broom. 'Doesn't look like anything on the water,' he said annoyingly, 'but they seem to go for it.'

    A little while later I did find a rising fish. For no good reason, I assumed that it was a small one; so was more than usually unprepared when it rose, hooked itself, tore across the stream with my reel howling, and rushed through a weedbed. By the time it came out the other side, the connection between fish and fly had been ended. Muttering grimly, I marched off to a distant part of the fishery where I was sure they would be feeding. Having torn my waders on a barbed wire fence, I got there to find that they were not feeding. I pressed on upstream, at almost every step disturbing wildfowl which flapped, quacking, into the air before bellyflopping into every possible fishholding spot. I returned to the fishing hut, wrote 'Fort - nil' in the damned book, and left. Back home, I eyed my golf clubs, recalling the sweet satisfaction of following the parabola of a cleanly-driven ball, the musical clunk of a birdie putt, the smell of a freshly mown fairway, the laughs, the comradeship. Perhaps ....

Chapter Sixteen - Kennet Days

The merry month of May, some clot called it. For me, it was anything but. A catalogue of misfortune would be nearer the mark, though I suppose the poet would complain about an absence of alliterative bounce.

Actually, I did not feel too mortified about the events of the first day of the month. One should not expect to catch fish on the opening day. The idea is to flex unused muscles, to oil rusty skills (if possessed), to resume the easy relationship with favourite rod and trusted reel, to admire the trees coming into leaf, to sniff the flowering of spring, to check if the river and its trout are as they should be.

This occupied me pleasantly enough through the morning, there being nothing else to do, since the fish were fasting. After lunch I left the main river, which was lifeless, to explore one of the side streams. There I found a genteel feast in progress. There was a fall of black gnats. A steady trickle of them was being washed downstream, and snouts were appearing to intercept them. I cast over a snout, and my fly disappeared in a delicate dimple. I tightened. There was a boil and a wave as the trout sped upstream. My faculties were still in winter atrophy, and I did nothing, and the fish got off.

I walked up to a turbulent pool below a little red brick bridge. Big fish live there - someone once took a seven-pounder on a spent mayfly - but the contrariness of the currents makes presentation a tricky business. I was congratulating myself on my finesse when there was a confident rise. I struck viciously, my cast broke, and I went home to play cricket with my son.

My next visit began atrociously. I found that I had left my scissors behind, and therefore had to carry out all the finicky snipping of nylon with a kitchen knife. This was not easy on the temper. Even worse were the protruding struts on my new, polarised spectacle shades, which dug into my nose in a manner which quickly became unbearable. The weather was lovely - for cricket, or drinking cold beer in a deckchair. It was lousy for fishing, with that piercing brilliance in the sunlight which discourages any fly from hatching, and seems to refine the trout's early warning system into a continual state of maximum alert.

The Far From Compleat Angler

This is all a roundabout way of explaining why, at three o'clock in the afternoon, I was asleep in the shade of a beech tree. I was not fishing because there was nothing to fish for. Revived by slumber, I thought it might be worth revisiting the spot where the black gnat binge had taken place the previous week. This time, there was no more than an occasional insect being taken by an occasional fish. I hooked one and he broke me. I hooked another, a little way upstream, and he broke me too. I then caught his grandson, who was five inches long. Above the little red brick bridge I hooked a third good fish, and he threw the hook. At this point the water suddenly acquired a strange milky appearance, and all signs of life ended. The keeper told me wearily that the water authority people were 'at it again' upstream, and the discoloration was likely to last for hours. Realising that my bankside snooze had been the highlight of the season thus far, I retired.

But early May was not always so barren. True, there was virtually nothing by way of hatches of olives. But the black gnat, and to a greater extent the hawthorn, did something to fill the gap. The hawthorn, of course, has nothing of the elegance and delicacy of the olive. But what it lacks in beauty, it more than makes up for in toothsomeness; for it is greeted with rare relish by the trout.

It takes its English name from the hedge, and its Latin one - *bibio marci* - from St Mark's Day, which is as early as you are likely to see it. Although it is a terrestrial rather than aquatic species, it likes to swarm and mate near or above water. Whether from absent-mindedness or amorous abandon, it frequently falls onto the surface, which is bad news for the hawthorn but splendid news for the trout.

A little way above the red brick bridge to which I have already referred was a spot much beloved by the hawthorn for reproductive antics. A line of soaring limes overshadowed the water, and beneath the spreading branches the fish would line up to snaffle the insects as they fell. It was a demanding place to fish, for you had to keep yourself down, and cast low beneath the branches, allowing the fly to come down within a few inches of the near bank. The rises were extremely delicate, but the fish were often good ones. One year,

Chapter Sixteen - Kennet Days

among the half dozen I had in two delightful sessions, was a trout of three pounds fourteen ounces.

The hawthorn season was brief, lasting barely three weeks. By the time the last of them was succumbing to sexual exhaustion, the first mayfly were taking wing, fluttering their huge, gauzy wings at the start of their apotheosis. It used to take the trout a few days to recover from the shock of seeing these exotic apparitions. Then they would begin to gorge themselves in earnest.

In my days on the upper Kennet I used to display a lofty indifference towards the mayfly. The insect did not appear there, and we would not have welcomed it if it had. We much preferred our modest hatches of well-mannered olives and dainty pale wateries. Our view of the mayfly was akin to that of monks on hearing reports of Roman orgies.

When I came to Benham, I took with me much of my old prejudice; and, though I developed a more flexible attitude, I cannot say that I have entirely shed it now. I cannot help thinking that there is something gross and undignified about the whole business, which is an affront to notions of flyfishing as the most refined and graceful of pastimes. This is mainly because of the behaviour of the fish. We like to think of trout as reasonably discriminating creatures, which help themselves in moderation at Nature's table and examine our imitations with a critical eye. But - on the Kennet at least - this went out of the window with the arrival of *ephemera danica*. Gluttony and piggishness ruled in the frenzy to swallow as many of these luscious titbits as possible. Our chalkstream trout became like schoolboys who had found the tuckshop left unlocked.

There is also the matter of the scale of the hatch. A hatch of fly should be a modest affair. It should not blot out the sun, obscure the meadows, form a hovering cloud over the river. The fisherman does not really wish to have huge insects settling on his ears, festooning his hat, creeping across the lenses of his spectacles. Nor, if he has any sensibility, does he care to see the water transformed into the aquatic equivalent of the classic French film, *La Grande Bouffe*. Afterwards, of course, excess is succeeded by biliousness and torpor. The fish, stuffed to the gills, sink dyspeptically to the bottom, contemptuous of anything as puny as a trickle of olives. 'If only,' one exclaims irritably as one surveys the unbroken surface in early July, 'if only Nature would organise matters more sensibly. Why cannot the mayfly be supplied little and often, instead of in this one colossal binge?'

I realise that I am overstating my case. The scenes of abandon which I have described are hardly the norm. And when they do occur, they tend to involve fisheries recently stocked with large numbers of greedy, uneducated fish whose ingrained instincts of caution have been nullified by the transfer from stewpond to river. On stillwaters, the mayfly hatch is likely to be as patchy and maddening as any other. I have done my time on the great Irish lakes like Corrib, where, more often than not, the surging hope which attends the start of the mayfly day is transformed into despair by the time a fishless evening is reached. And I know that I am quite unjustifiably blackening the reputation of the insect itself, an exquisite and fascinating creature whose appearance is one of the wonders of the angler's year.

What, above all, quickens the heart in the mayfly season is the matter of BIG fish. It is the time when the disciplined angler may legitimately put aside considerations of quantity and reasonably pursue the dream of the monster. It is the time when the five and six pounders which one has been told exist actually offer proof of the fact. It is the time for putting oneself to the test.

At Benham, one of the sidestreams left the main river via some hatches, and rejoined it some distance below. On its meandering journey it was connected to a shallow lake which used to be home to a very few, very large, wild brown trout. In the mysterious way of the mayfly, it hatched on the stream but not on the lake. When the hatch was at its height, the leviathans would migrate into the running water to dine.

One evening, I spotted one of the grandfathers feeding beneath a tangled gorse bush. There were sucking sounds, and ripples of a size to promote pounding of the heart. The luxuriance of the surrounding

Chapter Sixteen - Kennet Days

vegetation made proper casting impossible. On my knees, I thrust the end of my rod through the thicket, and lowered a French Partridge onto the water. It travelled slowly into the monster's lair, and there was a noise like a wet kiss. I tightened, and the drama moved to its climax at unnerving speed.

The fish went upstream, turned, came back past me, dived, broke me; and I never even got off my knees. Trembling and panting, like a mountaineer at high altitude without oxygen, I stumbled away. A little later I bumped into the keeper and recounted the terrible story. He endeavoured to console me by telling me that he himself had seen this fish; or enough of it to estimate its weight at eight pounds. In his view, I had done well to hook it. No man could have expected to land such a trout in such a spot.

In subsequent seasons, I pondered the theory of the mayfly, which is that one catches monsters. I found it wanting. The fact was that other people caught them, and I lost them. My final year at Benham, at least a dozen trout of over five pounds were caught. My own chance came on one of the carriers, where the water broke over a gravel bar. Just above the bar, it was deeper than one might have suspected, and a heavy fish advertised its presence close to the roots of a tree on the near bank by gulping down every fly that came its way.

The cast was an exceedingly awkward one, requiring the fly to be catapulted through a narrow gap between the branches of an alder, and the surface. At the third or fourth attempt, I delivered the fly to the right spot, and a huge mouth absorbed it. That fish behaved most provokingly. It seemed determined to show me exactly what the dimensions of the prize were, before snatching it from me. Five times it jumped clear of the water, showing a tail as wide as a garden spade and a great expanse of spotted flank. My initial estimate of four pounds had soared beyond five to six, when it tired of acrobatics and surged upstream.

I wouldn't say that I was confident of landing him, but I did have hopes. I knew he was well hooked, and I avoided my customary nonsense of getting my line caught round reel handle, rod butt, or wadered leg. I peered upriver, and saw my cast cutting through the water at a fearful lick with great waves spreading out behind. Then, incredulous, I spotted a massive clod of weed floating down the middle of the stream towards me. Clod met cast, out came hook, and off went my last Kennet giant.

17. OTHER CHALKSTREAMS

In 1994 I swapped Berkshire for Hampshire, forsook the broad waters of Benham for the limpid Itchen at Abbots Barton. It felt like the start of a new age, for a change of river at my time of life is a momentous thing. It was as if I had left the familiar surroundings of school, where I felt secure in my place; and was peering into the quadrangle of some institute of higher learning, a touch apprehensive at the demands which might be made of me.

The season on the Itchen starts on 1 April, which is too early for me. Forget about Chaucer and his 'Aprille with his shoures soote'. The problem these days is persuading winter that his time is up. He hangs around to flay hopeful spring-seekers with Arctic blasts, hailstorms and the like, and so it was last year. So, for the first half of the month, I cowered indoors, until at last the breeze swung into the south-west and I was moved to head for Winchester.

The countryside was caught between seasons. The grass was lush and deep green. Some of the trees were just alive again with their new foliage, while the oaks were bare and skeletal. The main river was lifeless, gunmetal grey. But the little feeder streams which crisscross the meadows were cheerful, the emerald of the ranunculus and starwort bright against the pallor of the chalk bed. Of hatching insect life, there was no sign at all, and by lunchtime I had hardly bothered to cast.

The primary reason for coming to Hampshire for my fishing was to encounter proper hatches of fly again. As I ate my bread and cheese, I pondered sceptically - and a trifle resentfully - on the reports I had read about the infallible appearance on April days of the Large Dark Olive; and the guarantee this presented of sport with trout. 'Ha,' I said to myself scornfully. 'So much for the marketing men. I should have known it was all snare and delusion.' Then, suddenly and

The Far From Compleat Angler

miraculously, they did begin to hatch. Down they floated towards me, dark smudges against the sheen of the surface. And up came the trout to snatch them.

I had two hours of utterly absorbing fishing. Being stocked fish, they were none too faddy and took a small hackled Greenwell readily enough. By mid-afternoon I had caught and returned three or four which did not quite make the fourteen inch size limit, and kept one handsome two pounder. At the fishing hut I met the keeper, a bluff, affable pipe-smoker who introduced himself as Mike. We exchanged pleasantries, and I wandered upstream for a final flurry. I noticed two fish feeding avidly on a bend. I caught one, then the other; each heavily spotted with a golden tummy, each just over two pounds.

I was shamingly pleased with myself as I returned to the hut. Mike took the pipe out of his mouth as I approached. 'That was very efficiently done,' he commented approvingly. 'Help,' I thought. 'He thinks I'm a proper fisherman. Wait till next time.'

I was right, of course. The dawning of the new age was too golden by half, and subsequent visits through May and June showed me how rapidly these Itchen trout informed themselves about anglers and their deceiving ways. By August I was seriously ravaged by the insidious infection known as self-doubt. I had had two successive blank evenings, and as the second drew to its maddening end - with the only trout I had managed to hook making its escape into the weeds with my fly in its mouth - I was wondering whether it might all be beyond me.

What made it worse was that other people were catching fish; every other member, apart from me, it seemed. Were they all, I asked myself gloomily, simply better fishermen than me? 'Probably' was the answer that hung heavily over my head. I knew that I had made a bad mistake, and one wholly typical of my defective approach to my sport (I fear it is the chief reason why I shall never be anything other than a mediocre angler). I had got it into my head that there was only one place I wanted to fish, which was towards the upper limit of our stretch of the main Itchen. The others had prowled around the feeders, picking up an odd fish here

Chapter Seventeen - Other Chalkstreams

and there. But I had skulked in this one spot, waiting for something which did not happen.

The Main, as it is known, is hardly classic Itchen. It was, the old-timers relate, barbarously dredged in the 1950s. As a result it flows sluggishly over a thick, dark, lifeless blanket of silt. Only in one or two short stretches is it shallow and narrow enough for the current to quicken sufficiently to keep the bottom clean and to nourish weed growth. One of these was where I stationed myself; for I knew that there were good trout there. The flaw was that the hatch of blue-winged olives which I thought I had every reason to expect never materialised.

Wiser after these failures, I returned, determined to give the Upper Main a miss. So, at quarter to nine, in blissful warmth with the sun sinking in a molten sky, I found myself on the Upper Main. Quite why this should have been, I cannot say. I certainly left the fishing hut with good intentions, heading for one of the little streams at the opposite end of the fishery from my place of temptation. But someone else was there, so I tramped across to the Lower Main - far away from the home of the siren - still fixed in my resolve. There I encountered a serious deterrent.

Now, I have nothing against birds in moderation. A couple of coots, a duck here and there, even the occasional family of swans - these I can view with equanimity, even smile on as they go about their absurd business of ducking and diving and swimming around in meaningless circles. With an effort I can even forgive them their atrocious habit of taking to the air for no good reason at all, and flopping down on proven trout lies, scaring every decent fish out of its wits. But the Canada goose is another matter.

I counted thirty of these oversized, stupid and ridiculous birds. As I approached the only promising run on the Lower Main from below, they sailed into it from above. Round and round they went, while their chums hastened to join them from all points near and far. Briefly I savoured a fantasy - a variation on the climax to Lindsay Anderson's *If* - in which the countryside idyll was shattered by automatic gunfire and the honking of wounded geese. Then I strode upstream towards the forbidden zone.

The Far From Compleat Angler

On the way I came upon fish, feeding fish. I was somewhat amazed, as on the previous occasions the trout had been engaged in some obscure ritual of self-denial. Now, though, this Ramadan had evidently expired, and they were hard at it, tails and backs breaking water as they slurped and guzzled. To begin with, I was not seen to full advantage. I wasn't sure what they were taking, so I put on a little cul-de-canard sedge. This was grabbed at once. I landed the fish, knocked him on the head, cast again, was taken again, and broken. I tied on another sedge, of deerhair, hooked a fish and lost it; rose another and missed it. This community of fishes then reached a consensus that it had had enough disturbance for one evening, and sank out of sight.

Around the next corner was the riffle from which I had promised to abstain. But it was too much for even my iron self-control; for there were even more trout, troughing away. There was about half-an-hour of fishing light left, and not a moment to be wasted. From the way they were rising, quietly and purposefully, I knew they weren't on the sedge. It must be the blue-winged olive, which is what it should have been the previous week, and the one before that. But this was no time for recriminations. I knotted on an Orange Quill, and set about disrupting this gormandizers' gala.

Innate modesty and the horror of being thought tedious, compel me to skip the details of the resulting display of dynamism and competence. I was, dare I say it, the embodiment of cool calculation. The expression 'fishing machine' springs to mind. I was... but enough. Back at the hut I bumped into the fellow member who had originally deflected me from the distant feeder stream. 'Nice fish,' he murmured as I tipped out my two brace. 'Very nice fish.' And they were - the two best reaching two-and-three-quarter pounds. As I skipped off down the path to my car, I heard a little warning voice in the darkness. Something about self-doubt being bad, but excess pride being worse, I think.

I know of no book which celebrates the joy of dry fly fishing for trout in a finer or more memorable manner than Plunket Greene's *Where*

Chapter Seventeen - Other Chalkstreams

The Bright Waters Meet. His profession was singing, his escape from it the river, and he wrote as I imagine he sang, with vigour and passion and beauty. It is a curious accident that, while his career as a baritone is now forgotten, his memory should survive through this one book, his song to the little Bourne.

The extraordinary charm of the book lies in the bond between writer and water. Although Plunket Greene strays from the Bourne - to the Test, to Germany, to the Kennet, to Blagdon - he is always drawn back to its music and its golden trout. The story he tells lingers in the mind because it has tragedy as well as delight and happiness. It is suffused with sunlight and shadow.

There is, too, an overwhelming nostalgia - 'of all the pains which a mortal has to suffer, the worst', Plunket Greene writes. The book is filled with an impossible yearning for a departed world, the Edwardian idyll which was shattered by the Great War. That tone is set at the start, with his discovery of the village of Hurstbourne Priors, one summer's day in the penultimate year of Queen Victoria's reign: 'In the middle (of the valley) lay the village in a golden sheet of buttercups, and through the buttercups under the beech woods of the deer park ran a little chalkstream, clear as crystal and singing like a lark. There was a church half hidden in the trees, and the people were just coming out after service, and there was an indescribable feeling of peace over the whole scene'.

Fleetingly, one wonders how real it was even then, with the cricket matches on the ground by the church, the dinners and the evenings of bridge, and the practical jokes, the fishing and the pigeon shooting. Was everybody, as Plunket Greene maintains, really 'full of high spirits and blessed with a sense of humour'? Well, perhaps not, and perhaps the little Bourne did not truly sing like a lark. But he still makes one wish one had been with him when he walked over from Whitchurch that Sunday morning.

According to Plunket Greene, that world had departed by 1924, when the first edition of the book was published. Seventy years later, one might have expected that it would have been utterly obliterated. But the village and its valley remain instantly familiar. Thus, the

The Far From Compleat Angler

Whitchurch road crosses the bridge, and turns right by the cricket ground, with its thatched pavilion and well-worn benches. The church stands beyond, its sturdy square tower wrapped in Virginia creeper. To the left is the Long House, which Plunket Greene rented. To the right stretches the field by the broad water - no buttercups, perhaps, but with the great spreading sycamores under which he doubtless sought shade on flaming August afternoons.

And what of the river? At first sight - as one peers over the Beehive bridge - it might seem much the same. The gravel is golden, the weed a rich green, and the bow waves of fleeing trout testify that life survives. But come a mile or so upstream, and look more closely. Still soaring above the valley is the viaduct which carries the railway from Basingstoke to Andover. Below, the Bourne is split into two tiny channels, in the left of which (looking down) Plunket Greene caught those three trout up to three and a quarter pounds on an August day in 1904, evidence of his contention that this was 'unquestionably the finest small trout stream in England'.

Early editions of the book have a photograph of the two channels, and now one can see the difference. The viaduct is there. The cottage rented by Plunket Greene's friends, Sharkey and Savage, is there. The channels are there. But in the photograph they are brimful of water. Now they are not, and the trout have gone. The Bourne, which was always tiny, is now shrunken. Beyond the viaduct is the cress farm, the acres of crop cultivated in severe concrete rectangles. Higher up still, the river no longer exists. Somewhere up there Plunket Greene caught his biggest Bourne trout, three and three-quarter pounds. It is not easy to imagine it now.

But enough of lamentation. No, it is not the same as it was in that golden age. The lustre has long gone and will not return. The wonder is that the Bourne is still as good as it is - that it remains a sight to gladden the fly fisher's heart and set the nerve ends tingling. I have fished it half a dozen times, thanks to the generosity of a friend whose father retained a rod; and on each occasion have been entranced by its charm, amazed by the numbers of fish, and unnerved by the amazing clarity of the water. One may count the spots on a fish, see the pink of the gills, make out the colour and shape of a stone on the bottom as if

Chapter Seventeen - Other Chalkstreams

it lay in the palm of one's hand.

The water from the church down to the bridge is the best of it, I think. It is minuscule in scale, heavily overgrown with high, tangled banks, phenomenally rich in feeding, and heaving with fish - mainly grayling, with a fair sprinkling of trout. It is exceedingly awkward to fish, because it has to be waded, and every step sends shoals scurrying in all directions. But they can be coaxed to take a small dry fly, and the clarity of the water makes the use of the nymph a challenge and a joy.

I spoke of tragedy in Plunket Greene's book. It arose from the decision - which he supported - to stock the little river. It was grossly overdone, to the tune of more than two thousand fish, and the consequence was starvation both for the immigrants and the native stock. This disaster virtually brought down the curtain on the active side of Plunket Greene's love affair with the Bourne, and he continued to reproach himself bitterly for his part in it. But it did recover, to an extent; and now, although it is still stocked, the wild fish are able to thrive.

In the church lies the body of Sir Robert Oxenbridge, Lord of the Manor of Hurstbourne Priors. When he died in 1574, the great yew to the south was a mere three or four hundred years old. It still stands there, and beyond its sombre mass is the grave of Harry Plunket Greene. On the one side is the cricket ground where he played; on the other, the river he fished. It is something that, come Saturday in summer, white flannels still stand out against the green, and that the trout are still rising.

It was a peach of a day, all the more glorious for confounding expectation. The man on the radio had forecast November chill and dankness. But as I bowled along the Roman road that points at Salisbury, the grey flannel above peeled away to reveal a soft, blue sky and a soft autumn sun. It shone down on the wide, bare spaces of the downs, and the foliage of the oak and beech copses glowed with coppery life.

In short, it was a grand day to be out and about, with a fishing rod in the back of the car and a long-held ambition to fulfill. As I rolled

The Far From Compleat Angler

down into the Test valley, I spared a thought - being a compassionate man - for the millions chained to their desks, eyes trained on screens, fingers skipping over keyboards, ears jammed to telephones. And I reflected that the sweetness of the song of the birds, and the healing quality of sunshine, were distinctly enhanced if you happened to be the only one around to enjoy them.

My ambition was to fish for grayling with a fly rod, in the grayling's proper season, which is autumn. I had caught them before on English rivers, but always unintentionally, when fishing for trout in summer. In such circumstances they are something of an annoyance. In general, the grayling's reputation has never stood as high here as in continental Europe. It tends to do best on our southern chalkstreams, where it competes with the trout for the angler's attention. As a result, it is regarded - at best - with something approaching condescension, occupying a position in the fishy world equivalent to that of the gentlewoman's companion in the human world. At worst, it has been the victim of persecution by ideologues and snobs who think it unworthy to share hallowed water with the noble trout.

The best thing about it is that it is in its prime when the trout season is done with, which is why my heart was light as I arrived at Timsbury, where the kind father of a kind friend had told me I was welcome to do my worst. Fishing the same place in high summer, I had caught a couple of big grayling during a hectic hatch of sedges. But in autumn, so I had read, the nymph was the way.

There are nymph fishers and non-nymph fishers, and by inclination I am of the second category. I like to see my fly float, and the nymph sinks; and I never have the least confidence that I know what is happening to it. The experts tell you that you should spot your fish under water, and strike when it opens its mouth to absorb the nymph. Now, there are doubtless men who can see a pair of small, white lips opening and closing through several feet of water, but I am not one of them. The alternative is to watch your leader, and strike when it behaves unnaturally. But I cannot see the leader either.

Chapter Seventeen - Other Chalkstreams

Luckily, some time before, a pleasant young man at the tackle shop in Stockbridge had given me a first-rate tip, which was to attach a tuft of thick orange wool treated with flotant to the leader to act as a bite indicator. I did as I was bid, and it worked splendidly. I spent a considerable proportion of the limited daylight afforded by a November day in watching my wool bob along over various likely grayling lies. But although it bobbed nicely, it never went under, and by early afternoon I was having serious doubts about the nymph.

The situation was saved by the mellowness of the weather, which encouraged a timely hatch of olives. Now, at last, I knew what I was doing. I came across a little shoal of grayling rising to the olives, and immediately caught one of them on a Kite's Imperial; and a gorgeous sight it was, with its silver flanks speckled with black, and bristling, red-membraned dorsal fin. Aha, I said to myself, I shall make a killing now. But the fish, as if hardly persuaded that rising to olives was a good idea after all, stopped doing so.

With the sun sinking fast, I went back to the nymph. There was insufficient time to fiddle around with wool, so I stared as hard as I could at the leader. Much to my surprise, it suddenly dropped out of sight, and I caught a grayling even lovelier than the first, a good pound-and-a-half. It would have been a crime to kill it, so I slipped it back. The 'lady of the stream' is how some felicitous writer dubbed the grayling; and I felt that, as a gentleman, I had paid my respects.

18. In Eden

Not that long ago, a lifetime or so, most of England was blessed with true, natural trout rivers; rivers with self-sustaining stocks of native brown trout. Our age, and the neglect and abuse we have fostered in our march towards the millennium, have seen the spoiling of much of this legacy. Pollution, water abstraction, and unthinking exploitation have picked off one river after another, leaving them ruined or corrupted.

Of course, there are sanctuaries where the wild brown trout survive. Those game, fierce little fellows of Exmoor and Dartmoor still thrive. There are streams in Derbyshire, Yorkshire, Northumbria, and Shropshire which have escaped the blight we have brought in the name of progress. Even in the chalkstreams of the south, the wild fish hang on, despite being outnumbered and eclipsed by stocked interlopers.

But think of what we have lost! Think of those tiny brooks which once threaded their bright way through the countryside of Hertfordshire - the Lea, the Gade and the rest of them, destroyed by having their waters sucked away. Think of the Darent in Kent, the Misbourne and the Chess in Buckinghamshire. Think of the way the proud Test has been reduced to the status of a stew water. We should hang our heads in shame when we consider how we have treated our inheritance.

Chapter Eighteen - In Eden

I am a southerner, and most of my trout fishing is done on the domesticated rivers of Berkshire and Hampshire. But the English river which engages my imagination, and nourishes the daydreams of the long winter months, does not belong to a gentle, downland valley. It belongs to the north-west, to a wide, open landscape of sweeping fields and treeless dun fells. It is the Eden of Cumberland (no right-minded angler recognises Cumbria); a grand, untarnished river whose trout are its own, and are wild.

My Eden is complemented by another river. The character of the big river is determined by its scale. Its breadth and power compel respect, though it is never forbidding. The lesser stream, the Eamont, has sweetness and charm. It flows north-east from Ullswater, by curiously named places like Honeypot and Udford, through a green, wooded valley; then meets the Eden at Watersmeet, under the distant frown of Cross Fell. The villages of this part of the world are sturdy settlements of stone houses and whitewashed cottages, with sturdy names: Langwathby, Lazonby, Salkeld and the like. But there is a softer sound to the name of the hamlet which lies across the river from Langwathby. It is called Edenhall, as is the estate which lies in the angle between the two rivers. Those four miles or so of water represent the closest I have yet come (together with the Irish Suir) to my ideal of what trout fishing should be.

It begins at the bridge at Langwathby, which I have mentioned elsewhere. The view remains as fine a sight to me now as when I first viewed it more than thirty years ago. I love the bubbly shallows, the dark channels between rosy sandstone boulders, the marbled runs fringed by emerald weed, and the calm depths shaded by beech and hazel.

When there is a hatch of fly - which there should be of a summer's morning, though they are by no means as reliable as once they were - it can take a full morning to do justice to this short stretch, from the bridge up to where the river bends to the right. A little way up from there is a steep bluff, thick with trees. The water runs deep and strong at its foot and is full of trout - although the testing nature of the wading and the proximity of the bank make getting at them something of a trial.

The Far From Compleat Angler

Above this stretch are wide, somewhat featureless flats; and then a tremendous fish-holding reach. It has to be fished in chest waders, and is best in low water, for there is a strength to the current which constantly threatens to pluck the legs from the bottom. There is a great head of trout here; I have stood at the height of a sedge hatch on a June night and lost my head and my nerve utterly at the spectacle of the surface boiling.

It was at the top of this section, very many years ago, that I endured one of the indelible, decisive traumas of my fishing career. In those days, I should explain, we (my brothers and I) knew nothing whatever of the dry fly, and almost nothing about entomology. We would arrive, and race off to the Penrith tackle shop, Charles R. Sykes, where a shrivelled and matchlessly pessimistic old boy would sell us made-up casts of wet flies: Partridge and Orange, Partridge and Yellow, Waterhen Bloa, Poult Bloa, Greenwell, Brown Owl, Black Spider, March Brown, and other time-honoured northern patterns.

The notion that any of these creations imitated a specific insect never occurred to us. We would simply tie on whichever of the casts first came to hand and fish across and down in the approved manner, until a break or a tangle forced us to attach a new one. On this occasion I was with my brother Matthew. It was late April. The sky was white, the wind raw, and soon it began to snow heavily. We were astounded to see that this blizzard coincided with a frenzied rise. Between the snowflakes as they hit the water we saw multitudes of dark, high-winged flies, and the trout slashing at them. We immediately became delirious with excitement. It seemed impossible that we would not catch fish, lots of fish. We flailed away with whatever flies we had on. Trout rose to the right, to the left, in front, behind, at our feet. But they would not take our flies. We were overwhelmed by the numbness brought on by the cold, and our despair. Eventually we stumbled away through the snow, unable to believe what had happened.

About ten years later I worked it out. What we had witnessed had been a classic hatch of iron blues. Had we used a dry imitation, or a wet Snipe and Purple, we would indeed have done great deeds. As it was, we were simply too ignorant to have any clue what to do. We always fished downstream, and when - by accident - we used the correct fly, we used to hook a lot of fish. And, because the method

Chapter Eighteen - In Eden

is so defective, we used to lose a lot. Of course, when the weather warmed up and the water fined down, the trout would not look at our flies, clumsily landed on their heads and dragged around in front of their noses. One hot day in June I watched a stranger extract two fish of over a pound each from what I would have regarded as an impossible little curl of water tucked in against the bank. I asked him what he was using, and he showed me a whisp of black. It was a black gnat; as far as I can recall, the first dry fly I had ever seen.

It took a little while for the lesson to sink in. But gradually I became a convert to the new method, and lost my faith in the three-fly casts dispensed by the gloomy man at Charlie Sykes (though never in the shop itself - the prophet of doom has now gone, but it remains first port of call in Penrith). In those formative years I mainly used a dry, winged Greenwell, which was - and still is - a most reliable imitation of the medium olives which make up the main daytime hatches. Then I became aware that, in the evenings, something called a sedge would sometimes appear and rouse the trout to a state of excitement, and I would use that.

One year we persuaded our Irish friend, Niall, to come over and join us, and he was so entranced by the water and the landscape that he became a regular visitor. We were given the run of the rivers by the kind friends who owned the estate, and would stay with the excellent Mrs James at Melmerby; roaming up and down Eden and Eamont as we willed, meeting to eat, drink, and swap adventures and abuse at the neat wooden hut which overlooked the surging pool known as the Boil Hole, with the smooth waters of the Tuck above, and Beach Dub to the right, where the river swung under a red-earthed bluff before straightening to receive the Eamont.

Niall's approach to this fishing was the antithesis to my own. Mine was simultaneously haphazard, in that my choice of fly was largely dictated by guesswork; and rigid, in that I was extremely reluctant to use anything other than the patterns which had caught me fish in the past, namely the Greenwell and the sedge. He, on the other hand, was educated in matters of trout and their food. He would observe, then determine tactics. I can remember being most impressed at seeing him take three nice fish from a little run just upstream from the hut, on a hawthorn. I had never heard of the fly;

The Far From Compleat Angler

but he had seen them hovering, then dropping on the water. It doesn't sound much, but it was an eye-opener for me.

There was one trip at around this time which I found particularly character-forming. We met right at the end of May, after I had had several productive days with the mayfly on the Kennet. I was rather full of myself, and talked over-confidently of baskets of trout, instead of individuals. If I could master the large, refined fish of the chalkstream, so my thesis went, these simple little northern creatures should be easy meat. In short, I was in a foolish state of mind, and riding for a fall.

The first evening was a beauty: a little cool, but still and clear. I had decided, in advance, that it would be an evening for the sedge. As Niall and I walked up from the hut to the lower Eamont, he told me he thought it would be a sedge evening, too. This last piece of the Eamont, before Watersmeet, contains some glorious water. Here, the river has escaped from its narrow valley, and runs broad and energetic between open fields. There is a big bar of gravel extending diagonally downstream to the far side, with a magnificent run by the near bank whose top is marked by a wild currant bush. A little way below, the stream breaks over rocky shallows before collecting itself to flow in a smooth orderly fashion into the Eden itself.

The light was dimming as Niall and I separated; he to fish this bottom pool, I to tackle the currant bush run. As I slipped quietly from the bank into the water, I spotted a rise or two. Then there were more: dimples in the shallows along the gravel bar, more decisive sucks in the main flow. I began to bang my sedge down on their heads. The fish ignored it, but went on rising. I felt that familiar sense of irritation, like not being able to understand a joke that everyone else is laughing at. I put on a different sedge, and caught a little trout of six ounces. Briefly, hope revived; then declined, as the sedge continued to float down towards me, untouched among the rises.

Enervated by this display of faddishness, I decided that I should really be fishing somewhere else; where the fish might show proper appreciation for a sedge. I strode downstream and spotted Niall, playing a fish. Instinctively, I knew that it was the latest of several.

Chapter Eighteen - In Eden

He proferred the information that it was not a sedge evening at all. It was a Blue-Winged Olive evening, and he was fishing an Orange Quill. Not knowing what an Orange Quill looked like, I snorted and marched on. By the time I reached my alternative station, it was completely dark and the river had gone quiet.

The next morning I started fishing at Langwathby bridge, and exhausted myself covering a vast distance in a vain attempt to find a spot sheltered from a relentless downstream gale. By evening, the wind had dropped, and having borrowed a couple of Orange Quills from Niall, I was ready for the rise to begin in the smooth run where he had scored the night before. There was no rise. My brother Matthew fished the currant bush run, and caught four good fish.

On the third day I despaired. I walked the same distance as the day before (four miles in chest waders is no joke), and fished into the same wind, with the same result - except that I rose the best fish I saw all weekend, to a mayfly, and yanked it out of his mouth. In the evening, thank God, we went out to dinner, so I was spared further humiliation.

Monday was our last day, and we had to leave after lunch. By this time, both Niall and Matthew had enjoyed a sufficiency of success. Blasé about their own efforts and unbearably condescending towards mine, they hardly cared whether they caught more fish or not. I did, very much, as I hurried off to the currant bush run which, thus far, had treated me so unkindly. I cast away for a while with no result, and then a decent fish took my Greenwell when I was looking the other way. A little ashamed, I netted it and rapped it over the head. There was still no proper rise, but a little way upstream I saw swallows dipping over a quiet little pool off the main flow. I approached and saw a sip at the surface. I caught that fish and then another. I hooked a third and lost it. Fifty yards above, I spotted another sip and caught the sipper.

I brought back the four fish, which Matthew fried in butter, and which we ate in our fingers. They were sweet to the taste, sweeter by far to catch. As I munched, I reflected on the nature of an obsession that enabled three days of failure to be redeemed by an hour when everything went right. And it occurred to me that the acquisition of humility was a painful, but necessary business.

The Far From Compleat Angler

The fishing on Eden and Eamont is never easy. The vagaries of weather, water levels, and wild trout ensure that. The general opinion is that the fish are much less plentiful than they used to be. In William Nelson's day in the last century (*Fishing in Eden*, first published in 1922), bags of thirty or forty were nothing exceptional. Stephen Johnson (*Fishing From Afar*) writes of April days on the Edenhall water between the wars, when he and his father would bring back anything from a dozen to twenty trout to the Edenhall hotel. I myself can remember an extraordinary morning on the flats below the Salmon Stream, during which I caught a dozen takeable trout, every one of them on a Partridge and Orange fished downstream.

I accept that the fish are fewer now, but the consolation is that they are bigger. Six ounces was a reasonable average in the old days; I would suggest that it is nearer ten ounces or even three-quarters of a pound now. What is more worrying is the way the hatches of fly have declined. In the past, the appearance of the medium olive around mid-morning could be pretty well relied upon, unless the weather was unusually vile or the river was in flood, and the hatch would often extend well into the afternoon. These days the hatch tends to be a niggardly, spasmodic affair if it happens at all. The sedge has become wholly unreliable, and the BWO disappoints at least as often as it rewards.

Very occasionally, as a result of some happy but utterly mysterious coincidence of factors, the fly appears all day, and the fish rise. I had one such four years ago. It was after mid-June, the latest I had ever been at Edenhall after trout, and it was deliciously, temperately warm. I strolled up from the hut, around the corner at Beach Dub, and looked up towards Watersmeet. On the far side, beneath a precipitous slope, the water runs deep and strong through a succession of salmon lies. But the near side is shallower, and when the level is down, you can wade out to midstream, and make your way up, casting left and right and straight ahead, and even across and down with plenty of slack to avoid drag.

This morning there was a nice, constant trickle of olives coming down, with the trout in a genial taking mood. I had with me a collection of lightly dressed, paleish olive imitations which I had bought at infinitesimal cost the previous summer at a little shop in Cracow. The

Chapter Eighteen - In Eden

sparseness of the dressing seemed to make them far more attractive than the Greenwells on which I would normally have relied; their only drawback being that they were tied on hooks of extremely dubious provenance, several of which snapped at the bend in fish.

That hatch lasted a full twelve hours. I fished up to the confluence with the Eamont, catching and releasing trout of up to a pound, the time slipping by at the gallop. And the evening I was on the same stretch of water, and still they rose to my Polish flies until twilight came, and then darkness. In between, as is the way, there was a disaster which, at the time, left me so numb with despair that I did not believe I could recover. It was a tribute to the quality of the day that, by nightfall, it was but a memory; painful, but manageable.

I had gone up the Eamont, past the currant bush run, past the flats at Udford, past a succession of inky deep holes where the red salmon like to lurk, to the very top of our allotted stretch, where two enticing pools can offer some marvellous fishing. It was my brother Matthew who discovered them, bringing back tales of big fish feeding hard on olives, and a two pounder - a big fish for these parts - as evidence.

The pools are similar in character. At the head of each the water tumbles over shelves of stones, and the current then swings away to the far bank, slowing where the willows trail their branches, then slackening altogether. The best fish inhabit the water shaded by the willows, where the olives swept down over the stones are held up and revolve temptingly. The first of the pools (heading upstream) seems to be the more productive, and when I arrived, I at once saw two or three good trout lunching with keen appetites. The rises were quiet and I was taken unawares by the strength and size of the fish which grabbed my light olive at the first cast.

In the early stages of the battle, I was sure I was going to lose it. It seemed inevitable that my Cracow hook would break, or that it would wriggle free. Then, little by little, I began to hope; until, when it lay beaten in the shallow water just below me, I felt a welling sense of triumph. It was unresisting as I drew it towards the rim of my net. Then I could see the fly in the skin at the extremity of the lower jaw. The fish tilted six inches from the net, and the fly came out. The trout faded from view, then vanished as I lunged at it.

The Far From Compleat Angler

An hour or so later, having found the uppermost pool quiet, I returned to the same spot. The fish were continuing to snaffle olives in the foamy water by the willow. I cast a slackish line across, my fly stood out for a moment, and disappeared in a little ring. This time there was no mistake. He weighed one pound five ounces, and I was much consoled by him, even though his fellow must have been a good half-pound bigger.

Only once have I hooked a bigger trout at Edenhall, and I lost that as well. It was the following year, and again Matthew and I went in June. It was just about the only hot weekend of a dismal summer. The river was high, the water cold, and the fishing as poor as it had been splendid twelve months before.

There was no fly during the day, and the only decent hatches came very late on the two evenings we were there. On the first of them I was in the wrong place doing the wrong thing, and missed out entirely. Twenty-four hours later I was in the right place, which was on the Eden. I had crossed the river by boat, and gone down to the smooth, flat water below the Salmon Stream, where the fish began to feed on a steady trickle of blue-winged olives. One rose above me, close to the bank, in the quiet way of a big fish, and he took my Orange Quill first go. Unfortunately, I had spent too much time among the portly, placid trout of the Kennet and was mentally unprepared for the explosive fight of the wild, northern fish.

He hurtled out into midstream, then down past me. I knew that I had to get onto the bank, and get below him. But I was paralysed by his strength and the violence of his resistance. So I stood like a fool where I was and gave him line, knowing that I would lose him. And so I did, but not until he had leaped. He was a two-pounder, a good two-pounder, and I was no match for him. My brother, fishing on the other side and a way below me, heard it all, and said he had turned pale at the passion of my language.

www.ingramcontent.com/pod-product-compliance
Lightning Source LLC
Chambersburg PA
CBHW032251150426
43195CB00008BA/405